Introduction to
MACROECONOMIC THEORY

THE IRWIN SERIES IN ECONOMICS

Consulting Editor
LLOYD G. REYNOLDS
Yale University

GAMBS & KOMISAR *Economics and Man* 3d ed.

GORDON *The Investment Financing and Valuation of the Corporation*

GRAMPP & WEILER (eds.) *Economic Policy: Readings in Political Economy* 3d ed.

GROSSMAN, HANSEN, HENDRIKSEN, MCALLISTER, OKUDA, & WOLMAN (eds.) *Readings in Current Economics* rev. ed.

GUTHRIE *Statistical Methods in Economics*

GUTHRIE & WALLACE *Economics* 4th ed.

HAGEN *The Economics of Development*

HARRISS *The American Economy: Principles, Practices, and Policies* 6th ed.

HERBER *Modern Public Finance*

HIGGINS *United Nations and U.S. Foreign Economic Policy*

JOME *Principles of Money and Banking*

KINDLEBERGER *International Economics* 4th ed.

KUHLMAN & SKINNER *The Economic System* rev. ed.

LEE *Macroeconomics: Fluctuations, Growth, and Stability* 4th ed.

LLOYD *Microeconomic Analysis*

LOCKLIN *Economics of Transportation* 6th ed.

LOW *Modern Economic Organization*

MEYERS *Economics of Labor Relations*

PEGRUM *Public Regulation of Business* rev. ed.

PEGRUM *Transportation: Economics and Public Policy* rev. ed.

PETERSON & GRAY *Economic Development of the United States*

PHILLIPS *The Economics of Regulation: Theory and Practice in the Transportation and Public Utility Industries* rev. ed.

REYNOLDS *Economics: A General Introduction* 3d ed.

RIMA *Development of Economic Analysis*

SCITOVSKY *Welfare and Competition: The Economics of a Fully Employed Economy*

SIEGEL *Aggregate Economics and Public Policy* 3d ed.

SIRKIN *Introduction to Macroeconomic Theory* 3d ed.

SMITH & TEIGEN (eds.) *Readings in Money, National Income, and Stabilization Policy*

SNIDER *Introduction to International Economics* 4th ed.

SPENCER *Managerial Economics: Text, Problems, and Short Cases* 3d ed.

VANEK *International Trade: Theory and Economic Policy*

WILCOX *Public Policies toward Business* 3d ed.

Introduction to
MACROECONOMIC
THEORY

GERALD SIRKIN, Ph.D.
Associate Professor of Economics
The City College of The City
  University of New York

Third Edition

1970 *RICHARD D. IRWIN, INC.*
Homewood, Illinois
IRWIN-DORSEY LIMITED
Georgetown, Ontario

Third Edition

First Printing, March, 1970

Library of Congress Catalog Card No. 73–110415

Printed in the United States of America

1603680

To
N.P.R.S.

PREFACE

"Macroeconomic" theory is often defined as analysis employing aggregates, in contrast with "microeconomic" theory, which deals with the interrelations of individual units or components of the economy. Actually, such a definition does not successfully distinguish between "macro" and "micro." Both branches of economics use various degrees of aggregation and disaggregation. Macroeconomic analysis, for example, will break down consumption or investment as finely as the problem at hand requires, while microeconomic analysis aggregates buying or selling units into markets or industries as broadly as the problem requires.

The difference between macro and micro lies not so much in their analytical methods as in the questions they aim to answer. Macroeconomics is concerned with the determination and behavior of certain aggregates—the total economic output and the price level. Microeconomics deals primarily with the allocation of resources among alternative uses and with the distribution of the product.

The division of theory into macro and micro compartments makes the subject more manageable to the student at the introductory level but also imposes serious limitations. These limitations are encountered in the more advanced areas of macroeconomics, where discussions of consumer and investor behavior, inflation, growth, and international aspects of income analysis call for the application of microeconomic tools. In this book I have made the cautious assumption that the student's acquaintance with microeconomic theory is slight, and I have, therefore, attempted to couch all expositions in terms which do not require a prior course in microeconomic theory. Eventually the evolution of theory texts will proceed to the point of full integration of macro- and microeconomics, but the day when undergraduate courses will be ready to use such a book is not yet in sight.

In this third edition the principal changes are extensive revisions of the investment and income-fluctuations chapters. The new treatment of investment includes a rigorous derivation of the investment-demand function, a critical view of the traditional accelerator models, and a normal-output theory of investment demand to replace the simpler accelerator theories. The analysis of fluctuations, building on those revisions, is oriented toward the view of a stable economy which fluctuates because of exogenous shocks, in contrast to the more prevalent view of an unstable economy inherently prone to fluctuate. Other revisions include changes in the theory of credit rationing and in the reconciliation between the liquidity-preference and loanable-funds theories of the interest rate. Among the new features of this edition are an exposition of the aggregate supply function and discussions of flexible exchange rates and wage-price guideposts.

This book owes much to the generous efforts of Dr. Arthur M. Okun, former Professor of Economics at Yale University and Chairman of the Council of Economic Advisers, and of Professor Lloyd G. Reynolds of Yale University, who read the manuscript of the first edition and made many excellent suggestions. It has also benefited from comments on the first edition by Professor M. O. Clement of Dartmouth College and from comments on Chapter 8 by Anna J. Schwartz of the National Bureau of Economic Research. The transformation of my manuscript into a book could not have been done without the assistance of my wife, Natalie Robinson Sirkin, who edited, criticized, encouraged, and indexed. The faults and errors that remain are due entirely to my own persistence.

New York, New York
February, 1970

GERALD SIRKIN

CONTENTS

PART II.   THE DETERMINATION OF AGGREGATE DEMAND

PART III.   PROBLEMS AND POLICIES

LIST OF ILLUSTRATIONS

FIGURES

CHARTS

TABLES

PART I

Fundamentals

Chapter
1

NATIONAL INCOME ACCOUNTING

National income accounting is important to students of income analysis for two distinct reasons. One is that it provides a structural picture of the economy and a set of definitions on which income theory is built. The other is that it provides a body of useful statistics.

Since this is a book on income theory, it is accounting as the foundation for the theory that occupies the center of the stage. But the second part of this chapter takes a brief excursion into the wings to consider some of the problems of compiling the statistics and to ask exactly what it is the statistics measure.

ACCOUNTING CONCEPTS

"Stocks" and "Flows"

At the start it is necessary to distinguish between two kinds of measures: the amount of a *stock* at a given point in time (for example, the water in a reservoir on July 1, 1969) and the amount of a *flow* over a period of time (say the quantity of water flowing into or out of the reservoir between July 1, 1969, and July 1, 1970).

In business accounting, the *balance sheet* is a statement of stocks —the amount of a firm's assets, liabilities, and net worth at a particular moment of time. The *income statement* of the firm is a measure of certain flows—the receipts and expenditures of the firm during a period of time.

In national income accounting, as the name suggests, we are primarily interested in something like an income statement—a set of flows. Our interest in stocks is secondary; they enter the theory at those points where they may exert an influence on the flows.

3

Income = Product

The total product of a nation during a year consists of the goods and services produced by it during that year. In the course of production, various claims upon the product are created. These claims are called incomes. A statement of total income shows how the total product is allocated among the different types of claims.

The total of claims on product, or incomes, cannot differ from the total product. If the producer allocates to others less than the total value of the product, then the residual becomes the producer's income—profits. If the producer allocates to others more than the total value of the product, then the producer's income becomes negative—a loss. No matter how incomes are divided, total income must equal total product.

In other words, product and income are the same total quantity looked at in two different ways—what was produced and who receives the claims on it.

Intermediate and Final Products

In a complex economy, most products will pass through several firms before they become finished or final products. A product sold by one firm to another which will use it for further production in the same income period is called an "intermediate product." Clearly, if all the production of all firms were added up, there would be multiple counting of those products that passed through the hands of more than one firm. To avoid such multiple counting, two approaches are possible.

The first takes the value of product of each firm and deducts the value of intermediate products (inputs purchased from other firms). This gives the *value added* by each firm, and the sum of values added equals total product.

Alternatively one can add up the value of final products.

Components of Output

A number of different ways of breaking down total output can be used. One way is to show value of output by industrial origin, as in Table 1–1. This tabulation is arrived at by deducting intermediate products from the production of each industry to obtain a value-added type of measure. Another method is to classify output according to the nature of the final use of the product. The choice is determined by the use to which the information is to be put; and while for certain purposes output data by industrial origin are valuable, for purposes of income analysis output grouped according to type of final demand is even more serviceable.

An important facet of income theory is to explain what determines the amount of output demanded, and for that task it is helpful to group together products for which the determinants of demand are broadly similar. Three categories, consumption, investment, and government purchases of goods and services, will be defined, each representing a different set of demand forces. A second reason for choosing this division of output is that consumption and investment differ in the impact they have on future levels of income. Consumption and investment may be further subdivided to take into account the differences in the determinants of demand that may apply to components of those categories.

TABLE 1–1

National Income by Industrial Origin, 1968
(billions of dollars)

All industries, total	714.4
Agriculture, forestry, and fisheries	21.9
Mining and construction	42.9
Manufacturing	215.4
Nondurable goods	82.9
Durable goods	132.5
Transportation	27.2
Communication	14.2
Electric, gas, and sanitary services	13.7
Wholesale and retail trade	105.2
Finance, insurance, and real estate	78.2
Services	86.1
Government and government enterprises	105.0
Rest of the world	4.7

Source: U.S. Department of Commerce, *Survey of Current Business*, July, 1969.

Consumption and Investment

Consumption and investment cannot be distinguished by the physical appearance of the commodity. The purchase of an automobile may be either consumption or investment. The purchase of a pair of shoes may be either consumption or investment. The distinction rests entirely on the use to which the product is to be put.

The uses of the product of the current accounting period can be divided into three categories. Those that are used up in further production in the same accounting period are intermediate products. They are eliminated from the national product accounts. Those that are acquired for the satisfaction they yield in the current period and are not to be used in production in future periods are called *consumption*. Those that are to be used in production in future periods are called *investment*.

The test for identifying investment is, in principle, simple: Does it add to the capital stock, the accumulation of products to be used in future production?[1] By this test, we can clear up the confusion created by the difference between the macroeconomic definition of investment and its everyday usage. People speak of "investing" in stocks or bonds, but such purchases do not, in themselves, constitute an addition to the capital stock and hence are not investment in the macroeconomic sense.

Certain transactions can result in a reduction in the capital stock. For example, if a producer sells a capital item to a consumer to be used up in the current accounting period, the capital stock is thereby reduced. The amount of the reduction is *disinvestment*. The transaction would appear in the accounts as an addition to consumption and a negative amount of investment. Since most capital goods are not readily adapted to consumption, disinvestment must ordinarily occur through two special processes. The chief process is not replacing capital goods as they wear out; the capital goods have become "embodied" in the goods which they produced and are thus consumed. The other important process is through the reduction of inventory stocks.

Government Purchases of Goods and Services

The simplest and most logical accounting approach to the government sector would be to treat government as a producer. Government is a producer of services. It produces with two kinds of inputs: product purchased from other producers and labor hired

---

[1] In statistical practice some thorny definitional problems are encountered, such as the treatment of consumers' durable goods and of education. These are discussed at a later point in this chapter.

directly. Some of the purchases from other producers will be used up in the current period and some will contribute to production of services in succeeding periods. The output of services will be either intermediate products going to other producers or will be final products going to consumers.

Statistical realities, however, have compelled a modification of this treatment. One important characteristic of government product is that it is not sold but given away. Its value cannot be measured, as private product is, by the prices at which it is sold. Furthermore, the beneficiaries of government services may be producers or consumers, and which they are cannot readily be determined, so that it is difficult to separate government product into intermediate goods and final goods.

For such reasons, most accounting systems follow the practice of treating government output as entirely final product, valued at cost (the cost of product purchased from producers plus the cost of labor services bought by the government). A consequence of this method is that all government purchases are charged to current production, i.e., treated as if they were all used up in the current period, so that there is no category of government investment.

In effect, then, "government purchases of goods and services" is actually "government production of consumer services." It is kept separate rather than lumped in with personal consumption because it responds to a different set of forces from those that explain personal consumption demand.

Gross National Product

The estimated total value of the output of an economy in an income accounting period (typically a year) is called the "gross national product." It is "gross" because no deduction has been made for the amount of capital stock that was used up in producing the national product. The capital stock of the economy is the collection of productive assets, accumulated through investment in previous periods, which last over a number of income periods. Some portion of the capital stock can be imagined to be used up in each period, and, to that extent, part of the capital stock becomes embodied in the current product. The gross national product is, therefore, an overstatement of current product, since it contains what was actually the product of some previous period. To adjust for this overstatement, an estimate of the capital used up is deducted from gross national product, giving what is called "net national product."

In Table 1–2 we have the 1968 estimate of U.S. gross national product, divided into consumption, investment, net exports, and government purchases, with finer subdivisions under each of these headings.

TABLE 1–2

U.S. Gross National Product, 1968
(billions of dollars)

Personal consumption expenditures		536.6
Durable goods	83.3	
Nondurable goods	230.6	
Services	222.8	
Gross private domestic investment		126.3
Fixed investment	119.0	
Nonresidential structures 29.3		
Producers' durable equipment 59.5		
Residential structures 30.2		
Change in business inventories	7.3	
Net exports of goods and services		2.5
Exports	50.6	
Imports	48.1	
Government purchases of goods and services		200.3
Federal	99.5	
State and local	100.7	
Gross National Product		865.7

Source: U.S. Department of Commerce, *Survey of Current Business,* July, 1969.

The subdivisions of consumption and government purchases are self-explanatory, but two of the components of investment will require some brief discussion: change in business inventories and net exports.

Change in Business Inventories

Inventories are stocks of materials, semifinished goods, and finished goods held by producers. They are part of a stream of goods flowing through the firm in the productive process, in contradistinction to fixed assets. Thus tractors, though producers' durables to farm operators, are inventory to tractor manufacturers and dealers.

A net increase of inventories in the economy does not differ, in the broadest sense, from investment in producers' durables. It is current product acquired on capital account. Producers want to invest in inventories for the same reason they want to invest in durables: They are assets that will make a productive contribution to the operations of the enterprise. But "change of inventories" has certain distinctive characteristics which make it advisable to separate it from investment in producers' durables.

First, the flexibility of inventories in a *downward* direction is high compared to that of producers' durables. Disinvestment in producers' durables must take place through the wearing out of those assets (with the exception of a negligible part of the capital stock that might be shifted to consumer use in its existing form). The time rate of such disinvestment is fixed by technical conditions. Disinvestment in inventories, on the other hand, occurs when the flow of production is less than the flow of sales; the rate at which disinvestment in inventories can proceed has wide latitude for variation.

Second, investment (or disinvestment) in inventories may be unintentional. Since "change in business inventories" depends upon the relationship between production and sales, any surprises about the rate of sales will leave the producer with more or less inventory than he had intended to hold. We can generally presume that the investments made in producers' durables were intended.

Third, there is a special difficulty about computing change in business inventories which, since it gives rise to an additional item in the national income accounts, will be taken up here rather than in the later sections of this chapter devoted to measurement problems.

Change in inventories is measured by comparing the value of the inventory stock at the beginning and the end of the accounting period. That measure is equivalent to subtracting the amount of outflow of inventories from the amount of inflow. If prices are unchanged during the period, the figure for inventory change will measure the physical change in inventories. But changing prices can obscure the actual physical inventory change, the result depending on the method used to value the inventory.[2]

---

[2] One method of valuing inventories is the so-called "first-in, first-out" or "Fifo" procedure, which treats inventories as though they flow out in the same order as they flow in, so that the stock at the end of the period is priced at the

The figure which appears in the product accounts for "change in business inventories" has been adjusted from the value of the change in inventories as it appears on the books of businesses to an estimate of the current value of the physical volume of change in inventories. The amount of the adjustment, called the "inventory valuation adjustment," must also appear as a correction to the measure of income created by the production process—a point which will be reintroduced shortly.

Net Exports

The relationship of the foreign sector to the national accounts will be covered in detail in the next section, but a few general remarks on the nature of net exports should be introduced at this point.

Goods and services produced by this country and exported are part of the national product of this country. So is the output of factors of production owned by residents of this country but used in production abroad. The output of domestically owned factors used abroad is measured by their income receipts.

Conversely, some part of the expenditures listed under "consumption," "investment," or "government purchases" may have been imported and should not be counted as part of this country's product. Likewise, any output produced with foreign-owned factors, as measured by income payments to those factors, is not part of this country's product.

The deduction for imports and for factor payments to abroad

most recent prices. In a period of rising prices, an inventory which is unchanged in physical amounts will have a higher value at the end than at the beginning of the period. The problem for the statistician is to determine whether there has been a physical change in inventories and then to value that change at current prices (since the rest of gross national product is also being valued at current prices). The calculation consists of expressing the end-of-period inventories in constant prices, through the use of appropriate price indexes, and subtracting this figure from beginning-of-period inventories in constant prices to get an estimate of physical volume change. The volume change in constant prices is then converted to current prices.

An alternative technique used by some firms for inventory accounting is the last-in, first-out or "Lifo" method, in which inventories are treated as though they flow out in the reverse order from that in which they flow in. Stable or increasing volumes of inventories are correctly measured under this system by the change in the book value of inventory. But if there is a decrease of inventory volume, the Lifo method measures the decrease, not in current prices, but in some precurrent prices, and an adjustment is required.

is made from the total of exports and factor payments from abroad, giving net exports.

Components of Income

The process of production generates a flow of incomes which, in the aggregate, is equal to the total value of output. Total income can be broken down in a variety of ways. The classifications used in national income accounting attempt to meet the needs of both aggregative income theory and those areas of economic analysis which utilize data on functional distribution of income.

Table 1–3 shows, in the left-hand column, the components of gross

TABLE 1–3

U.S. Gross National Income and Product Account, 1968
(billions of dollars)

Compensation of employees	513.6	Personal consumption expenditures	536.6
Proprietors' income	63.8		
Rental income of persons	21.2	Gross private domestic investment	126.3
Corporate profits and inventory valuation adjustment	87.9	Net exports of goods and services	2.5
Corporate profits before tax	91.1	Government purchases of goods and services	200.3
Inventory valuation adjustment	−3.2		
Net interest	28.0		
Capital consumption allowances .	73.3		
Indirect business tax and nontax liability	77.9		
Business transfer payments	3.4		
Current surplus of government enterprises less subsidies	−0.8		
Statistical discrepancy	−2.5		
Gross National Income	865.7	Gross National Product	865.7

Source: U.S. Department of Commerce, *Survey of Current Business*, July, 1969.

national income, while the right-hand column repeats the production data from Table 1–2. Such income items as "compensation of employees" and "net interest" need no further explanation. "Proprietors' income"—the income of all unincorporated private enterprises—appears as a classification because, though it is actually made up of compensation for labor and returns to property, the accounting methods of unincorporated enterprises make it difficult, if not impossible, to separate them.

Under "corporate profits" we make a deduction for "inventory valuation adjustment." On the production side, investment has already been corrected for an overstatement of change in inventories as measured by the book value of inventories. This same adjustment is made on the income side, reducing corporate profits which were overstated by the amount of the fictitious increase in inventories. (An adjustment for inventory valuation of unincorporated enterprises is also included in proprietors' income.)

"Capital consumption allowances" are an estimate of the amount of the capital stock used up during the income period.

"Indirect business tax" refers to all taxes which are not on income, such as excise taxes, customs duties, and property taxes. The "nontax liability," an insignificant element, refers to such charges as fines, penalties, and forfeitures.

"Business transfer payments" consist mainly of corporate gifts to nonprofit institutions and consumer bad debts. Other ingredients are personal injury payments of business to persons other than employees, unrecovered thefts, and cash prizes.

"Government enterprises" are defined as government agencies which sell their output of goods and services to cover a substantial part of their operating costs. "Government subsidies" can be looked at as just the reverse of indirect business taxes and are, therefore, a deduction from the income side of the Gross National Income and Product Account. The "surplus of government enterprises" is net of any losses of government enterprises; and, since such losses represent subsidies to government enterprises, one form of government subsidy has already been deducted. To complete the deduction, other government subsidies are also subtracted from surplus of government enterprises.

Since gross national income and gross national product must be equal by definition, any difference that arises between the separate statistical measurements of those two totals is entered under "statistical discrepancy." The product estimate is treated as correct, and the discrepancy is entered as an adjustment to the income estimate. The figure is generally trivial.

Gross National Product, Net National Product, and National Income

In the section on gross national product, it was pointed out that gross national product is in reality an overestimate of current output since it includes some product of a previous income period, in the form of a portion of the capital stock used up in producing the current product. The deduction of the capital consumption allowance from both sides of the Gross National Income and Product Account would, in principle, correct the overestimate. The resulting figure, net national product, is conceptually superior to gross national product as an evaluation of current output. In practice, however, our view of the comparative merits of the two measures must be related to the confidence we feel in the capital-consumption-allowance estimate. Capital consumption allowances are based on the depreciation calculations of businesses which allow not only for the decline in physical productivity of capital assets but also for the decline in money value of assets due to obsolescence. For national income purposes, only the using up of capital as its productivity declines is relevant, so that capital consumption allowances as presently calculated are too large.

Net national product is measured in terms of the market value of current product. Alternatively, it can be measured in terms of the cost of the factors of production put in. But not all of the items appearing in the income column of the National Income and Product Account are factor costs. Specifically, "indirect business taxes," "business transfer payments," "surplus of government enterprises less subsidies," and "statistical discrepancy" are not payments to factors for productive service. When they are deducted, we have net national product at factor cost, also called "national income," which is less than net national product at market prices. Actually the distinction between them makes very little difference. The figure for net national product is meaningful only in a comparative sense (for example, in a comparison of one year with another). If the relationship between net national product at market prices and at factor prices remains unchanged between the two years, then it makes no difference which concept is used. If, between the two periods, NNP at market prices increases by a greater proportion than NNP at factor prices, perhaps because of an increase in indirect business tax rates which raised market prices, it still does not matter which concept is used; a valid comparison requires that an adjustment be made for price changes between the periods being compared, and that adjustment wipes out the discrepancy introduced by the change in indirect business tax rates.

The choice between NNP at market prices and at factor prices is of consequence only in the case of an examination of NNP by industrial origin. In that case, the picture of the relative contribution of the various industries to total output may differ substantially when output is measured by market prices or factor costs.

SECTOR ACCOUNTS

In broadest terms, the flows of current income in an economy can be described in this way. The production process generates a set of income receipts which we can call the *original* income allocation. Subsequently, there will be some reallocations of income to other recipients *which are not payments for current products or services.* These reallocations are known as "transfer payments."

The original allocations are shown in the Gross National Income and Product Account (Table 1–3). To show the transfer payments, the economy is divided into a number of sectors. The accounts of these sectors can then reveal, in addition to current product and the original income allocations, the transfers *between* sectors. Transfers within sectors are not shown and are ignored. For this reason the choice of the sectors into which the economy is to be divided is made so as to display those transfers that are of interest in income analysis and to leave out those that are not.

Each sector account shows the current receipts of the sector and how those receipts are allocated. Since these accounts show transactions between sectors, one sector's allocation is another sector's receipt. Each transaction appears twice, as a receipt in one sector and as an allocation in another.

The U.S. system of sector accounts consists of the National Income and Product Account and four sector accounts. The domestic economy is divided into the personal sector and the government sector. A fourth account, the Foreign Transactions Account, lists the transactions between the domestic economy and foreign economies. The system is completed with a sector account called the "Gross Saving and Investment Account," which will require a brief explanation.

Some transactions are current charges against current income, such as consumption expenditures (an allocation of the personal sector, a receipt of the production sector) or personal income taxes (a transfer payment which is an allocation of the personal sector, a receipt of the government sector). But what accounting disposition shall be made of any receipts of the personal sector over and above what are allocated to consumption or to tax payments to the government? Such a residual, called "personal saving," represents current income which is allocated, not to current use, but to a capital use. As such, it is not a transaction with either the business, government, or rest-of-the-world sector. Hence the Gross Saving and Investment Account is set up for capital transactions, and personal saving becomes an allocation of the personal sector and a receipt of the gross saving and investment sector. The same principle holds for all transactions which are current to one party and capital to the other. Current income allocated to capital use becomes a receipt under "saving" in the Gross Saving and Investment Account. Exchanges of *product* which are current to one transactor and capital to the other are a receipt of the business sector and an allocation of the gross saving and investment sector.

The system of sector accounts is illustrated in Table 1–4. The double entry of each item is shown by the number in parentheses which indicates the account and line of the corresponding entry.

Personal Income and Outlay Account

On the income side, the personal sector account records the factor incomes from the National Income and Product Account which go directly to persons, i.e., all factor incomes except employer contributions to social security, corporate profits tax, and undistributed corporate profits. To these personal incomes from factor services are added the transfer payments from the government and business to the personal sector. The employee contribution to social insurance is deducted. The total is personal income.

On the outlay side of the account, the personal income tax liability is entered first. The remainder, known as *disposable income,* is allocated between personal outlays and personal saving.[3]

---

[3] Previous to the revisions of definitions in 1965 (see *Survey of Current Business,* August, 1965), personal saving was defined as disposable income minus personal consumption expenditures. The revised definitions treat interest payments by consumers as a transfer payment (like government interest payments), and they are no longer counted in gross national product. Also, private gifts to abroad, formerly treated as consumption expenditures, are now shown separately as a transfer payment. Personal saving, therefore, is now defined as disposable income minus personal outlays. (Personal outlays consist of personal consumption expenditures plus interest paid by consumers plus personal transfer payments to foreigners.)

TABLE 1–4

U.S. Sector Accounts, 1968*
(billions of dollars)

1. National Income and Product Account

Line			Line		
1	Compensation of employees	513.6	24	Personal consumption expenditures (2–3)	536.6
2	Wages and salaries	465.0	25	Durable goods	83.3
3	Disbursements (2–7)	465.0	26	Nondurable goods	230.6
4	Wage accruals less disbursements (5–4)	0.0	27	Services	222.8
5	Supplements to wages and salaries	48.6	28	Gross private domestic investment (5–1)	126.3
6	Employer contributions for social insurance (3–14)	24.4	29	Fixed investment	119.0
7	Other labor income (2–8)	24.2	30	Nonresidential	88.8
8	Proprietors' income (2–9)	63.8	31	Structures	29.3
9	Rental income of persons (2–10)	21.2	32	Producers' durable equipment	59.5
10	Corporate profits and inventory valuation adjustment	87.9	33	Residential structures	30.2
11	Profits before tax	91.1	34	Change in business inventories	7.3
12	Profits tax liability (3–11)	41.3	35	Net exports of goods and services	2.5
13	Profits after tax	49.8	36	Exports (4–1)	50.6
14	Dividends (2–11)	23.1	37	Imports (4–2)	48.1
15	Undistributed profits (5–5)	26.7	38	Government purchases of goods and services (3–1)	200.3
16	Inventory valuation adjustment (5–6)	–3.2	39	Federal	99.5
17	Net interest (2–13)	28.0	40	National defense	78.0
18	**National Income**	**714.4**	41	Other	21.5
19	Business transfer payments (2–17)	3.4	42	State and local	100.7
20	Indirect business tax and nontax liability (3–12)	77.9			
21	Less: Subsidies less current surplus of government enterprises (3–6)	0.8			
22	Capital consumption allowances (5–7)	73.3			
23	Statistical discrepancy (5–9)	–2.5			
	Charges against Gross National Product	**865.7**		**Gross National Product**	**865.7**

2. Personal Income and Outlay Account

1	Personal tax and nontax payments (3–10)	97.9	7	Wage and salary disbursements (1–3)	465.0
2	Personal outlays	551.6	8	Other labor income (1–7)	24.2
3	Personal consumption expenditures (1–24)	536.6	9	Proprietors' income (1–8)	63.8
4	Interest paid by consumers (2–15)	14.2	10	Rental income of persons (1–9)	21.2
5	Personal transfer payments to foreigners (net) (4–4)	0.8	11	Dividends (1–4)	23.1
6	Personal saving (5–3)	38.4	12	Personal interest income	54.1
			13	Net interest (1–17)	28.0
			14	Net interest paid by government (3–5)	11.9
			15	Interest paid by consumers (2–4)	14.2
			16	Transfer payments to persons	59.2
			17	From business (1–19)	3.4
			18	From government (3–3)	55.8
			19	Less: Personal contributions for social insurance (3–15)	22.6
	Personal Taxes, Outlays, and Saving	**687.9**		**Personal Income**	**687.9**

3. Government Receipts and Expenditures Account

1	Purchases of good and services (1–38)	200.3	10	Personal tax and nontax payments (2–1)	97.9
2	Transfer payments	57.9	11	Corporate profits tax liability (1–12)	41.3
3	To persons (2–18)	55.8	12	Indirect business tax and nontax liability (1–20)	77.9
4	To foreigners (net) (4–3)	2.1	13	Contributions for social insurance	47.0
5	Net interest paid (2–14)	11.9	14	Employer (1–6)	24.4
6	Subsidies less current surplus of government enterprises (1–21)	0.8	15	Personal (2–19)	22.6
7	Surplus or deficit (–), national income and product accounts (5–8)	–6.7			
8	Federal	–5.2			
9	State and local	–1.5			
	Government Expenditures and Surplus	**264.2**		**Government Receipts**	**264.2**

TABLE 1-4 (Continued)

4. Foreign Transactions Account

	Receipts from Foreigners			Payments to Foreigners	
1	Exports of goods and services (1-36)	50.6	2	Imports of goods and services (1-37)	48.1
			3	Transfer payments from U.S. Government to foreigners (net) (3-4)	2.1
			4	Personal transfer payments to foreigners (net) (2-5)	0.8
			5	Net foreign investment (5-2)	-0.3
	Receipts from Foreigners	**50.6**		**Payments to Foreigners**	**50.6**

5. Gross Saving and Investment Account

1	Gross private domestic investment (1-28)	126.3	3	Personal saving (2-6)	38.4
2	Net foreign investment (4-5)	-0.3	4	Wage accruals less disbursements (1-4)	0.0
			5	Undistributed corporate profits (1-15)	26.7
			6	Corporate inventory valuation adjustment (1-16)	-3.2
			7	Capital consumption allowances (1-22)	73.3
			8	Government surplus or deficit (—), national income and product accounts (3-7)	-6.7
			9	Statistical discrepancy (1-23)	-2.5
	Gross Investment	**126.0**		**Gross Saving and Statistical Discrepancy**	**126.0**

* Numbers in parentheses indicate accounts and items of counter-entry in the accounts.

Source: U.S. Department of Commerce, *Survey of Current Business*, July, 1969.

The derivation of the other aggregate income and product concepts from gross national product can now be summarized, using the 1968 data in the sector accounts:

	Billions of Dollars
Gross national product	865.7
Less: Capital consumption allowances	73.3
Net national product	792.4
Less: Indirect business taxes	77.9
Business transfer payments	3.4
Current surplus of government enterprises less subsidies	−0.8
Statistical discrepancy	−2.5
National income*	714.4
Less: Corporate profits taxes	41.3
Contributions for social insurance	47.0
Undistributed corporate profits plus inventory valuation adjustment	23.5
Plus: Government transfer payments to persons	55.8
Interest paid by government (net) and consumers	26.1
Business transfer payments	3.4
Personal income	687.9
Less: Personal income taxes	97.9
Disposable Income	590.0

Government Receipts and Expenditures Account

Only one point of clarification remains to be made about the items in this Account and that is with respect to the treatment of government interest payments. Government interest, in the U.S. accounting system, is considered not to be a factor payment but rather a transfer payment. It is not counted, therefore, in gross national income but appears as a transfer from government to households in the sector accounts.

The reasoning behind the handling of government interest is briefly this: All government purchases are considered to be on current account so that the government owns no capital stock. Hence, there can be no output from government property on the product side of the national accounts and no factor payments to capital, such as interest, in the allocations of national product.

To treat all government purchases as if they were consumed in the same period in which they were produced is obviously artificial, and the adoption of that accounting practice can only be explained in terms of the difficulties that confront the statistician who must decide which government purchases are capital-forming and which are not, and who must estimate the addition to national product to be ascribed to government capital. Current discussion suggests that accounting methods will be eventually modified to recognize government capital formation, but the change may be considerably delayed.

Foreign Transactions Account

This Account shows the sales of current products and current factor services to abroad and the current purchases of products and factor services from abroad. Neglecting unilateral transfers for the moment, one can say that after these exchanges of goods and services have been netted out, any excess of sales to abroad represents a part of domestic product that has been *lent* abroad.

However, the presence of unilateral transfers (gifts to abroad by the government or households) affects this picture. The transfers to abroad represent an amount of product which has not been lent but given. By deducting net unilateral transfers from the excess of sales to abroad, the amount that has been lent abroad, labeled "net foreign investment," is computed.

Until recently, net foreign investment appeared in the national product account. However, because of the unilateral transfer items, net foreign investment was not quite consistent with the other items in the national product account. The other items in the product account measure a flow of goods and services. Government unilateral transfers are made up of grants of goods and services (foreign aid in kind) and grants in cash. Hence net foreign investment is, in part, a financial flow, rather than a product flow. The revisions made in the U.S. accounts in 1958 are an attempt to come closer to a consistent treatment.[4]

In the present system, military grants and nonmilitary grants in kind are omitted from exports and omitted from unilateral transfers in the national income accounts. They are included in U.S. government purchases of goods and services. Exports, therefore, consist only of sales to abroad and unilateral transfers consist only of cash grants by the U.S. government to foreign countries. In the Foreign

---

[4] See U.S. Department of Commerce, *U.S. Income and Output* (1958), pp. 57–58.

Transactions Account, net foreign investment is shown as exports sold minus imports and minus unilateral transfers in cash.

In the national product account, net foreign investment no longer appears. The foreign transactions shown are export sales and imports. Thus the product account shows only the flow of product: to consumption, to domestic investment, to government purchases, and to net exports. The total gross national product is not changed since the revision represents only a rearrangement of items within the product account.

Gross Saving and Investment

Saving is the part of current income not allocated to consumption. In the sector accounts, total saving is subdivided among the three domestic sectors. Gross business saving is the retained income of business, i.e., capital consumption allowances and undistributed corporate profits. Personal saving is disposable income minus personal outlays. Government saving is government receipts, net of transfers, minus government consumption expenditures. The particular form in which savers may hold their savings (cash, savings accounts, reduced indebtedness, blast furnaces, etc.) is of no consequence to income accounting.

For every dollar of income there is a dollar of current product, and, so, for every dollar of income not consumed (saving), there is a dollar of product not consumed, which is investment. Total investment, composed of business purchases on capital account (producers' durables), change in business inventories, and net foreign investment, must equal total saving.

NATIONAL INCOME ACCOUNTS AS MEASURES

To this point we have been concerned with national income accounts primarily as a framework on which to build the theory of income analysis. But income accounts are also used as measures when statisticians make estimates and put numbers into the accounts. Since these numbers are likely to be widely used, some attention to what they measure is worthwhile.

Inclusions and Exclusions

A completely comprehensive measure of gross output would include the results of all activity in the nation that produces something of value. Actual measures are a considerable compromise with the completely comprehensive concept.

The type of product which is easiest to include is product that is sold, since the amount for which it is sold provides a figure at which it can be valued.

In addition, the U.S. accounts contain an estimated amount of product (and a corresponding amount of income) which was either given to the consumer or consumed directly by the producer. There being no market valuation for these products, a value must be imputed to them. Imputed products in the American statistics cover payment in kind (food, certain types of clothing, and lodging) to employees, net rent of owner-occupied dwellings, services of financial intermediaries (banks, investment trusts, and life insurance companies), and food and fuel produced and consumed on farms.

But these imputed items which are included are small compared to the excluded output for which some case can be made for imputing a product. First, we have the vast amount of productive activity carried on by members of households for themselves—cooking, housekeeping, child care, transportation in private passenger cars, and the whole range of "do-it-yourself" projects like clothes-making, carpentry, and house-painting. This output in households is produced not by labor alone, but by labor working with a variety of equipment which we classify under "consumers' durables," but which would be called "investment" if we counted its product in national product. Second, there is the product of government-owned durables which could be imputed if the government acquisition of those durables were treated as investment rather than consumption.

The likelihood that the handling of government durables will someday be revised has already been mentioned. What of the excluded items of household production?

The difficulty of estimating the value of these household products is certainly great, though perhaps not much different in nature from the problem of estimating farm production consumed by farmers. A more serious question arises when we ask where the process of imputation is to end. If we include housekeeping, should we not also include combing one's hair, swinging in a hammock, or any other activity producing consumer satisfaction? A line must be drawn somewhere. Wherever it is drawn, it will reflect not watertight logic but pragmatism.

One aspect of the choice between inclusion and exclusion is consistency. If a particular kind of product, say the housing service of a dwelling, were to be excluded from national product when it is occupied by the owner but included when occupied by a tenant, the inconsistency would be glaring. So it is with the omission of personal production of transportation service while counting transportation produced in the business sector. Our present practice of including the services of hired housekeepers but excluding the housekeeping services of members of the household is inconsistent, but not glaringly because paid housekeeping is such a small proportion of total housekeeping. In excluding swinging in a hammock, there is no inconsistency.

More important than inconsistency is the correctness of the picture conveyed by the data. It must be kept in mind that the absolute amount of some figure, gross national product for example, means little if anything. It takes on meaning only in a comparison. If you were told that last year the GNP of country X was 642, you would be entitled to look blank. But if you were also told that, in the previous year, GNP had been 700, your eyes would gleam with intelligent curiosity about the decline.

Two kinds of comparison of national income data are possible—with other time periods and with other countries. In each case, the excluded production creates a potential source of misinformation.

If an economy is undergoing structural changes which shift significant amounts of production between the included and excluded category, income data can give a misleading impression of trends through time. For example, in a country which is moving from a condition in which food, clothing, home furnishings, and entertainment are produced in the household to one in which these items are largely produced in the business sector, income data which exclude home production will show an exaggerated rate of growth. The reverse movement of production from the business sector to households is illustrated by the relative decline of passenger transportation by public carriers and the rise of transportation by private automobiles in the United States.

International comparisons are similarly obscured. The difference in per capita income between two countries, one of which produces in the home a great deal which the other produces in the business sector, will be overstated. Comparisons of rates of investment may be falsified if one country includes government investment and the other does not; or if neither recognizes government investment, and purchases of such government durables are relatively more important in one country than the other; or if "consumer investment," ignored in both, is substantial in one and small in the other.

It may be that for most of the uses to which national income data will be put, the incomplete coverage will make a negligible difference; but an awareness of the limits of the statistics should keep the user alert for those cases where comparisons are vitiated by the accounting methods employed.

National Income and Welfare

That no direct relation can be inferred between the level of national income, as now measured, and the level of national welfare is fairly obvious. The omission from income data of certain outputs that add to satisfaction has just been mentioned. The distribution of national income has much to do with the welfare it affords. Furthermore, the prices at which product is valued may not reflect its contribution to the community's satisfaction, as might be the case with lavish public monuments or surplus agricultural products consigned indefinitely to storage.

Beyond these sources of discrepancy between income and welfare, there are some that are not quite so obvious. One such has to do with output which is produced solely to meet the needs created by the complexities of an enlarged and increasingly specialized economy. The transportation of goods and of workers is a large output item in a modern economy, where in a primitive economy the proximity of workers, producers, and consumers may keep transport activity small. In welfare terms, the greater transport of the modern economy represents not an output but a *cost* and, in a comparison of welfare between the two countries, a corresponding deduction from the output of the modern economy (or an addition to the output of the primitive economy) should be made. A great deal of packaging, advertising, clerical, and administrative costs also falls into this category. A crude comparison of national income statistics between two quite different types of economies may exaggerate the welfare difference.

Another cost for which some deduction should be made in welfare estimates is "human cost." A reduction in the arduousness of labor, in the disagreeableness of working conditions, or in the danger of injury or illness from work ought to be reflected in the increased welfare value of a given output. Likewise, a shortening of hours worked means a decrease in the human cost of output, or, if one prefers, an increased output of "leisure," which ought to appear in any net output figures that are intended to bear on national welfare.

Income Comparisons and the Index Number Problem

Some difficulties of income comparisons arising from accounting definitions and methods have been mentioned. Now a difficulty of another sort, inherent in the problem regardless of the accounting methods used, must be introduced.

The sum of a great variety of different products can be obtained only by using some common unit of measure for each, which in practice means valuing each product at its market price or some approximation to a market price if the product is imputed. A national product figure, therefore, is compounded of a set of product quantities and a set of prices, and the analyst must wrestle with the problem of sorting out the influence of each.

Intertemporal Comparisons

To interpret intelligently a change in national income between two points in time, it is necessary to know how much of the change is attributable to quantity variation and how much to price variation. The two can be separated if we can hold prices constant, i.e., multiply quantities by the prices that prevailed in the first (or base) period or the prices of the second (or current period) or by some other given set of prices. An income series measured in constant prices is generally referred to as a measure of "real income."

Unfortunately, it can make a considerable difference which set of prices is chosen. In Table 1–5 we have figures for a hypothetical

TABLE 1–5
Measurement of Output Change (Alternative Constant Prices)

| | Units of Product | | Price | | Value of Product | | | |
| | Period 1 | Period 2 | Period 1 | Period 2 | Period 1 Prices | | Period 2 Prices | |
	(Q_1)	(Q_2)	(P_1)	(P_2)	(P_1Q_1)	(P_1Q_2)	(P_2Q_1)	(P_2Q_2)
Steel	10	100	$10	$10	$100	$1,000	$100	$1,000
Wheat	10	20	10	30	100	200	300	600
					$200	$1,200	$400	$1,600

economy producing only two products, steel and wheat. The total value of output increased eightfold between periods 1 and 2:

$$\frac{P_2Q_2}{P_1Q_1} = \frac{\$1,600}{\$200} = 8,$$

but part of that increase resulted from a rise in prices. To measure the change in real output, we can measure output in the constant prices of period 1. Then output in the first period is valued at $200 ($= P_1Q_1$) and in the second period at $1,200 ($= P_1Q_2$), a sixfold increase. Or we can use constant prices of period 2, giving a value of $400 ($= P_2Q_1$) in period 1 and $1,600 ($= P_2Q_2$) in period 2, a fourfold increase.

Did real product increase by six times or four times? The difference arises because wheat, which had a much smaller increase in quantity of output than steel, is given more weight in the final average when it is valued at the higher price of period 2 than when it is valued at the lower price of period 1. The two measures of the increase of product are equally correct, for, since both sets of price weights are equally defensible logically, there is no basis on which to choose between the two outcomes.

In this index of volume of output or in any other index in which two or more items must be averaged, the choice of weights must have an element of arbitrariness, and more than one "correct" answer can emerge. This is the index number problem. The example given in Table 1–5, however, is an extreme case; in practice, base and current period weights will often yield very similar index numbers, so that the horns of the statistician's dilemma are considerably blunted.

Another difficulty in making index numbers arises from the introduction of new products, or changes in the quality of existing products. If, for example, products in the index are replaced by others of superior quality, the quantity of the improved product ought, ideally, to be adjusted to reflect the increased capacity of the product to yield satisfaction. Index makers of the U.S. government do attempt to make an adjustment for quality changes, but comparisons of quality are often very difficult. The difficulty is particularly acute in the case of services; ordinarily no adjustment is attempted. In an economy which tends generally in the direction of quality improvement, there is likely to be an insufficient allowance for that improvement and a downward bias in the index of aggregate output.

Intercountry Comparisons

Let us suppose that the data in Table 1–5 pertain to some country A which we want to compare to country B having the following outputs and prices in period 2:

	Units of Product (Q₂)	Price (P₂)	Value of Output (P₂Q₂)
Steel	20	100 pesos	2,000 pesos
Wheat	80	50	4,000
			6,000 pesos

How can these incomes be compared? One method often used is to employ the official exchange rate of currencies to convert the national product of one country into the currency of the other. In this example, if the exchange rate were six pesos to $1, the income of country B in period 2 could be expressed as $1,000 and compared to the income of A of $1,600. But the conversion by application of exchange rates does not inspire confidence because exchange rates are often very far from reflecting the relative purchasing power of each currency in its own economy.

An alternative method that has been tried is to value the output of one country by the prices that apply to the same commodities in the other. In the example above, we could value B's output of steel (20 units) by A's price of steel ($10) and B's output of wheat (80 units) by A's price of wheat ($30), giving a total value of output for B of $2,600, which exceeds the value of A's output of $1,600. Or we might value A's steel (100 units) and wheat (20 units) at B's prices of 100 and 50 pesos respectively, reaching a total value of output for A of 11,000 pesos—almost twice B's 6,000-peso income.

Thus A appears to have either a lower or a higher income than B, depending on which set of weights is applied. Again, actual comparisons will ordinarily not present such extreme results, though the discrepancies will often be quite large.

Intercountry-Intertemporal Comparisons

It is often desired these days to compare rates of growth among countries. Here, again, one of the numerous obstacles is the index number problem.

Assume that countries A and B have identical production data, represented by the quantities in Table 1–6, but the price structures differ.

As Table 1–6 illustrates, two countries with the same production quantities will appear to have quite different rates of increase in value of product if the prices we use weight the more rapidly growing outputs more heavily in one country than the other. This am-

TABLE 1-6
Intercountry Comparisons of Output Change

| | Units of Product in Country A or B | | Prices in Period 2 | | Value of Product | | | |
| | | | | | Country A | | Country B | |
	Period 1 (Q_1)	Period 2 (Q_2)	Country A (P_{2A})	Country B (P_{2B})	Period 1 ($P_{2A}Q_1$)	Period 2 ($P_{2A}Q_2$)	Period 1 ($P_{2B}Q_1$)	Period 2 ($P_{2B}Q_2$)
Steel	10	100	$10	100 pesos	$100	$1,000	1,000 pesos	10,000 pesos
Wheat	10	20	30	50	300	600	500	1,000
					$400	$1,600	1,500 pesos	11,000 pesos
Percent increase ..						300%		633%

biguity can be avoided if the quantities in both countries can be weighted by the same price structure. In the case just cited, A and B will show the same rate of growth, 300 per cent, if quantities in both countries are priced at country A's prices. Of course, a question about the rate of growth remains, since, in country B's prices, both countries have increased value of product by 633 per cent. But at least the same rate of growth will be shown for two countries with the same quantity statistics.

RECOMMENDED READINGS

GILBERT, MILTON, and KRAVIS, IRVING B.   *An International Comparison of National Products and the Purchasing Power of Currencies.* Paris: Organisation for European Economic Co-operation, 1954.

KUZNETS, SIMON. *Economic Change; Selected Essays in Business Cycles, National Income and Economic Growth.* New York: W. W. Norton & Co., Inc., 1953.

NATIONAL BUREAU OF ECONOMIC RESEARCH. *Studies in Income and Wealth, Vol. 22; A Critique of the United States Income and Product Accounts.* Princeton, N.J.: Princeton University Press, 1958.

RUGGLES, RICHARD and NANCY D.   *National Income Accounts and Income Analysis.* 2d ed. New York: McGraw-Hill Book Co., Inc., 1956.

STUDENSKI, PAUL.   *The Income of Nations.* New York: New York University Press, 1958.

U.S. DEPARTMENT OF COMMERCE, Office of Business Economics.   *National Income, 1954.*

QUESTIONS

1. Explain why the following transactions are not included in investment in national income accounting:
   a) The purchase of bonds or common stocks.
   b) The purchase of land.
   c) The purchase of used machinery.
2. What is the difference between the purchase of intermediate goods and investment?
3. Is the position of the government sector in the flow of national income and product more like that of the producing sector or the consuming sector? How does the treatment of the government sector in the U.S. income accounting system differ from the treatment of the producing (business) sector?
4. Why do certain transactions such as personal income tax payments appear in the sector accounts but not in the Gross National Income and Product Account? What kinds of transactions do not appear in the sector accounts?

5. What is the difference between net exports of goods and services and net foreign investment?

6. Compute gross national product, disposable income, personal saving, government purchases of goods and services from the following data:

Total factor incomes	200
Total taxes	40
Consumption	150
Capital consumption allowances	20
Government transfer payments	8
Business transfer payments	1
Total investment	35
Undistributed corporate profits	5
Indirect business taxes	7

Chapter 2   SOME BASIC CONCEPTS

As the analysis proceeds, a variety of concepts pertaining to income theory will be introduced. There are, however, certain quite fundamental ideas which apply not merely to income theory but to economic analysis in general, and which, because of their important role in economic thinking, must be clearly understood at the outset.

Equilibrium

When something movable or changeable (a dependent variable) is affected by a given set of forces, the net effect of those forces, so long as they are constant, may be a position of rest for the dependent variable. That position of rest is called an "equilibrium." For example, a person on a scale and the counterweights of the scale are forces acting on the pointer which moves to an equilibrium.

In economic behavior, each decision-making unit, e.g., a household or a business firm, in response to a given set of forces, seeks the best level for the thing it is deciding about, a level which will be an equilibrium position for itself. The combined efforts of all the individual units, each seeking its own equilibrium, will determine the equilibrium positions of aggregate economic magnitudes (quantities demanded and quantities supplied of each good, consumption, investment, income, etc.). But the aggregate cannot be in equilibrium unless the individual units are in equilibrium; for, if any unit is in disequilibrium, it will make adjustments, disequilibrating other units and changing the aggregate. An overall equilibruim can exist only if there is a position in which each of the separate units can have attained its equilibrium.

Those to whom these ideas are abundantly clear should skip the following few paragraphs which present a simple illustration of the concept of equilibrium.

Imagine a couple owning only one lamp by which both want to read while sitting in chairs fixed at points H and W in Figure 2–1. The equilibruim condition for each is that the lamp shall be within two feet of the chair.

FIGURE 2–1

Illustration of Equilibrium

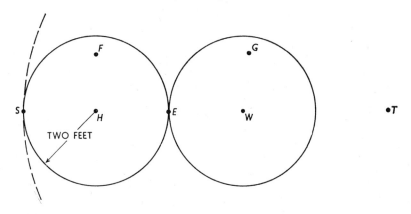

If the lamp is at F, in the husband's circle, he is in equilibrium while the wife is in disequilibrium. She could reach equilibrium by moving the lamp to G, which would disequilibrate her husband. Overall equilibrium can be reached only by putting the lamp at E.

In this example, a possible equilibrium position is assumed, but it need not be so. If the two circles did not intersect, then as long as the assumed conditions prevailed, no equilibrium would be possible.

Identifying the equilibrium position, E, is not the same thing as saying the lamp will move to E. With certain couples, it is conceivable that the lamp will fluctuate between F and G indefinitely. To reach equilibrium, the adjustment process must be subject to conditions which ensure that the adjustments will be in an equilibrating direction.

Furthermore, designating an equilibrium position such as E in no way implies that the lamp, having gotten to E, will remain there forever. E is an equilibrium position only as long as the conditions by which the equilibrium position was determined remain unchanged. Should they change, a new equilibrium may be determined. Thus suppose that the wife decides to stop reading and watch the television set at T, and her equilibrium condition becomes that the lamp be at least 10 feet from T. A circle of 10-foot radius centered on T touches the husband's circle at S, so that an overall equilibrium is possible at that point. Should the wife decide to watch the programs but read during the commercials, the lamp could alternate between E and S yet always be in equilibrium (assuming instantaneous adjustment).

Statics and Dynamics

The terms "statics" and "dynamics" refer to two different *methods of analysis*. Each has its appropriate applications, and a clear understanding of the difference between the two will prevent a certain amount of confusion as the theory unfolds.

Statics is a method which assumes that all the forces operating on the dependent variable act simultaneously and determine the position of the dependent variable in that same moment of time. Another way of putting this is that all of the relevant variables in the analysis relate to the same time period.

Dynamic analysis does not make that assumption; the relevant variables may relate to different time periods. Rather than occurring at a single moment of time, the process of determining the position of the dependent variable is seen as taking place over a span of time or a series of time periods, a process in which things that happen in one time period are related to things that pertain to other time periods.

Perhaps our disequilibrated lamp can throw some light on the distinction between statics and dynamics. If we imagine that the couple are on speaking terms, that each announces his equilibrium requirement, that they observe the equilibrium solution, E, and put the lamp there, we have used static analysis.

If, on the other hand, we assume that they are not speaking, then we may anticipate a process, pictured in Figure 2–2, in which the lamp being at F, the wife moves it to G, causing the husband to move it to J, leading the wife to put it at K, resulting in the husband's moving it to E, where it comes to rest. This process would be anticipated if the position of the lamp in each period bore some specified relation to its position in the previous period. In other words, the behavior of the lamp has been predicted by a form of dynamic analysis.

Which analysis is more suitable to the problem? In this case, both

FIGURE 2–2

Dynamic Path to Equilibrium

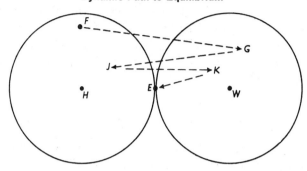

static and dynamic analysis indicate the same equilibrium. The path to equilibrium, it is true, is different in the two models; and, if the path is of interest to the analyst, he will want to choose the model that will more exactly describe its actual path, i.e., the dynamic model. But if the path is of no direct concern and the equilibrium position is the only part of the solution desired, then the appropriate technique, where both lead to the same equilibrium, is the one which is simpler, i.e., statics.

Where static and dynamic analysis indicate *different* outcomes, it obviously matters a great deal more which method is applied. In our lamp example, a change in the assumptions about the behavior of the participants can produce a model in which the lamp, starting at *K*, then moves successively to *J*, *G*, *F*, and so on, in a disequilibrating direction, culminating in divorce. The static model continues to show an equilibrium position, but the dynamic model is now explosive. In such cases, dynamic analysis is the correct technique.

There is nothing inherently superior or inferior in either statics or dynamics; it is entirely a matter of choosing the proper technique for the problem at hand. The exposition of income analysis can go a long way on purely static assumptions. But at certain points dynamic analysis becomes appropriate. Those points are:

1. Where "lags" become important, i.e., where the effects of an occurrence in one period are spread over one or more future periods.
2. Where "expectations," in which present actions are influenced by data pertaining to some future period, are important.
3. In "growth" situations, where future magnitudes depend on present actions.

Ex Ante and *Ex Post*

These terms refer to two different ways of defining any economic quantity such as demand, supply, saving, or investment.

Let us start with an example. A store advertises that tomorrow at 9 A.M. 100 refrigerators will go on sale at $25 each. The next day at 10 A.M., when the combatants have been dispersed and order restored, it is found that 100 refrigerators have been sold. Did supply equal demand?

In one sense we can say that supply and demand were equated: 100 refrigerators were supplied; 100 were bought.

But to the many would-be buyers who were turned away unsatisfied, supply and demand do not appear to have been equated. The buyers demanded many more than were supplied.

These disparate points of view arise from the use of different definitions of demand and supply. In the case where we say demand and supply were equated, we are using an *"ex post"* definition. That is, we are looking at the amounts that were actually supplied and actually bought. *Ex post* amounts are frequently referred to by such terms as "actual" or "realized" magnitudes.

When we say the demand for refrigerators exceeded the supply, we are using those words in the *"ex ante"* sense. We are speaking not of what actually happened, but of what the participants *intended* or *desired* to do. At a price of $25, the buyers intended to buy more than the seller intended to supply. "Intended" can be used as a synonym for *ex ante*.

Ex ante demand is the amount which, given the determinants of buyers' behavior, will be an equilibrium quantity for the buyers. A corresponding statement can be made for *ex ante* supply, saving, etc. The things individuals "intend" to do and their efforts to "reach equilibrium" are really one and the same, so that *ex ante* demand is the quantity that will equilibrate buyers, and *ex ante* supply is the quantity that will equilibrate sellers.

Certain things such as demand and supply must, in the *ex post* sense, be equal. The quantity bought must equal the quantity sold; they are, in fact, just two ways of looking at the same transaction.

But these same things need not be equal in the *ex ante* sense. Intended demand and intended supply can be unequal and remain so unless some variable (e.g., price) is adjusted to bring them into equality.

Chapter 3 ┊ AN ECONOMIC SKELETON

Studying an economy, like studying a living body, requires the systematic investigation of a large number of separate parts. If one first has some idea, however crude, of how the parts fit together and what functions each performs in the assembled product, it then becomes a good deal easier to learn about the individual parts. For that reason, just as medical schools use skeletons, economics uses highly simplified "models" of the economic system at the introductory stage of income analysis. Like skeletons, these models are valuable aids to learning. Like skeletons, their value arises from the simplification and elimination of detail which permits selected components to be exposed. And, like skeletons, they should not be mistaken for, nor repudiated for not being, the real thing.

Equilibrium Income

The core of income analysis is the question of what determines movements in the level of aggregate income. The basic model, therefore, is one which shows how the equilibrium level of income is determined and which tells something about the movement of income toward the equilibrium.

We have seen that one requirement for overall equilibrium is that the individual decision-making units shall have achieved equilibrium. In income analysis we are dealing with two groups of decision-making units. One is the consuming sector, which has two choices with respect to current income: to consume it or to save it. The other group is the producing sector, which decides how much of the current product to acquire on capital account, i.e., it chooses the amount of investment. A necessary condition for equilibrium, therefore, is that savers reach equilibrium by actually saving the amount they intend to and producers reach equilibrium by investing the amount they intend to. This equilibrium condition can be summarized:

Intended saving = Actual saving
Intended investment = Actual investment.

A glance back at the discussion of national income accounting reminds us that actual saving must always equal actual investment. By definition, saving is the part of current product not consumed, and investment is the part of current product not consumed. *Ex post*, saving and investment are names that reflect two different ways of looking at the same portion of current product. We have, then, by definition:

Actual saving = Actual investment.

Ex ante, saving and investment are not necessarily equal, that is, the amount that savers *intend* to save need not equal the amount that investors *intend* to invest. But, in *equilibrium*, where intended saving equals actual saving and intended investment equals actual investment, it must follow from the identity of actual saving and actual investment that:

Intended saving = Intended investment.

It is not difficult to see that both savers and investors cannot be in equilibrium unless intended saving equals intended investment. Suppose that national product is 100, that consumers intend to consume 80 and save 20, and that intended investment is 10. Two possible outcomes of this state of affairs are these:

(1)
Intended saving = Actual saving
National product 100
Consumption 80
Saving 20
Investment 20

(2)
Intended investment = Actual investment
National product 100
Investment 10
Consumption 90
Saving 10

In the first alternative, the consuming sector is in equilibrium, having fulfilled its intentions. But the investing sector must be in disequilibrium. It intended to invest only 10 but actual investment has been 20. What has happened is this: producers turned out 100 of product but only 90 was demanded, 80 by consumers and 10 by investors. The remaining 10 was left with the producers and became part of inventories. They had not, however, intended to invest that amount in inventories. The total investment of 20, therefore, consists of intended investment of 10 and unintended investment (in inventories) of 10.

In the second alternative, the investors are in equilibrium, having actually invested what they intended. But the consumers are then in disequilibrium since they must have acquired 90 of consumer goods and saved only 10. Unintended consumption may occur during the interval between a fall of income and the time when consumers have completed adjusting their consumption to the level intended at the lower income.

A necessary condition for overall equilibrium is, therefore, that intended saving equal intended investment.

Saving decisions and investment decisions are, by and large, made independently by two separate groups of individuals. Why should it happen, except by chance, that these two groups should intend to save and invest the same amount? The answer is that the economy must contain some mechanism which equates the two if equilibrium is to be reached. In the simple model which we are about to construct, it is the level of income which acts as the sole adjusting mechanism that brings intended saving and investment into equality. The *equilibrium level of income* is the level that equates intended saving and intended investment.

Hereafter, all statements about saving, consumption, and investment will refer to intended magnitudes unless otherwise specified.

Saving, Consumption, and Income

Three kinds of saving have been defined—personal, government, and business saving. The amount each of these sectors intends to save is influenced by a number of variables, of which income is one. Initially, we will assume that the variables other than income all remain unchanged so that we may isolate the relation of saving to income. For the time being, we will make the further simplifying assumption that government and business saving are not affected by income. This leaves only personal saving to consider.

Households, after the deduction of personal income taxes from personal income, have their disposable income to allocate between consumption and saving. Since disposable income can only be consumed or saved, whatever is said about the relation between personal consumption and disposable income also says something specific about the relation between personal saving and disposable income.

Two hypotheses about the relation between personal consumption and disposable income will be employed in this model. One is that intended personal consumption is a positive function of disposable income, which means that it increases when disposable income increases and falls when disposable income falls. The second hypothesis is that the change in intended personal consumption will be less than the change in disposable income which causes it. Both of these propositions are sufficiently reasonable that there should be no difficulty about accepting them provisionally until the empirical evidence that supports them can be introduced at a later point.

The Consumption Function

The way in which consumption depends on disposable income is called the "consumption function." Such a function is illustrated in Figure 3–1 by the line CC'. Our first hypothesis, that consumption is a positive function of disposable income, is shown by the upward slope of line CC'. Thus, an increase of income from Y_1 to Y_2 will raise consumption from gY_1 to iY_2.

FIGURE 3–1

The Consumption Function

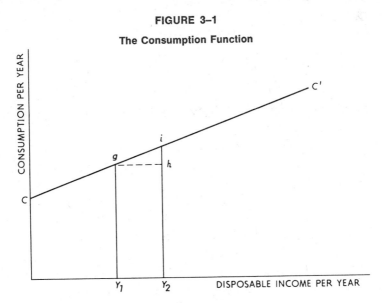

Our second hypothesis, that the change of consumption will be less than the change of disposable income, is shown by the degree of slope of CC'. The increase of the disposable income gh $(= Y_1Y_2)$ raises consumption by an amount ih. The ratio of the change of consumption to the change of disposable income is then ih/gh. The hypothesis states that ih/gh will be smaller than one. But ih/gh is also a measure of the slope of the consumption function in the segment between g and i. So the hypothesis is incorporated by drawing the consumption function with a slope smaller than one at all points.

The Marginal Propensity to Consume

The slope of the consumption function has been given a name— the *marginal propensity to consume*. In symbols, where Y stands for disposable income, C for consumption, and $\triangle$ attached to any item indicates the amount of *change* of that item,

$$\text{Marginal propensity to consume} = \frac{\triangle C}{\triangle Y}$$

In Figure 3–1, CC' is a straight line or a line of constant slope. In other words, it is drawn on the assumption that the marginal propensity to consume is the same at all levels of disposable income.

The Average Propensity to Consume

The ratio of consumption to disposable income is called the average propensity to consume. Using the symbols just defined,

$$\text{Average propensity to consume} = \frac{C}{Y}$$

The difference between the marginal and the average propensity to consume should be kept clearly in mind. The marginal propensity measures the *change* in consumption that a *change* in disposable income will produce. The average propensity measures the proportion of disposable income that is consumed.

The geometric measurement of the average propensity to consume is shown in Figure 3–2. Choose any level of income such as OY_1. Consumption at that level of income will be aY_1. The average propensity to consume, already defined as C/Y, is equal to aY_1/OY_1, a ratio which is measured by the slope of the line Oa. The slope of a line from the point O to a point on the consumption function will

FIGURE 3–2

Average Propensity to Consume

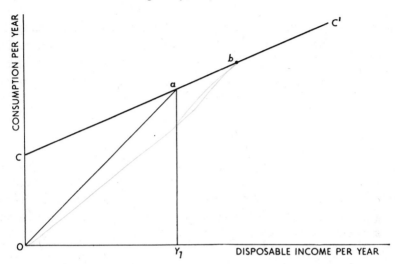

measure the average propensity to consume at that point of the consumption function. A line connecting O and b would have a smaller slope than Oa, indicating that the average propensity to consume is lower at b than at a. In fact, we note that from zero disposable income, where C/Y equals infinity, the average propensity to consume declines constantly as income increases.

The Saving Function

Once the personal consumption function is drawn, the personal saving function can be automatically derived. Subtracting consumption from disposable income at each level of disposable income gives saving as a function of disposable income (Figure 3–3).

The slope of the saving function measures the marginal propensity to save. The average propensity to save can be measured by the same method as was used for the average propensity to consume —by the slope of a line from O to the saving function.

Saving and Consumption Related to Gross National Product

Relating saving and consumption to disposable income is only an introductory step. The income, the equilibrium position of which we are investigating, is not disposable income but some measure of total

FIGURE 3–3

Consumption and Saving Functions

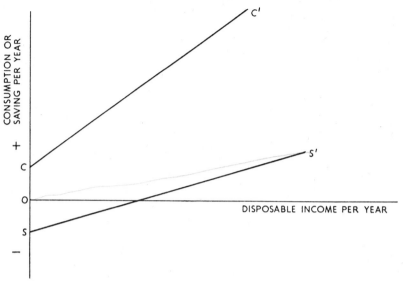

national output such as gross national product. Saving and consumption must then be related to gross national product. If the relationship between consumption and disposable income is known and if there is some given relationship between disposable income and gross national product, it is a simple mechanical operation to relate consumption to gross national product.

For the purposes of this first income model it was assumed that gross business saving, government receipts (taxes), and transfer payments are not affected by the level of income and remain constant. Since

> gross national product − disposable income = gross business
> saving + tax receipts − government transfer payments

we have, in effect, assumed that the difference between gross national product and disposable income is some constant amount.

To illustrate, assume that gross national product is 50 greater than disposable income at all levels. Then the conversion from consumption as a function of disposable income to consumption as a function of gross national product is shown in Figure 3–4. On the horizontal axis of Figure 3–4*a* the level of GNP that corresponds to each level of disposable income is given in parentheses. The con-

FIGURE 3–4

Consumption-GNP Function

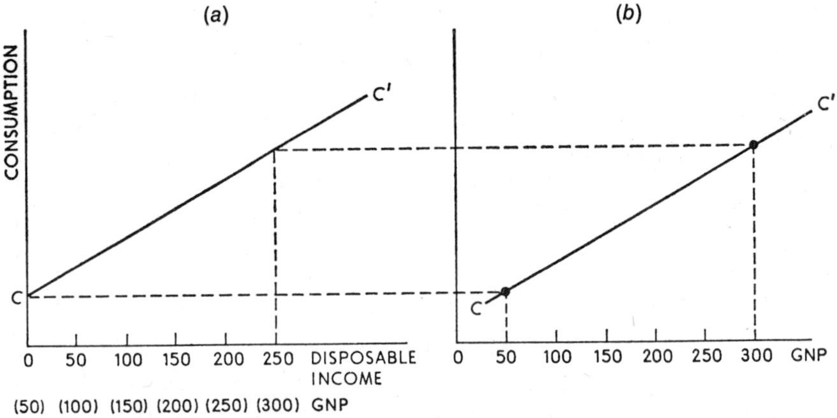

sumption function is then transferred to Figure 3–4b by entering the level of consumption that goes with each level of gross national product. The slope of the consumption function is not changed, because the gap between GNP and disposable income has been assumed to be constant.

The Total Saving Function

Personal saving as a function of gross national product can be arrived at by the same procedure that was applied to the consumption function. If to personal saving are added gross business saving and government saving, both of which have been assumed constant, *total saving* as a function of gross national product will emerge. Taking the personal saving function which can be derived from Figure 3–4 and adding assumed values for gross business saving and government saving, say 20 and −2 respectively, we obtain the total saving function in Figure 3–5. The slope of the total saving function remains the same as that of the personal saving function, on the assumption that business saving and government saving are constant.

Investment

The level of intended investment is determined by a number of variables, of which income is one. Unlike consumption, however, no

FIGURE 3–5

Personal and Total Saving Functions

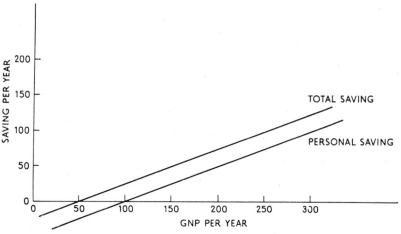

simple relationship between investment and income may reasonably be assumed. One could, of course, assume that investment is a positive function of income and draw an investment function rising with the level of income; but as a description of reality, if that is the objective, such a function is at least as far off the mark as the much simpler assumption that investment is independent of income. This simpler assumption, that investment is not affected by the level of income, will therefore be adopted until at a more advanced stage the influence of income and other variables on investment can be more fully discussed.

Equilibrium Income Determination

When the saving and investment functions are combined, as in Figure 3–6, an equilibrium level of income is determined.

The income level, Y, that equates intended saving and intended investment is, by definition, the equilibrium income. The equilibrium position having been determined, the question then arises: Will income move toward the equilibrium position? A mechanism which moves income toward equilibrium is supplied by the behavior of the individual units in the economy. If, for example, gross national product in Figure 3–6 were greater than Y, producers would have to be investing more than they intended or consumers would

FIGURE 3–6

Determination of Equilibrium Income

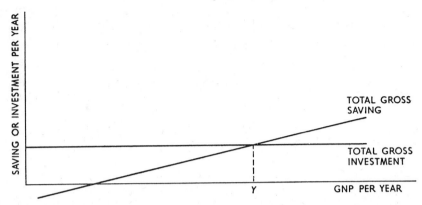

have to be saving less than they intended. Producers will attempt to eliminate unintended investment (which is in the form of accumulated inventories) by reducing production below sales so as to dispose of some of their inventory. Consumers will reduce consumption so as to get their saving up to the intended level. The effect of producer and consumer efforts to reach equilibrium will be to lower income toward the equilibrium level.

The reverse process would hold if income were below the equilibrium level. At a subequilibrium level of income, intended investment exceeds intended saving, which means that the amount of product demanded for investment exceeds the amount of product which would be available for investment if consumer demand were satisfied. Either investors or consumers or both must obtain less than they intend. The unsatisfied demand of buyers causes producers to want to produce more and exerts upward pressure on output until the equilibrium position is reached.

This same equilibrium can be described by an alternative diagram which will prove useful. First, the equilibrium condition, saving equals investment, can be restated in different terms. Saving is gross national product which is not consumed. Thus

saving = gross national product − (personal consumption + government expenditures on goods and services).

In equilibrium, where saving equals investment, then

investment = gross national product − (personal consumption + government expenditures on goods and services).

This can be written

> personal consumption + government expenditures on goods and services + investment = gross national product.

In other words, when saving equals investment, total demand for product (personal consumption plus government expenditure on goods and services plus investment) is equal to total product. *Total demand equals total product* can be substituted for saving equals investment as the equilibrium condition.

Diagrammatically, total demand as a function of income is shown by adding to the consumption function the constant amount of government expenditure and investment that have been assumed (Figure 3–7). The equilibrium income can be observed more easily if a

FIGURE 3–7

Aggregate Demand and Equilibrium Income

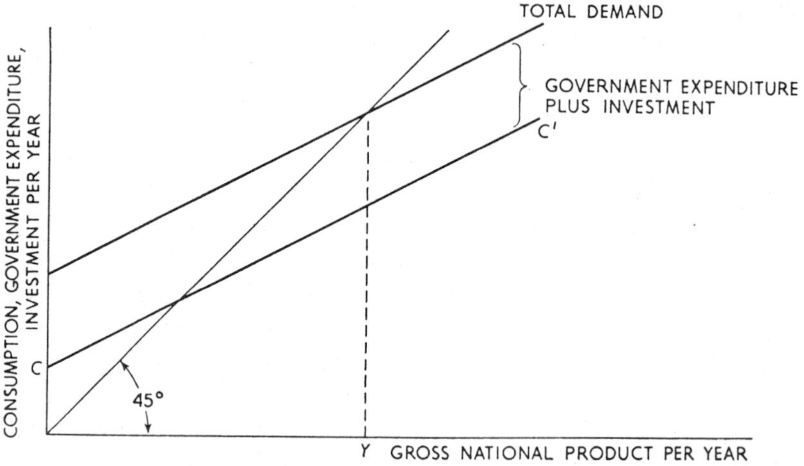

"visual aid" is drawn in, in the form of a line made up of all points at which the distance to the horizontal axis (total product) is equal to the distance to the vertical axis (total demand). If the scale on both axes is the same, such a line will make an angle of 45 degrees with either axis. The equilibrium level of gross national product is then indicated by the intersection of the total demand function and the 45-degree line, since only at that gross national product are total demand and gross national product equal.

Induced and Autonomous Changes in Demand

The things that affect consumer, government, and investment demand have been divided into (1) income and (2) all other variables. It becomes convenient to have terms which distinguish between demand changes which are due to income variation and those arising from other causes.

An increase or decrease of demand brought about by a movement of the income level will be called an *induced* change. Diagrammatically, induced changes are shown by a movement *along* a function. In the model we have developed, the only induced change that occurs is in consumption, shown by a movement along the consumption function. It was assumed that there were no induced changes in investment or government expenditures.

A change in demand for any reason other than income variation will be referred to as an *autonomous* change. Such changes are shown in a diagram by a *shift* of a function. Consumption, government expenditure, or investment may each change autonomously.

Autonomous Changes in Demand and Equilibrium Income

It is clear from Figure 3–7 that a shift of the total demand function will change the equilibrium position of income. In fact, the *only* way the equilibrium income can be changed is by a shift of the total demand function. That shift can be brought about by an autonomous change in consumption or government expenditure or investment, or some combination of the three.

In Figure 3–8, the total demand function, $D_1D'_1$ has been raised to the position $D_2D'_2$. The consumption function has not shifted, so the autonomous increase in demand (A) has been in government expenditure or investment. The equilibrium income is raised from Y_1 to Y_2.

If income increases from Y_1 to Y_2, consumption will be induced upward by an amount c. The total additional income, $\triangle Y$, will consist of the autonomously added expenditure, A, plus the induced increment of consumption, c.

The Multiplier

In Figure 3–8 we note that an autonomous increase in demand, A, causes an increase of income which is greater than A. The num-

FIGURE 3–8

Autonomous Changes in Demand and Equilibrium Income

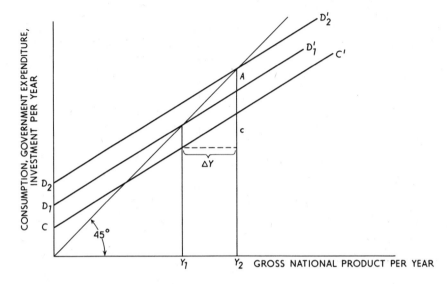

ber of times by which the change of income is greater than A is called "the multiplier." In symbols the multiplier is expressed:

$$\frac{\triangle Y}{A}$$

In the simple model represented by Figure 3–8

$$\triangle Y = A + c$$

The induced change in consumption, c, is equal to the marginal propensity to consume times the change of income. Letting b stand for the marginal propensity to consume, we have

$$c = b\triangle Y$$

which when substituted into the previous equation gives

$$\triangle Y = A + b\triangle Y$$

or

$$\frac{\triangle Y}{A} = \frac{1}{1-b} = \text{the multiplier.}$$

Since the marginal propensity to consume and the marginal propensity to save must add up to 1, $1 - b$ is equal to the marginal propensity to save. The multiplier, $1/(1 - b)$, can be written $1/s$, where s is the marginal propensity to save.

An alternative method of explaining the multiplier may be helpful. When an autonomous increase of demand occurs, investment will initially exceed saving by the amount of the autonomous increase. Whether the autonomous increase is in investment demand or whether it is an increase in consumer or government demand which reduces intended saving by a corresponding amount, the excess of investment over saving is equal to the autonomous addition to demand. On the assumptions of the simple model, income can reach equilibrium by rising until it has induced saving upward to equality with the level of investment. If income rose only by the amount of the autonomous increase of demand, saving would rise only by a fraction of the autonomous increase, whereas, to reach equilibrium, saving must rise by exactly the amount of the autonomous change. Hence the increase of income must be some multiple of the autonomous change.

Thus, in equilibrium,

$$\triangle S = A$$

and, by assumption,

$$\triangle S = s \triangle Y$$

Therefore,

$$s \triangle Y = A$$

and the multiplier

$$\left(\frac{\triangle Y}{A}\right) = \frac{1}{s}$$

Autonomous Changes in Tax Receipts and Government Transfer Payments

Autonomous changes in tax receipts or government transfer payments differ from the previously discussed autonomous changes in that they are not, in themselves, changes in demand, but they will lead to changes in demand. The analysis then proceeds from the change of tax receipts or transfer payments to the resulting change of demand to the change in the equilibrium income.

Assume that tax rates are lowered so that tax receipts are reduced by 10. That means that at any level of gross national product, disposable income will be 10 greater than before. The reduction of tax receipts has raised consumption as a function of gross national product, though consumption as a function of disposable income is unchanged. Figure 3–9 will serve to bring out the mechanics of this shift more clearly.

FIGURE 3–9

Tax Changes and Consumption Function

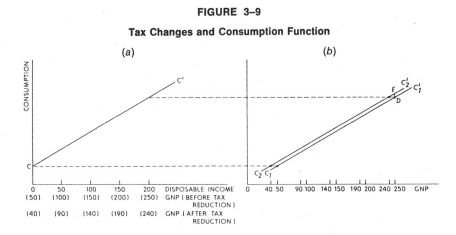

Because of the reduction of the difference between disposable income and gross national product by 10, the consumption function in Figure 3–9b is moved from $C_1C'_1$ to $C_2C'_2$. Measured horizontally, the consumption function has shifted leftward by 10. Measured vertically, the consumption function has shifted upward by a fraction of 10. The proportion which the vertical distance DE is to 10 can readily be seen to be the slope of CC', i.e., the marginal propensity to consume.

To summarize, a reduction of tax receipts of 10 raises disposable income, at every level of gross national product, by 10 and therefore raises consumption at every level of gross national product by the marginal propensity to consume times 10.

An important assumption underlying this analysis needs to be made more explicit. When it is said that the change in tax receipts does not change consumption as a function of disposable income (Figure 3–9a), it is being implicitly assumed that the tax change does not so alter the distribution of income as to shift the consumption function. Another way to put this is that it is being assumed that the marginal propensity to consume that applies to the increment to disposable income resulting from the tax change is the same as the marginal propensity to consume that applies to variations of disposable income in general.

The multiplier effects of the tax change can be analyzed in the same way as previously. The reduction in tax receipts raises consumption autonomously by some amount, $\triangle C$. Then the increase in income, $\triangle Y$, is given by

$$\triangle Y = \triangle C \frac{1}{1 - b}$$

The multiplier principle gives the appearance of being different in the case of taxes, however, if we want to relate $\triangle Y$ to the change in tax receipts, $\triangle T$. In the preceding analysis the autonomous increase in consumption was found to be equal to the marginal propensity to consume times the tax decrease. Letting b_t stand for the marginal propensity to consume that applies to the tax cut, we have

$$\triangle C = -b_t \triangle T$$

Substituting in the previous equation,

$$\triangle Y = -b_t \triangle T \left(\frac{1}{1 - b} \right) = -\triangle T \left(\frac{b_t}{1 - b} \right)$$

Ordinarily, it is assumed that b_t is less than one. The multiplier that applies to the change in tax receipts is thus smaller than the expenditure multiplier by the fraction, b_t. $\triangle T$ affects income indirectly through causing a change of demand. But the change of demand that it causes is a fraction of $\triangle T$. Hence $\triangle T$ has a smaller multiplier effect than an equal-sized direct change of demand.

This analysis holds true also for autonomous changes in government transfer payments, since transfer payments, at least in their effect on demand, can be viewed as taxes with the algebraic sign reversed.

The "Balanced-Budget" Multiplier

If the multiplier applicable to an increase in government purchases is larger than the multiplier applicable to an increase in tax receipts, it follows that the net effect of an identical increase in both government purchases and tax receipts will be to raise the equilibrium level of income. The expansionary effect of the increase of government purchases exceeds the contractionary effect of the increase of tax receipts, and the net result is an expansion of income. This outcome holds provided b_t is less than one.

To illustrate, assume b is 0.8 and b_t is 0.7, and government purchases and tax receipts are each increased by 10. The multiplier applicable to the increase of government expenditures is $1/(1 - b)$, which is 5. Therefore, the increase of government expenditures alone raises the equilibrium income by 50. The multiplier applicable to the increase of tax receipts is $-b_t/(1 - b)$, which is -3.5. The increase of tax receipts of 10 reduces the equilibrium income by 35. The net effect of both changes is $50 - 35$ or an increase of equilibrium income of 15.

A shorter route to the solution is to subtract the tax multiplier from the expenditure multiplier to obtain the net, or balanced-budget, multiplier. Thus, $1/(1 - b) - b_t/(1 - b) = 5.0 - 3.5 = 1.5$. An increase of government purchases and tax receipts by 10 each, raises equilibrium income by 10×1.5 or 15.

More Complex Multipliers

The simple multiplier, $1/(1 - b)$, is based on the assumption that the only induced change in the system is in personal consumption (and its Siamese twin, personal saving). Actually, we can expect economies to have certain other induced variables, which, when introduced, will change the size of the multiplier.

Tax receipts from both indirect and income taxes will rise as income rises and fall as income falls. Certain government transfer payments, such as unemployment compensation, will increase as income falls (and fall as income rises). Gross business saving will ordinarily rise and fall with income because corporations tend to adjust dividends up or down by less than the increase or decrease of corporate profits. Net foreign investment will vary inversely with income because imports will be induced upward or downward by the rise or fall of income. (Note, however, that this effect also depends on what happens to exports. If an induced fall of imports causes foreign economies to contract, their imports, which are our exports, will also be induced downward. Exports will not fall so much as imports, so that net foreign investment is still increased but by less than if exports had been constant. There is the further possibility that the balance-of-payments problem of foreign countries will "induce" them to put restrictions on our exports, lowering them by as much as the fall of our imports, and leaving net foreign investment unchanged.)

To obtain the multiplier when these additional induced changes are permitted, we use the same procedure by which we arrived at the simple multiplier. Some autonomous increase in demand, A, raises the equilibrium level of income by an amount $\triangle Y$. $\triangle Y$ will be made up of A plus the induced increase in consumption ($\triangle C$) plus the induced change in investment ($\triangle I$). Thus,

$$\triangle Y = A + \triangle C + \triangle I$$

$\triangle C$ is equal to the marginal propensity to consume (b) times the change in disposable income ($\triangle Y_d$). But, because of the induced changes in taxes, transfer payments, and business saving, $\triangle Y_d$ is less than $\triangle Y$. Disposable income will not rise so much as gross national product because of the induced rise of taxes, the induced fall of transfer payments, and the induced rise of business saving.

Let t stand for the fraction of additional income which will go into taxes ($= \triangle T/\triangle Y$), and p for the proportion of reduction in government transfers to increase of income ($= -\triangle$ transfers$/\triangle Y$), and z for the fraction of additional income that will go into business saving ($= \triangle$ business saving$/\triangle Y$). Then,

$$\triangle Y_d = \triangle Y - t\triangle Y - p\triangle Y - z\triangle Y = \triangle Y \, (1 - t - p - z)$$

and

$$\triangle C = b\triangle Y_d = b\triangle Y \, (1 - t - p - z)$$

Next, consider $\triangle I$. It is still assumed that there are no induced changes in investment in producers' durables or inventories. But net foreign investment will fall as income rises. Assuming exports unchanged, net foreign investment will fall by the amount of the induced rise of imports.

Let m stand for the ratio of induced imports to change in income (the marginal propensity to import). Then

$$\triangle I = -m\triangle Y$$

Returning to our original equation for the change of income ($Y = A + \triangle C + \triangle I$) and substituting for $\triangle C$ and $\triangle I$, we have

$$\triangle Y = A + b\triangle Y \, (1 - t - p - z) - m\triangle Y$$

Transposing terms and factoring out $\triangle Y$:

$$\triangle Y \, [1 - b \, (1 - t - p - z) + m] = A$$

Dividing by $\triangle Y$ and taking the reciprocals we have

$$\frac{1}{1 - b \, (1 - t - p - z) + m} = \frac{\triangle Y}{A}$$

which is the ratio of the change in income to the autonomous change in demand, or the multiplier.

To illustrate the effects of these induced changes, we can assume for the unknowns in the multiplier formula some conceivable values $(b, 0.8; t, 0.1; p, 0.05; z, 0.05; m, 0.1)$.

With these figures the simple multiplier, $1/(1-b)$, is equal to 5. The multiplier with all the additional induced variables becomes

$$\frac{1}{1 - 0.8\,(1 - 0.1 - 0.05 - 0.05) + 0.1} = \frac{1}{0.46} = 2.17$$

The introduction of the additional induced changes has made the multiplier smaller.

Diagrammatically, the effects of these induced changes are shown in Figures 3–10, 3–11, and 3–12. In Figure 3–10a, consumption as

FIGURE 3–10

Consumption-GNP Function

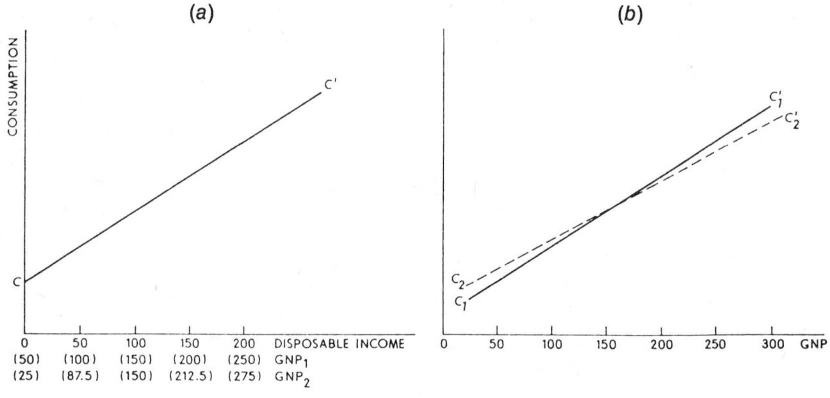

a function of disposable income is seen again. On the horizontal axis the row of figures labeled GNP_1 gives the gross national product corresponding to each level of disposable income, when personal consumption is the only induced variable. The figures are repeated from Figure 3–4a. The row of figures labeled GNP_2 shows gross national product at each level of disposable income, when all of the induced changes discussed above are introduced. GNP_2 was calculated in this example by arbitrarily choosing as a starting point the relationship: gross national product equals 150 when disposable income is 100. Then gross national product at each level of disposable income was computed in both directions from that point. We previously defined the relationship:

$$\triangle Y_d = \triangle Y \, (1 - t - p - z)$$

which, with our assumed values for t, p and z, gives

$$\triangle Y_d = 0.8 \triangle Y$$

or

$$\triangle Y = \frac{\triangle Y_d}{0.8}$$

Each change of disposable income ($\triangle Y_d$) of 50 will correspond to a change of gross national product ($\triangle Y$) of 50/0.8 or 62.5. If, when disposable income is 100, gross national product is 150, then when disposable income is 150, gross national product will be 150 + 62.5 or 212.5 and so on.

When the consumption function is transferred from Figure 3–10a to 3–10b, it is seen that consumption as a function of gross national product when the additional induced changes are included ($C_2C'_2$) has a smaller slope than the original consumption function ($C_1C'_1$). The marginal propensity to consume with respect to gross national product has been reduced.

In Figure 3–11, investment and government expenditure are

FIGURE 3–11

Aggregate Demand Functions

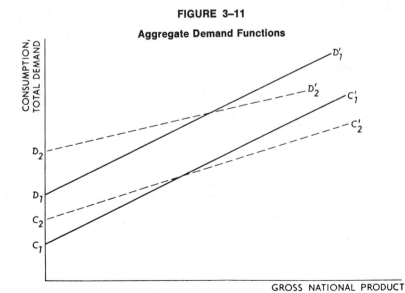

added to the consumption function to obtain the total demand function. The slope of the total demand function $(D_2D'_2)$, which was reduced by the flattening of the consumption function, is still further reduced by the induced change in net foreign investment.

The multipliers, with and without the extra induced variables, are compared in Figure 3–12. Assume an autonomous drop of de-

FIGURE 3–12

Comparison of Multiplier Effects

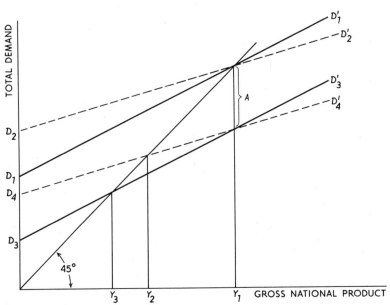

mand by an amount, A. If the total demand function originally is $D_1D'_1$, and falls to $D_3D'_3$, the equilibrium income decreases from Y_1 to Y_3. If the original demand function is $D_2D'_2$ and it falls to $D_4D'_4$, equilibrium income falls only to Y_2, indicating the smaller multiplier effect.

Instantaneous and Period Income Adjustments

The change in income produced by an autonomous change in demand has been analyzed by comparing the equilibrium income position "before" and "after." That analysis is not concerned with the path followed by income as it moves to the new equilibrium. Time is ignored and the adjustment of income is spoken of as if it occurred instantaneously with the autonomous change. This analytic method is "statics."

Recognition can be given to the fact that the movement of income, when disequilibrated, to a new equilibrium actually takes place over an interval of time by constructing a model employing "dynamic" analysis. The model presented next makes no claim to being an accurate description of the functioning of a real economy but is purely illustrative.

To simplify let us return to an earlier assumption that the only induced changes in the system are in personal consumption and personal saving. Time will be divided into a series of discrete periods. It will be assumed that there is a lag in consumer behavior such that the disposable income received in any period determines the level of consumption in the *next* period. No other lags are assumed. Production in each period adjusts to equal the demand in that period.

For purposes of a numerical illustration the marginal propensity to consume will be set at 0.8 and an initial autonomous increase of investment demand of 10 per period will be assumed. Table 3–1 shows the effects, in succeeding periods, of the autonomous change. Note that the figures represent, *not* the level of income, consump-

TABLE 3–1

A Period Income-Adjustment Model
(marginal propensity to consume = 0.8)

		Amount of Change from the Initial Position			
Period	Investment	Consumption	Intended Saving	Unintended Saving	Income
0	0	0	0	0	0
1	10	0	2.0	8.0	10.0
2	10	8.0	3.6	6.4	18.0
3	10	14.4	4.9	5.1	24.4
4	10	19.5	5.9	4.1	29.5
5	10	23.6	6.7	3.3	33.6
6	10	26.9	7.4	2.6	36.9
7	10	29.5	7.9	2.1	39.5
8	10	31.6	8.3	1.7	41.6
9	10	33.3	8.7	1.3	43.3
10	10	34.6	8.9	1.1	44.6
11	10	35.7	9.1	0.9	45.7
12	10	36.6	9.3	0.7	46.6
13	10	37.3	9.5	0.5	47.3
14	10	37.8	9.6	0.4	47.8
·	·	·	·	·	·
·	·	·	·	·	·
∞	10	40	10	0	50

tion, etc., in each period but the *change* from the original position in period 0. Thus, the series of 10's in the first column shows that in every period investment *per period* is 10 greater than it was in period 0.

The increase of investment in period 1 increases income in that period by 10. Consumption is not yet affected. In period 2, consumption rises by 8 (0.8 of the rise of income in period 1). Income in period 2 is thus up by 18 over period 0, 10 because of the increase of investment and 8 because of the increase of consumption. In period 3, the induced consumption has risen to 0.8 of 18 or 14.4, and income in period 3 is 24.4 above the level of income in period 0. As this process continues the increase in income is seen to converge on 50.[1]

Until income has risen by 50, the system cannot be in equilibrium since, before that point, consumers will be continuously in disequilibrium. In period 1, where income has increased by 10, consumers have not yet adjusted their consumption to the higher income level; they are consuming 8 less and saving 8 more than they intend to. In period 2 they adjust their consumption upward by 8 but, since income also rises by 8 more, they are still in disequilibrium, consuming 6.4 less and saving 6.4 more than they intend to.

In this model the equilibrium position arrived at by the period multiplier is the same as the one produced by the instantaneous multiplier. If it is the final outcome one is interested in, then it makes no difference, in this case, whether one uses static or dynamic analysis. However, we will eventually examine models in which it makes a considerable difference.

The Aggregate Supply Function and the Concept of Full Employment

Thus far, equilibrium income has been determined by the aggregate demand function. Nothing has been said explicitly about the

----

[1] It can be easily shown that, after an infinite number of periods, the increase of income will reach 50. A glance at Table 3–1 will show that income rises in successive periods by 10 plus 0.8 of 10 plus 0.8 of 0.8 of 10, etc. Thus

$$\triangle Y = 10 + (0.8)10 + (0.8)^2 10 \ldots (0.8)^n 10$$

or

$$\triangle Y = 10 [1 + 0.8 + (0.8)^2 + \ldots (0.8)^n]$$

The term in parentheses is a geometric progression, the sum of which when n is infinitely large, is equal to $1/(1-0.8)$ or 5. That the sum of $1 + 0.8 + (0.8)^2 + \ldots (0.8)^n$ approaches $1/(1-0.8)$ can be readily shown by multiplying the progression by $(1-0.8)/(1-0.8)$.

aggregate supply function. In place of the aggregate supply function, we have used the simple assumption that the economy will supply whatever quantity is demanded. Such an assumption is obviously unsatisfactory, since there is a limit to an economy's capacity to produce which will prevent it from supplying any amount demanded beyond that limit. The introduction of an aggregate supply function will provide the missing upper limit. It will also introduce the matter of the price level at which output is supplied, a variable which has so far been omitted from our analysis.

We will assume that capital and technology are fixed and the only variable input is labor. The supply function, therefore, will pertain to the short run. (In the long run, capital accumulation, growth of the labor force, and technological progress will shift the aggregate supply function to the right.)

The derivation of an aggregate supply function will be explained with the assistance of the four-quadrant diagram shown in Figure 3–13.

FIGURE 3–13

The Aggregate Supply Function

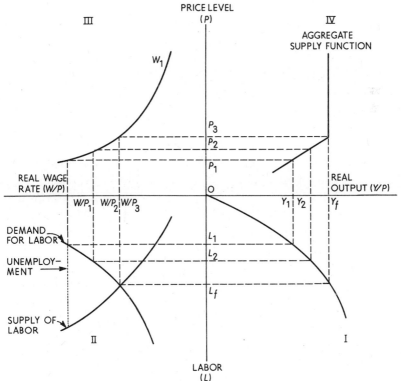

In quadrant IV will appear the supply function which is to be derived.

Quadrant I shows the short-run production function, or output as a function of labor input, with other inputs fixed. Real output is shown on the horizontal axis, labor input on the vertical axis, and the shape of the curve shows the marginal product of labor decreasing as labor input increases.

In quadrant II, with labor input on the vertical axis, and, on the horizontal axis the real wage rate (W/P, or the money wage rate W deflated by a price index P), we have a supply-of-labor function and a demand-for-labor function. The demand-for-labor function is drawn on the competitive assumption that employers will demand labor to the point where the marginal product of labor is equal to its real wage rate.

In quadrant III, the real wage rate is related to the price level. Assume that the wage rate is kept fixed at some particular wage rate, W_1. Then the real wage rate W_1/P is a function of the price level P. The curve labeled W_1 shows the real wage rate as a function of the price level on the assumption that the money wage rate remains at W_1.

Now we shall follow through the diagram sequentially. We begin in quadrant I with the economy producing output Y_1 which requires labor input L_1. We then find in quadrant II that with employment L_1 the marginal product of labor determines the real wage rate, W/P_1. In quadrant III we observe that the real wage rate W/P_1 requires the price level P_1. Finally, in quadrant IV, the association of P_1 with Y_1 gives us one point on the aggregate supply function.

We assume now an increase of aggregate demand so that output rises from Y_1 to Y_2. Tracing through sequentially, we see in quadrant I that employment rises to L_2, in quadrant II that the marginal product of labor and the real wage rate fall to W/P_2, and in quadrant III that the price level rises to P_2. P_2 and Y_2 in conjunction give us another point on the supply function in quadrant IV.

Further increases of output will be accompanied by further increases of employment and prices until employment L_f is reached. At that point, the demand for and supply of labor are equated, and the unemployment (shown by the vertical distance measuring the excess of labor supply over labor demand at each real wage rate) has disappeared. Any further increase of aggregate demand cannot increase employment and output. Y_f is, therefore, the full employment level of output.

The aggregate supply function in quadrant IV has been derived from the locus of points showing the price level which is associated with each level of real output.[2] At the full employment output Y_f, the supply function becomes vertical, indicating that the limit to increases of real output has been reached.

The term "full-employment output" has come to be used to mean the maximum potential output. In many economies the two actually are synonymous; but since there are also economies in which full employment of labor and maximum output are not the same thing, the terminology is somewhat unfortunate.

In the United States' economy the intensity with which the capital stock and land can be employed is limited by the quantity of labor available. In some countries, however, labor is so abundant relative to capital and land that it is the stock of the latter factors which limits the intensity with which labor can be employed. In such economies, unemployment or underemployment of labor can coexist with maximum output. For that reason it appears advisable to avoid the confusing implications of the expression "full employment" and to substitute the term "full potential."

Full-potential income or product will hereafter refer to the upper limit of national product when the supply of inputs and technical knowledge are given.

Equilibrium Income and Full-Potential Income

Full-potential income bears a dual relationship to equilibrium income. Full potential is both a goal of equilibrium and a restraint on it. To produce the largest output possible with the given factor supplies and knowledge is an obvious and generally accepted objective of an economy; and, by that criterion, an equilibrium income below full potential is an unsatisfactory condition.

On the other hand, if equilibrium income is greater than full potential, equilibrium is unattainable. That is, if equilibrium requires a level of income which is larger than the maximum possible, then it is impossible to reach an equilibrium position. The aggregate demand function represents demand in "real" terms as a function of "real" income. Prices may rise and increase income in money

---

[2] It should be kept in mind that this supply curve has been developed on the assumption that the money wage rate remains at W_1. At a later point, in Chapter 9, the supply function when the money wage rate is a variable will be discussed.

terms, but equilibrium requires the equality of real demand and real income.

These alternative positions are illustrated in Figure 3–14. Y_f is the assumed full-potential level of gross national product. $D_1D'_1$ and $D_2D'_2$ are two possible total demand functions. If the demand function is D_1D_1, then the equilibrium gross national product is

FIGURE 3–14

Inflationary and Deflationary Gaps

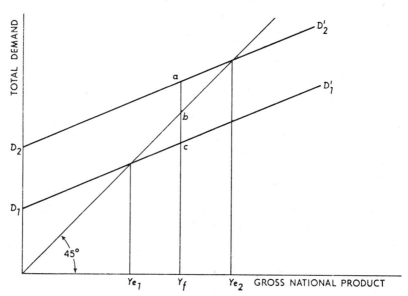

Y_{e1}, which lies below Y_f. Equilibrium can be brought up to full potential if the demand function is shifted upward by an amount bc; bc is often referred to as the "deflationary gap," or the amount of autonomous increase in total demand required to raise the equilibrium level of income to full potential.

If, however, the total demand function is $D_2D'_2$, then the equilibrium income, Y_{e2}, lies above Y_f. Since real gross national product cannot rise above Y_f, equilibrium cannot actually be attained. The system must continue in disequilibrium with either consumers, or investors, or both, consuming or investing less than intended, until the amount ab, which is the excess of demand over product at full potential, has been eliminated. Hence ab is often called the "inflationary gap."

There is, then, a fundamental asymmetry between equilibrium incomes below and above full potential. Equilibrium below full potential is attainable but undesirable. Equilibrium above full potential is desirable but unattainable.

QUESTIONS

1. If, last year, consumer expenditures were 200, total gross investment was 60, government purchases of goods and services were 40, and gross national product was 300, was gross national product at an equilibrium level? Explain your answer.
2. Assume: The marginal propensity to consume is 0.75; consumption will change by 0.75 of any change in tax receipts; except for consumption and saving, there are no induced changes in the system. If government purchases of goods and services and tax receipts are each increased by 10, what is the effect on the equilibrium level of income? Compare this outcome with the effect of increasing government purchases by 10 while tax receipts are left unchanged.
3. Assume: Consumption is equal to 10 plus 0.75 of disposable income; taxes plus gross business saving are equal to 0.3 of gross national product; investment is constant at 17.5 per year; government purchases of goods and services are constant at 20 per year; there are no transfer payments.
   a) What is the equilibrium level of gross national product?
   b) If investment increases autonomously by 5, what is the equilibrium level of gross national product?
   c) Diagram the aggregate demand function with the above assumptions. Draw in another aggregate demand function on the assumption that the sum of taxes and gross business saving is a constant 30 (not subject to induced change). Assume an autonomous increase in demand of 5 and compare the multiplier effects with the two demand functions.
4. What determines the elasticity of the aggregate supply function?
5. Show the effect on the aggregate supply function of an increase in the money wage rate.

PART II

The Determination of
Aggregate Demand

Chapter 4 | PERSONAL CONSUMPTION

The consumption function used in the income model in Chapter 3 is a highly simplified statement of the determination of consumer demand. A true understanding of consumer demand requires that we go much more deeply into consumer theory. We begin with a consideration of the consumption decisions of the individual household or consuming unit. We then aggregate the units to determine the total consumer demand of the economy.[1]

THE LIFETIME PLAN OF THE HOUSEHOLDER[2]

Our starting point is an idealized view of a householder's consumption plan. This model will then serve as a base for successive closer approaches to reality.

Imagine a householder who (a) begins his career with a given quantity of net worth (assets minus liabilities); (b) knows what his stream of earned income (nonproperty income) will be over his lifetime; (c) knows the utility his household will derive from consumption in all time periods; (d) knows the length of his lifetime; (e) wants to leave an estate of a given amount; (f) wants to distribute his total consumption among the time periods of his life in such a way as to maximize total utility.

With the information in items a through d the consumer can plan his lifetime consumption pattern so as to satisfy objectives e and f.

In the typical case, the householder's earned income will rise from the beginning of his earning years to the period at or near

---

[1] The approach to consumption theory that follows derives from F. Modigliani and R. Brumberg, "Utility Analysis and the Consumption Function: An Interpretation of Cross-Section Data," in K. K. Kurihara (ed.), *Post-Keynesian Economics* (New Brunswick, N.J.: Rutgers University Press, 1957).

[2] "Householder" will refer to the head of the household, who makes the consuming unit's decisions about consumption and saving.

retirement age and then fall off sharply after retirement. For the moment, assume that his utility function—the relation between his total utility and additions to his total consumption per period— remains the same in each period. Assume, also, that the rate of interest is zero. Total lifetime utility will then be maximized by consuming the same amount in each period, since the utility derived from the marginal unit of consumption will be the same in each period and total utility cannot be increased by consuming more in one period and less in another. The optimum annual consumption pattern of the household is arrived at by taking the initial net worth plus total lifetime income minus the estate to be left and dividing this total expendable amount equally over the number of years of life. If the householder's "needs" are expected to change over his lifetime—say, rising in his middle years and declining in his late years—the optimum consumption path is altered accordingly.

This picture of a consumer possessing perfect information about the future and pursuing a rational plan to maximize lifetime utility is obviously not completely realistic. However, complete realism of the assumptions is not a prerequisite for a useful theory. If the assumptions come close enough to reality to permit the theory to make good predictions of how consumers will behave, the theory is useful. In other words, if we determine what kind of consumer behavior is implied by our theory and then find that consumers do behave approximately that way, we can conclude that the assumptions are realistic enough for our purposes.

The remainder of this chapter examines the theory's implications about the variables that affect the consumption of the individual unit, the implications about the behavior of aggregate consumption, and the comparison of these implications with empirical observations.

VARIABLES AFFECTING CONSUMPTION OF THE HOUSEHOLD

1. Age of the Householder

The most obvious implication of the hypothesis of a lifetime consumption plan is that the average propensity to consume of a householder will be systematically related to his age. We would expect to find, as the typical pattern, the lowest propensity to consume in his middle years when his income is above his expected lifetime annual average and the highest in his late years when his income is below his average. In his late years we would expect to find that his average propensity to consume is greater than one, i.e., that he is dissaving. In the early years of the householder, his income is also likely to be below his expected average, with the result that his propensity to consume will be high, possibly greater than one. Dissaving in his early years may be restricted, however, by lack of assets and limited availability of credit. Data in the United States relating saving to the age of the householder bear out these expectations, showing on the average some dissaving before the age of twenty-five, net saving until the late sixties, and dissaving thereafter.[3]

2. Other Noneconomic Characteristics of Householders

The time-paths of the utility function can differ significantly among householders. Some may prefer higher levels of consumption in their middle years and sharply curtailed expenditures in their old age. Others may prefer a more even distribution.

The number of dependents in the family may be a factor in determining the time-path of its utility function: the larger the number of dependents, the more may saving be postponed until the number of dependents declines. The usual preconception is that the larger the number of dependents, the smaller the proportion of income saved, other things being equal. Surprisingly, the data do not support this notion. A recent investigation finds that there appears to be no significant difference in the propensity to consume between families without children and families with three or more children, other things being equal.[4] However, upon further thought we may feel that this finding is not so surprising after all. The number of children affects the family's mode of living, for example by substituting home activities for travel and entertainment, so that the difficulty of saving may not increase much as the size of the family increases. Moreover, the need to save is not reduced by having children (unless children are regarded as assets that will contribute to consumption in one's old age). An increase in the size of the

---

[3] See, for example, W. Eizenga, *Demographic Factors and Saving* (Amsterdam: North-Holland Publishing Co., 1961), pp. 76–81.

[4] See Harold W. Watts, "Long-Run Income Expectations and Consumer Saving," in T. F. Dernburg, Richard N. Rosett, and Harold W. Watts, *Studies in Household Economic Behavior* (New Haven, Conn.: Yale University Press, 1958), pp. 101–44.

family may actually increase the motivation to save by increasing the size of the estate which the householder wants to leave.

Householders will also differ in their capacity to foresee the future benefits of saving or in their ability to adhere to a rational saving program. In postulating that the typical householder approximates a consumption and saving pattern that maximizes his lifetime utility, we do not deny that because of irrationality, some householders will fail to a significant degree to attain the optimal saving path.

3. The Rate of Interest

The previous description of a lifetime consumption plan was simplified by assuming a zero rate of interest. We now consider the effect of introducing a positive rate of interest.

One consequence of a positive rate of interest is that the postponement of one dollar of consumption now will make possible the enjoyment of more than one dollar of consumption in the future. If the consumer has been aiming to equalize the marginal utility of consumption in each time period, introducing a rate of interest on his saving will cause him to reduce his consumption in the present, to the point where the marginal utility of present consumption equals the marginal utility that will be obtained in the future by consuming the savings plus the interest earned by the savings. This effect, known as the "substitution effect," will cause the consumer to save more (or dissave less) as the rate of interest rises, substituting future consumption for present consumption.

However, the interest rate also has an "income effect." For the householder who is currently saving, a rise of the interest rate will mean an increase in expected future incomes and therefore a rise of lifetime income. The rise of lifetime income will cause the householder to consume more of current income and to save less. For the householder who is currently dissaving, a rise of the rate of interest will reduce future expected incomes, reduce lifetime income, and reduce current dissaving. For the householder who is currently neither saving nor dissaving, there will be no income effect.

The combined result of the substitution and income effects when the rate of interest rises will then be: (1) for current dissavers, both the substitution and income effects will tend to reduce current consumption (reduce dissaving); (2) for householders consuming the whole of their current income, the substitution effect will tend to reduce consumption and the income effect will be nil; (3) for current savers, the two effects will work in opposite directions, the substitution effect tending to reduce consumption and the income effect tending to increase consumption, and the net effect may be either an increase or a decrease in current consumption.

Empirically it is difficult to detect any sign that changes in the rate of interest affect the proportion of current income consumed. Both the substitution and the income effects are evidently weak, and the rather small changes in interest rates that provide the material for our statistical tests are not sufficient to produce a measurable effect on the propensity to consume.

It is possible that rates of interest substantially higher than those which appear in empirical studies would produce a measurable effect on saving. One piece of evidence that hints at such an outcome is the higher propensity to save of entrepreneurs compared to nonentrepreneurs. The fact that entrepreneurs, putting their savings into their own enterprises, have a much higher prospective rate of return than the rate of interest received by nonentrepreneurs may explain the higher entrepreneurial propensity to save. The evidence is inconclusive, however, since it might also be explained by the hypothesis that entrepreneurship attracts people with personality characteristics which make for a high propensity to save, such as foresight, self-control, or a preference for making large current sacrifices in order to have a higher income in the future.

4. Uncertainty

Householders are uncertain, to varying degrees, about their lifetime income and their future needs. If a householder bases his consumption decisions on his most probable expectations, he runs some risk that he will save less than the optimum and some risk that he will save more than the optimum. If the penalties of exceeding or falling short of optimum savings are considered equal, the householder will obey the most probable expectation. But if, as seems plausible, the penalties of having saved too little are considered harsher than the penalties of having saved too much, the typical householder will add a precautionary margin to his current savings; and the greater the householder's uncertainty, the higher will be his propensity to save.

The higher propensity to save of entrepreneurs than of non-entrepreneurs may be evidence of the effect of uncertainty about income. The dispersion of income, and therefore the uncertainty about income, is considerably greater among entrepreneurs than among nonentrepreneurs.[5]

Uncertainty about the length of life also tends to increase saving by inhibiting dissaving during old age and adding to the amount of the estate left. This form of uncertainty can be avoided by putting one's assets into a pension or annuity plan; but to the extent that people prefer not to put all their assets into such plans, we can expect that uncertainty about the length of life will tend to raise lifetime saving.

5. Net Worth

The typical householder, by our hypothesis, plans to accumulate and then use up net worth according to some schedule determined by his expected lifetime income, his expected lifetime utility function, his intended estate, and the rate of interest. It follows that any *unplanned* change of the householder's net worth which may occur will affect his propensity to consume. An unplanned addition to net worth increases his potential lifetime consumption and tends to increase the proportion of his current income consumed; an unplanned fall of net worth tends to reduce the proportion of his current income consumed. Unanticipated inheritances or windfall gains or losses of assets are possible causes of unplanned changes of net worth.

One much-discussed cause of an unplanned change of net worth is an unanticipated change in the price level of consumer goods. A rise of the price level not matched by a corresponding rise in the price of assets will reduce the real value of net worth below the planned level and cause the householder to reduce his consumption. A fall of the price level will have the reverse effect.

6. Expectations about Prices

The expectation of a rise of the price level of consumer goods is commonly thought to lead to an increase in current consumer pur-

---

[5] Friedman points out that among entrepreneurs, farmers and nonfarmers have approximately the same dispersion of income, which suggests equal degrees of uncertainty. But the propensity to save tends to be higher among

chases. This effect, however, is not so certain as might at first appear.

To examine the effect of price expectations, we divide consumer expenditures into two categories: purchases to be actually consumed in the current period and purchases to be held in inventory for future consumption. (Technically the latter category belongs in investment theory, but there is no harm in dealing with it here.)

With regard to the former category, there is only one reason for current consumption to be affected by price expectations. An expected increase of the price level reduces the expected real rate of interest earned on assets or paid on debts. For example, if an asset yields 5 percent per year and the price level rises 2 percent per year, the rate of return to the asset-holder is actually 3 percent per year. If the rate of interest should rise by as much as the expected price increase—in the preceding example, if the yield of the asset rises to 7 percent—the expected real rate of interest would be unchanged and consumption would be unaffected. If the rate of interest does not rise by as much as the expected price increase, the expected real rate of interest will be reduced and consumption will increase, *provided that consumption tends to rise when the interest rate falls.* We have already noted the theoretical and empirical grounds for doubting that small reductions in the interest rate can cause a noticeable increase in consumption. However, if expectations of a big change in the price level can be shown to affect consumption, this relationship can be taken as evidence that similarly large changes in the interest rate would affect consumption.

The purchase of consumer goods for inventories in expectation of a price increase depends on whether the purchaser expects the gain to exceed the rate of interest he could earn on other assets. The expected speculative gain is the expected rate of price increase minus the costs of risk and of storage. Unless the expected rate of price increase exceeds the prevailing rate of interest, it will not lead to the purchase of inventories of consumer goods. (The popular attachment to the idea that expected price increases cause an increase in consumer expenditures is probably strengthened by the observation of increased purchases when a price increase is an-

nonfarm entrepreneurs than among farmers. This difference may be due to the higher prospective rate of return of nonfarm entrepreneurs. See M. Friedman, *A Theory of the Consumption Function* (National Bureau of Economic Research, General Series 63) (Princeton, N.J.: Princeton University Press, 1957), p. 78.

nounced to take effect in a short time. A price increase of 5 percent effective one week from today is equivalent to an *annual* rate of increase of 5 percent × 52 or 260 percent, a rate of return which may well stimulate buying. By contrast, an expected price increase of 5 percent *per year*, when compared to prevailing interest rates of about the same amount, will not increase consumer inventory holdings.)

On the whole we can reasonably conclude that expectations of price changes at moderate annual rates can be ignored as a determinant of consumer demand.[6]

7. Expectations about Income

One form of income expectation—the consumer's expectation of his lifetime income—has already been explicitly postulated as a major determinant of consumption. There remains to be considered the idea that current consumption may be affected by shorter term expectations, such as expectations about next year's income.

Whether this year's consumption will vary with an expected change in next year's income depends on whether the expected change has already been included in the householder's calculation of lifetime income. If the expected change of income has already been included, the householder's expected lifetime income will not be changed; and, according to the hypothesis that current consumption is geared to lifetime income, current consumption will not be changed. If the expected change of income next year exceeds the variation included in the lifetime calculation, current consumption will be affected, but only in proportion to the change in expected lifetime income. A change in the expected income of one year will ordinarily have a rather small effect on the income which a householder expects over his lifetime.

---

[6] A somewhat different case of expectation arises if prices are expected to be sticky upward or controlled, so that they do not rise freely to clear the market. Expectations then run in terms of "shortages" and of the replacement of price rationing by some other form of rationing. Since any nonprice system of rationing is inevitably more uncertain and inconvenient than price rationing, consumer inventory accumulation may occur to avoid the expected uncertainty and inconvenience. In a situation where no consumer inventory accumulation would occur if prices were free to rise—say when a 3 percent price rise per year is expected—it is possible nevertheless that such an accumulation will occur if prices are held down and consumers attach a high cost to the expected uncertainty and inconvenience. It follows that suppressed inflation can make demand more excessive than it would be under open inflation.

These considerations help to explain why information on householders' near-term expectations about income and general economic conditions contribute little to explaining current consumer expenditures.[7]

8. Relative Income

The hypothesis has been advanced by Duesenberry[8] that a householder's consumption is interdependent with the consumption of other householders in his society. The lower income householder, stimulated by the standard of living demonstrated by the higher income members of his social group, has his propensity to consume pulled upward. Conversely, the higher income householder may have his propensity to consume pulled downward because of his relatively high position in the income scale. Duesenberry offers data which are consistent with this relative income or "demonstration effect."

It is difficult to reconcile the relative income hypothesis with the hypothesis of a rational lifetime consumption plan. Two householders who are alike in all respects except for their relative positions in the scale of lifetime incomes will consume the same proportion of their normal incomes in any year, if they are adhering to the plan that maximizes total lifetime utility. Nevertheless, we cannot ignore the contribution which the relative income effect may make to consumer irrationality, leading those at the lower end of the income scale to save less than the optimum in their preretirement years and to make inadequate provision for their old age. Those at the relatively higher income levels may find it easier to be more rational about saving than they otherwise would be, so that the relative income effect may raise their propensity to save during preretirement years.

9. Fluctuations of Disposable Income

Up to now we have been relating consumption to the trend of expected lifetime disposable income. Our final question about the

---

[7] See James Tobin, "On the Predictive Value of Consumer Intentions and Attitudes," *Review of Economics and Statistics*, Vol. XLI, No. 1 (February, 1959), pp. 1–11.

[8] James S. Duesenberry, *Income, Saving and the Theory of Consumer Behavior* (Cambridge, Mass.: Harvard University Press, 1949).

determination of a householder's consumption concerns the effect of fluctuations of disposable income about the trend.

First, consider the case where the fluctuation has been anticipated and has been included in the expectations about lifetime income. A householder will ordinarily, depending on his occupation, anticipate some short-term instability of income, and his expected lifetime income will be influenced by these anticipated fluctuations. If fully anticipated, the current income fluctuations will leave expected lifetime income unchanged and will not, therefore, affect current consumption.

Second, take the case where the current fluctuation of income exceeds what has been allowed for in the householder's conception of his lifetime income. The current fluctuation will then change the expected lifetime income; but, provided the fluctuation is considered temporary, the percentage change in expected lifetime income will be much smaller than the percentage change in current income. Consumption will be affected, but in proportion to the change of lifetime income rather than in proportion to the change in current income.

These predictions about the impact of income fluctuations on consumption must be qualified to the extent that householders do not adhere to a rational lifetime plan. In such households, consumption will be more closely dependent on current income. In addition, following a lifetime plan may require a householder to dissave when he has not as yet accumulated sufficient liquid assets or capacity to borrow to permit optimum dissaving. For example, a young householder experiencing a temporary drop of income may be unable to finance the level of consumption indicated by a lifetime view of an optimal consumption pattern and may have to tie his current consumption more closely to his current income than the lifetime income model suggests. However, despite these qualifications, we should expect that a given percentage change in current disposable income will produce a considerably smaller percentage change in consumption. This expectation is borne out by the data which are presented below in this chapter.

AGGREGATE CONSUMPTION

By adding up the consumption and incomes of the individual householders, we can relate total consumption to total disposable income. In general, the same principles that apply to the individual units apply to the aggregation of units, but there are several special points that are raised by aggregation.

1. Age Distribution

Because of the relation between the age of the householder and his average propensity to consume, the aggregate propensity to consume will be affected by the age distribution of householders. The larger the proportion of householders in the age range between "apprenticeship" and retirement, the lower we would expect the average propensity to consume of the economy to be.

2. The Price Level and Net Worth

A change in the consumer price level, if not foreseen, will cause an unplanned change in the real net worth of individuals. An unplanned increase in real net worth will tend to increase the individual's consumption; an unplanned decrease will tend to lower his consumption. The aggregate effects of the price level on consumption must now be examined.

The money value of those assets whose price is not fixed in money terms will tend to fall or rise, on the average, with the price level. In the absence of any reason to expect the contrary, we will assume that the aggregate real value of such assets will not be affected by changes in the price level, and they will be eliminated from the analysis.

Assets having fixed money values will rise in real value as the price level falls and fall as the price level rises. In most economies, the only assets with fixed money values are debts.

A fall of the price level increases the real value of the assets of the holder of debt. It increases by the same amount the real liability of the debtor. The movement of the price level leaves unchanged the real value of aggregate net worth. However, it does not leave unchanged the *distribution* of net worth. A fall of the price level will increase the net worth of those in a net-creditor position and decrease the net worth of those in a net-debtor position. The consumption of the gainers will be increased, the consumption of the losers decreased, and the sum of these changes will determine the movement of total consumption.

As far as redistribution of net worth within the private sector is concerned, we have no *a priori* reason to expect that the consumption variations of gainers and losers will not cancel out. With the present state of our knowledge, the assumption that redistribution of real net worth within the private sector will have no net effect on consumption appears to be as good as any.

There will also be a net redistribution between the private sector and the public sector, which will *not* have symmetrical effects on consumption in each sector. The public sector, on balance, is in debt to the private sector. The private sector as creditor will have an increase in real net worth when the price level falls, at the expense of the public sector as debtor. The increased net worth of the private sector will tend to increase private consumption. Public consumption, being independent of the net-worth position of the public sector, will not be reduced by the fall of public real net worth. Total consumption will be increased.

The impact of a given change in the price level, therefore, depends in the first instance on the size of the net indebtedness of the public sector to the private sector. In the United States, the net indebtedness of the public sector (including the Federal Reserve System) consists of currency in circulation plus bank deposits in the Federal Reserve System plus privately held government debt minus Reserve bank credit to the private sector minus Treasury deposits in commercial banks.

The link between the price level and consumption that has just been described is generally called "the Pigou effect" after the economist who, in the debates over the Keynesian system, first insisted on its place in income analysis. How strong the effect is we need not conjecture here; it is sufficient to know the direction of the change in consumption. The Pigou effect will cause consumption to move inversely to the price level.

3. Income Distribution

The idea is widely held that the proportion of aggregate income consumed is higher the more equal the distribution of income among households. This idea is derived from budget studies which show that when households are grouped according to income bracket, the average propensity to consume declines as the income bracket rises. However, great caution is required in using budget data to draw conclusions about the effects of income distribution.

First, we note a relatively simple point. The effect that a change in income distribution will have on the proportion of total income consumed depends on the *marginal*, not the average, propensity to consume of the individual householders. A shift of income from a low to a high marginal-propensity-to-consume householder will increase total consumption, but a shift of income between two householders with equal marginal propensities will reduce the consumption of the one by the same amount it adds to the consumption of the other, leaving total consumption unchanged.

For illustration, suppose that budget survey data relating the average income and consumption of householders grouped by income brackets are plotted in Figure 4–1.

FIGURE 4–1

Hypothetical Budget Data

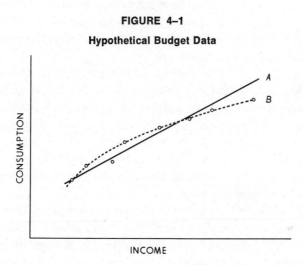

Line *A*, a straight line fitted to the observed points, shows a declining average propensity to consume but a constant marginal propensity to consume as income increases. In other words, if line *A* is taken to indicate the effects of a redistribution of income, it yields the conclusion that redistribution will not change the proportion of total income consumed, despite the fact that the average propensity to consume is lower for the higher income households. If, on the other hand, a line like *B* is fitted and is taken to represent the effects on consumption of moving households from one income level to another, the declining marginal propensity to consume as income rises implies that the more equally income is distributed, the higher will be the proportion of total income consumed. The empirical evidence from budget studies suggests that a line of type *B* is probable but that the degree of divergence from a straight line is sufficiently small that a redistribution of income would have a very small effect on the aggregate propensity to consume.[9]

In any event, too much reliance should not be put on budget data as a predictor of the effect of redistribution. Budget data present a cross section of householders' incomes and consumption in one year. However, a concept of income covering a longer term, preferably as long as a lifetime, is required for a fuller explanation of consumption. It is quite possible that the curved consumption line in budget data (Chart 4–1) would become a straight line, or nearly

CHART 4–1

Income and Consumption, Budget Data, 1950

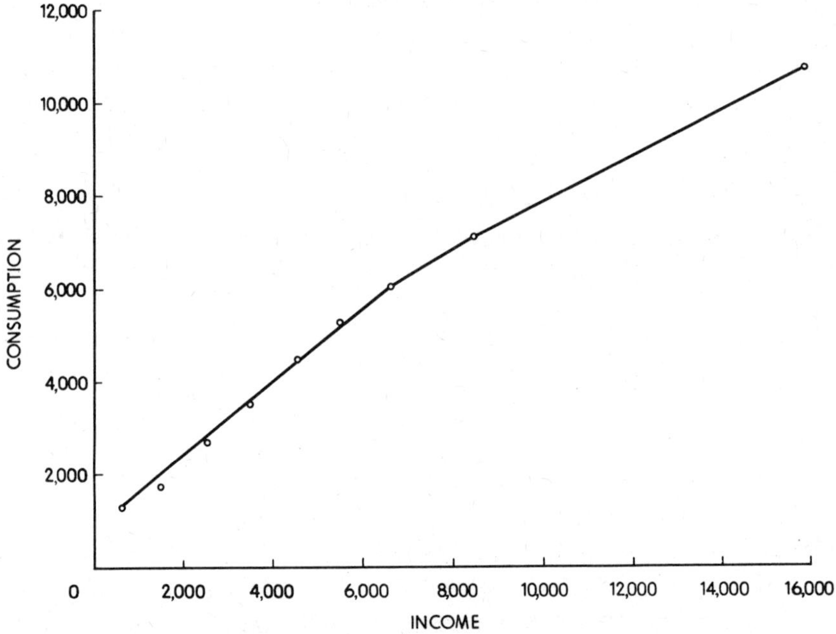

Source: See Table 4–1.

so, if consumption could be plotted against lifetime income. To foresee the effect of a redistribution of income on the aggregate propensity to consume, it would be desirable to know the effect of the

---

[9] See Harold Lubell, "Effects of Redistribution of Income on Consumers' Expenditures," *American Economic Review*, Vol. XXXVII, No. 1 (March, 1947), pp. 157–70; and further comments by J. M. Clark and Lubell, *ibid.*, No. 5 (December, 1947), pp. 930–31.

redistribution on lifetime income, and the relation between lifetime income and consumption. If the consumption line with respect to lifetime income is a straight line from the origin, the redistribution of lifetime income would not affect the aggregate propensity to consume. Thus, ordinary budget data may exaggerate the effect of a redistribution of income on aggregate consumption.

Another limitation on inferences about the effects of income redistribution is imposed by the relative income effect. A redistribution of income toward equality reduces the upward pull exerted by upper income households on the consumption of lower income households and reduces the downward pull of lower income households on the consumption of higher income households. Given the existence of interdependence among households, it is impossible to predict from budget data whether a more equal distribution of income would raise, lower, or leave unchanged the average propensity to consume of the economy.

4. Some Empirical Data

Data on the income-consumption relationship are of two types. One is the budget data previously mentioned—information on a cross section of households in one time period. The other is time-series data, showing the behavior of aggregate income and consumption over a series of time periods.

Budget Data   The general shape of the picture obtained from budget data is shown in Chart 4–1, which graphs the data in Table 4–1. The data show a declining average propensity to consume as

TABLE 4–1

Income and Consumption, Budget Data, 1950

Income Group	Average Income	Average Consumption	Consumption-Income Ratio
Under $1,000	$ 614	$ 1,278	2.08
$ 1,000–$1,999	1,532	1,768	1.15
$ 2,000–$2,999	2,534	2,718	1.07
$ 3,000–$3,999	3,487	3,570	1.02
$ 4,000–$4,999	4,462	4,450	1.00
$ 5,000–$5,999	5,449	5,257	0.96
$ 6,000–$7,499	6,618	6,043	0.91
$ 7,500–$9,999	8,434	7,108	0.84
$10,000 and over	15,914	10,773	0.68

Source: *Study of Consumer Expenditures, Incomes and Savings: Statistical Tables Urban—U.S.—1950;* tabulated by the Bureau of Labor Statistics of the U.S. Department of Labor for the Wharton School of Finance and Commerce, University of Pennsylvania (Philadelphia: University of Pennsylvania, 1956), Vol. I.

income rises. On the basis of this type of information alone, one would expect that as householders' incomes increase over the long run through the growth of the economy, the aggregate average propensity to consume will decline.

Time-Series Data When we turn to time-series data, we find instead that, despite the rise of incomes, the average propensity to consume has tended to remain constant over the long run. Chart 4-2 shows that the ratio of consumption to disposable income, while

CHART 4-2

Propensity to Consume and Per Capita Disposable Income
(constant dollars), 1897–1963

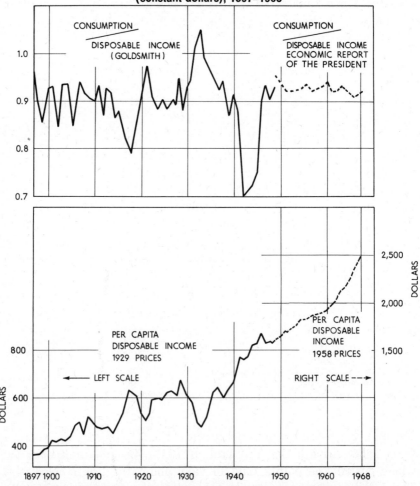

Source: 1897–1949—Raymond W. Goldsmith, Dorothy S. Brady, and Horst Mendershausen, *A Study of Saving in the United States* (Princeton, N.J.: Princeton University Press, 1956), Tables T–6, N–1, N–2. 1949–68: *Economic Report of the President*, 1969, Table B–16.

subject to short-run fluctuations, has fluctuated about an approximately constant level.

Chart 4–2 reveals another characteristic of consumption behavior. If one relates the fluctuations of the average propensity to consume shown in the upper part of the chart to the fluctuations of income shown in the lower part of the chart, one notes that the propensity to consume tends to rise when income declines and fall as income recovers. In effect, consumption is sufficiently sustained, during periods of cyclical decline of income, that the consumption-income ratio rises above the long-run average.

The relation between the cyclical and the long-run behavior of consumption is illustrated in Chart 4–3 by data which include the recession of 1957–58. The points numbered 1 to 14 mark the

CHART 4–3

Consumption and Disposable Income, 1956–59*

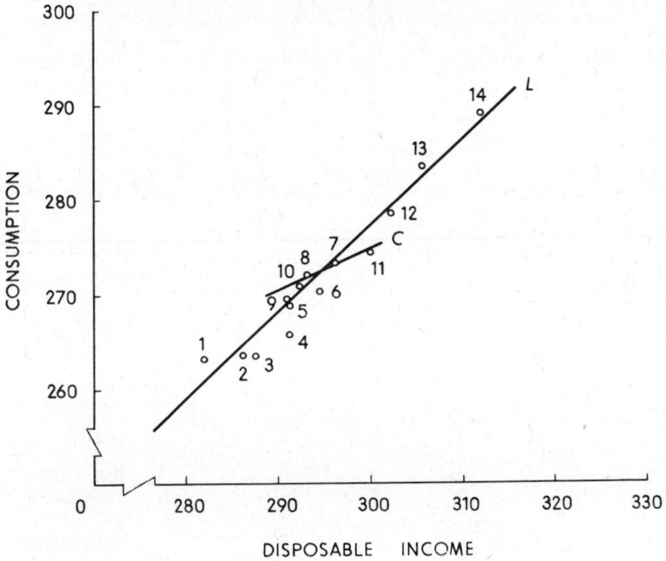

Source: U.S. Department of Commerce, *Survey of Current Business,* July, 1960 and July, 1961.
* Quarterly data at annual rates, seasonally adjusted, in 1954 prices.

consumption-income relationships for the 14 successive quarters from 1956 through the first half of 1959. We note that over the whole period, the points tend to vary about the line labeled *"L."* The *L* line depicts a constant consumption-income ratio of 0.925, approximately the long-run average.

From a peak at point 7, income falls and recovers. Points 8 and 11 indicate that when income falls cyclically, consumption does not fall back along the *L* line, but is sustained somewhat above it. In other words, the average propensity to consume tends to be higher than the long-run average during the period when income is below the previous peak. When income recovers and surpasses the previous peak, the average propensity to consume tends to be below the long-run average for a short time. Then, as income continues to grow, consumption rises rapidly and the average propensity to consume rises to its long-run average. The line labeled *"C"* approximates the cyclical behavior of consumption.

5. Long-Run and Cyclical Consumption Functions

From our time-series data it becomes apparent that in a discussion of consumption as a function of income, it will be helpful to distinguish between a long-run and a cyclical consumption function. The long-run function can be represented by a straight line from the point of origin, like the line *L* in Figure 4–2. Such a function

FIGURE 4–2

Long-Run and Cyclical Consumption Functions

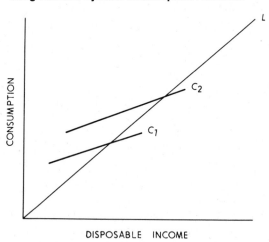

indicates a constant average propensity to consume, equal to the marginal propensity to consume, over the long run. As income grows, consumption will tend to rise along the long-run function. During a cyclical downturn, however, consumption will fall back along a cyclical consumption function like C_1. The recovery of income beyond the previous peak may leave consumption below the long-run ratio for a brief period but consumption will then rise to the L line again, and will tend to move up along the L line until the next downturn. Then fluctuation along a line like C_2 will occur, followed by a return once more to the L line as long-run growth of income is resumed. Thus we have the C lines representing the cyclical consumption function, which can be visualized as shifting upward as aggregate income grows. The marginal propensity to consume, as the slope of the C line shows, is smaller for cyclical fluctuations of income than for long-run changes.

6. The Treatment of Consumer Durables

In empirical investigations of consumption, an important decision that must be made concerns the treatment of consumer durables. The purchase of consumer durables is not the same thing as the consumption of those goods. Purchases of consumer durables can be increased to build up consumers' stocks of durables, or purchases can be postponed and the stocks allowed to run down. Obviously, expenditures on consumer durables can and do swing more widely than the actual consumption of durables.

Rather than include durables in consumption (as in the data presented above), it may be more accurate to treat them as capital goods. The consumption of durables would then be measured by their depreciation in each period. In addition, the value of the services of the consumer durables (measured by the rate of return on capital) would be included in consumption and in disposable income. When consumption is defined in this way, the fluctuations of consumption are considerably reduced and the fit of the calculated consumption function to the data is improved.

THEORIES OF THE CONSUMPTION FUNCTION

The preceding data confront us with several phenomena which any satisfactory theory of the consumption function must be able to explain. First, there is the seeming conflict between budget and time-series data. From budget data, which show a declining average propensity to consume as income rises, we would expect a long-run decline of the aggregate propensity to consume because of the growth of household incomes. Yet time-series data reveal a long-run constancy of the aggregate average propensity to consume. Second, time-series data show that the marginal propensity to consume is smaller for cyclical fluctuations of income than for long-run changes of income.

Several varieties of theories which are consistent with these observations will be discussed.

1. "Normal Income" Theories

Until recently, analyses of the consumption function attempted to relate consumption to income actually received in the same period or a previous period. This income variable has been termed "measured income." The newer theories view consumption as dependent on the consumer's notion of his "normal" income. The several versions of this approach differ mainly in their concepts of what determines normal income.

One variant of the normal income theory is the "life cycle" hypothesis.[10] The conceptual basis of this hypothesis is the attempt of the consumer to maximize his lifetime utility from consumption, subject to the resources he expects to have available over his lifetime. (The main elements of the lifetime consumption plan were presented at the beginning of this chapter.)

The total resources available to a consumer at a given point in time consist of his net worth plus current income plus the present value of nonproperty income which he expects to earn over the remainder of his earning life. In the Ando and Modigliani hypothesis, consumption in any period is said to be proportional to these total resources. This proposition can be put in "normal" income terms by defining normal income as the annual annuity that can be bought with the total resources available for consumption. The hypothesis, then, is that consumption is proportional to normal income.

If consumption depends upon normal income, then budget data will give a misleading prediction of the effect of income growth on the average propensity to consume. Budget data relate consumption to *measured* income, not to normal income. In budget data the average measured income of the lower income groups will, for several reasons, be below their average normal income. A large proportion of the lower income householders are the old and the very young,

---

[10] Albert Ando and Franco Modigliani, "The 'Life Cycle' Hypothesis of Saving: Aggregate Implications and Tests," *American Economic Review*, Vol. LIII, No. 1 (March, 1963), pp. 55–84.

whose measured incomes tend to be below their normal incomes. Furthermore, because of transitory variations of measured income, in any one year many of the low-income householders will have incomes below their normal incomes, while far fewer will have incomes above their normal incomes. At the higher end of the income scale, average measured income will be above average normal income. The householders found at the higher end of the scale in any one year will include many who are at the most productive stage in their life cycle, as well as a number who are there because of transitory gains of measured income. If consumption is proportional to normal income, householders whose measured income is below normal will consume an above-average proportion of their measured income, and householders whose measured income is above normal will consume a below-average proportion of their measured income. Thus budget data can show a declining average propensity to consume as income rises, even if the ratio of consumption to normal income is the same at all income levels. Consequently, though budget data suggest that the aggregate average propensity to consume will decline as household incomes grow over the long run, the normal income hypothesis suggests that the long-run growth of income (which is a growth of normal income) will leave the aggregate average propensity to consume unchanged.

The life cycle hypothesis provides an interesting explanation of what determines the aggregate propensity to consume. This explanation, in turn, by yielding a prediction of the propensity to consume, provides an empirical test of the life cycle hypothesis. A householder's lifetime consumption is equal to his total lifetime resources minus his estate. If, over the long run, the accumulation of assets through inheritance is negligible, lifetime consumption equals total resources, and lifetime saving is zero. The accumulation of capital in the economy then occurs solely because, through the growth of aggregate income, the amount being saved by householders in the prime of life constantly grows faster than the amount of dissaving by the older householders. Modigliani and Brumberg[11] have tested the life cycle hypothesis by calculating the proportion of income that would be consumed if saving occurred only because of the growth of aggregate income. They found that in the U.S. economy the calculated proportion is very close to the long-run average propensity to save. The results, in other words, are consistent with

---

[11] *Op. cit.*

the proposition that lifetime income is entirely consumed, and the long-run constancy of the average propensity to consume is explained by the relative constancy of the long-run rate of growth of aggregate income.

The implication of the Modigliani-Brumberg study, that bequests are zero or negligible, is difficult to accept. However, since the study deals with aggregate data for the long run, a more acceptable interpretation can be put upon the results: that the heirs tend to consume their inheritance so that over several lifetimes, net saving approaches zero.

The proposition that the long-run accumulation of capital through inheritance is zero is interesting and provocative, but it is not essential to the life cycle hypothesis. A possible alternative proposition is that the proportion of lifetime income consumed and the proportion bequeathed are uncorrelated with the level of income. That is, in all income groups, the average consumption-to-lifetime-income ratios are the same. In this case, the long-run growth of income will not affect the aggregate average propensity to consume, and, hence, the life cycle hypothesis is consistent with the observed long-run constancy of the propensity to consume.

Another version of the normal income theory is the "permanent income" hypothesis advanced by Milton Friedman.[12] It differs from the life cycle hypothesis chiefly in that, instead of a lifetime plan, it postulates that the householder's concept of his normal or permanent income is based on his income received during a shorter period, such as the most recent three years. Friedman postulates that consumption depends upon permanent income and that the proportion of permanent income consumed is uncorrelated with the level of permanent income, so that the proportion of permanent income consumed in all income groups is the same. On the basis of this hypothesis, one would predict that the long-run growth of income will not affect the average propensity to consume. Or, to put the matter conversely, the constancy of the long-run average propensity to consume may be taken as support for the hypothesis that consumption is the same proportion of permanent income at all levels of permanent income.

This "proportionality" hypothesis—that consumption is the same proportion of permanent income at all income levels—while consistent with time-series data, is not completely supported by budget

---

[12] *Op. cit.*

data. Permanent income is not directly measurable. But it can be estimated if it is assumed that a householder's notion of his permanent income is equal to an average of his measured income in the latest three years. For example, a group of householders whose incomes were unchanged in the past two years and who expect the same incomes in the coming year will, then, presumably, have measured incomes which closely approximate their permanent incomes. Using the measured incomes of this group of householders as estimates of their permanent incomes, we should find that the budget line shows a constant average propensity to consume, according to the Friedman hypothesis. The results of one study of this type[13] are shown in Chart 4–4. The consumption lines for the constant-

CHART 4–4

Budget-Data Test of the Permanent Income Hypothesis*

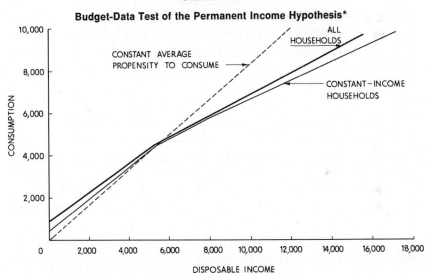

Source: Irwin Friend and Irving B. Kravis, "Consumption Patterns and Permanent Income," *American Economic Review*, Vol. XLVII, No. 2 (May, 1957), Table 1.
* Consumption excludes durables.

income group and for all households are compared to a line of constant average propensity to consume. At the lower end of the income scale, the line for the constant-income group is closer to the constant-propensity-to-consume line than is the line for all households. At the upper end of the scale, the opposite result is found. In gen-

---

13 Irwin Friend and Irving B. Kravis, "Consumption Patterns and Permanent Income," *American Economic Review*, Vol. XLVII, No. 2 (May, 1957), pp. 536–55.

eral, the test does not support the hypothesis of a constant ratio of consumption to permanent income.

The failure of this test to support the proportionality hypothesis may mean only that three years is too short an estimate of the householders' planning period and, therefore, the measured income of the constant-income group is not a good estimate of their permanent (normal) income. We can only say that evidence of the budget-data type appears to be against Friedman's form of the proportionality hypothesis. This test does not tell us anything about the proportionality thesis in the life cycle form of the normal income theory.

We turn now to the question of how the normal income theories explain the distinction between the long-run and the cyclical consumption functions. Consider first the long-run period. Normal income is based on the measured income experienced over the long run. Over the long run, aggregate normal income and measured income are equal, and consumption as a proportion of measured income and as a proportion of normal income are the same. Now introduce a cyclical decline. Measured income falls. Since the householder's idea of his normal income is only partially related to his measured income during the cycle, normal income will fall by a fraction of measured income. Consumption, according to the normal-income theories, is some constant proportion of normal income. Since measured income has fallen more than normal income, the ratio of consumption to measured income rises. When income recovers from the slump and rises above the previous peak, measured income is likely to exceed normal income, and the ratio of consumption to measured income will then fall below the long-run average. But, as income continues to grow, normal and measured income become equal once more and the ratio of consumption to measured income returns to the long-run level. Thus, the distinction between the cyclical and long-run consumption functions which we observe when we relate consumption to measured income is explained by the divergence of measured and normal incomes during cyclical fluctuations.

2. The Relative Income Hypothesis

The relative income hypothesis, which was described earlier in this chapter, is also capable of explaining the consumption data.

Take first the problem of reconciling budget and time-series data.

According to the relative income hypothesis, the declining average propensity to consume in budget data is due to the interdependence of consumption among householders, the upper income householders exerting an upward pressure on the consumption of the lower income householders and the lower income householders exerting a downward pull on the consumption of the upper income householders. Long-term growth raises income at all income levels. Householders in the same relative position in the income scale consume the same proportion of income as before, despite the increase in the absolute level of incomes. Thus, in the aggregate, the average propensity to consume is unchanged as total income grows.

With regard to the difference between the cyclical and long-run consumption functions, the relative income proponents suggest that the consumption of a householder is related not only to the consumption of others but also to his own recent consumption experience. As his income rises to new heights, his consumption tends to increase proportionately. But when his income falls cyclically, his consumption is partially sustained by the upward pull of the peak consumption level he recently enjoyed. During the cycle, therefore, the average propensity to consume rises above the long-run average. When incomes recover and growth is resumed, the consumption-income ratio returns to the long-run level.

At present we have no empirical tests which will enable us to choose between the normal income hypothesis and the relative income hypothesis. Nor do we necessarily want to do so, since both may have something to contribute to our understanding of the determination of consumer demand. The normal income hypothesis partially reconciles budget data with the constancy of the propensity to consume observed in time-series data. But it cannot complete the reconciliation if we reject the proportionality hypothesis. The relative income effect can supply the remainder of the explanation of why the propensity to consume does not fall as income grows.

RECOMMENDED READINGS

ANDO, ALBERT, and MODIGLIANI, FRANCO.   "The 'Life Cycle' Hypothesis of Saving: Aggregate Implications and Tests," *American Economic Review*, Vol. LIII, No. 1, Part I (March, 1963), pp. 55–84.

DUESENBERRY, JAMES S.   *Income, Saving and the Theory of Consumer Behavior*. Cambridge, Mass.: Harvard University Press, 1949.

FARRELL, M. J. "The New Theories of the Consumption Function," *Economic Journal,* Vol. LXIX, No. 276 (December, 1959), pp. 678–96.

FERBER, ROBERT. "Research on Household Behavior," *American Economic Review,* Vol. LII, No. 1 (March, 1962), pp. 19–63.

HAGEN, EVERETT E. "The Consumption Function: A Review Article," *Review of Economics and Statistics,* Vol. XXXVII, No. 1 (February, 1955), pp. 48–54.

PATINKIN, DON. "Price Flexibility and Full Employment," *American Economic Review,* Vol. XXXVII, No. 4 (September, 1948), pp. 543–64, reprinted in American Economic Association, *Readings in Monetary Theory,* pp. 252–83. Homewood, Ill.: Richard D. Irwin, Inc., 1951. Also, "Comment" by H. STEIN and "Reply" by DON PATINKIN, *American Economic Review,* Vol. XXXIX, No. 3 (June, 1949), pp. 725–28.

TOBIN, JAMES. "Asset Holdings and Spending Decisions," *American Economic Review,* Vol. XVII, No. 2 (May, 1952), pp. 109–23.

QUESTIONS

1. How do the normal income theories of consumption explain the tendency for the average propensity to consume to rise during periods of falling income? How does the relative income theory explain this phenomenon?

2. How do the normal income theories and the relative income theory reconcile budget data and time-series data?

3. What factors, according to the normal income theories, would explain why the average propensity to consume might differ among countries? How would the relative income theory explain it?

4. "If consumption responds to expectations of price changes of 1 percent to 2 percent per year, it ought to respond similarly to changes in the interest rate of 1 percent to 2 percent per year." Comment.

5. Why is the marginal propensity to consume of the various income brackets, and not the average propensity to consume, relevant to the analysis of the effect of income redistribution on aggregate consumption?

6. What is the significance of the relative-income hypothesis to the question of the effect of income redistribution on aggregate consumption?

Chapter 5 PRIVATE DOMESTIC INVESTMENT

The discussion in this chapter of what determines investment is restricted to private domestic investment. Public investment will be touched on in the next chapter. Foreign investment must await the treatment of international economic relations in Chapter 10.

THE RETURN ON INVESTMENT

Investment is undertaken for the sake of the return the investor expects to receive. Defining the rate of return, therefore, is a natural starting point.

Suppose you could buy a certificate which would entitle you to receive $100 one year from today. The price of the certificate is $95.24. If you bought the certificate, what rate of return would you receive on your purchase? Letting r stand for the rate of return, the $100 you receive at the end of the year represents the principal you invested ($95.24) plus a percentage earned on the principal ($r \times$ $95.24).

Thus

$$\$95.24 + (r \times \$95.24) = \$95.24\,(1 + r) = \$100$$
$$1 + r = \frac{\$100}{\$95.24} = 1.05$$
$$r = .05$$

Now, let us put a slightly different question. The certificate entitles you to $100 a year from now. Suppose the price of the certificate is not specified but you do know that you will not buy it unless it yields a return of at least 5 percent. What is the most you would pay for the certificate?

In order for the certificate to yield 5 percent, its price (P) must be such that P plus $0.05P$ adds up to $100.

Then

$$P\,(1.05) = \$100$$
$$P = \frac{\$100}{1.05}$$
$$P = \$95.24$$

You would pay $95.24 today for the right to receive $100 one year from today. Therefore $95.24 is the present value of next year's $100 when that $100 is discounted at 5 percent. The amount which you would pay now for a future receipt, in order to get some given rate of return, is known as the *present discounted value* of that future receipt.

Putting these two numerical illustrations together we note that the rate of return, 5 percent, which is received when one buys for $95.24 the right to receive $100 a year later is also the rate of discount which makes the present discounted value of $100 a year from now equal to its present cost, $95.24. The rate of return on an asset can, therefore, be defined as *the rate of discount which makes the present discounted value of the asset equal to its price.*[1]

This analysis of an asset with a life of one year can be extended to assets with lives of more than one year. If a certificate were offered which entitled the holder to receive $100 after one year and another $100 after a second year, those receipts, discounted back to the present, would measure the present value of the certificate. The $100 after one year has been shown to have a present value (P_1) of $100/(1+r)$. The present value of $100 to be received two years from now is equal to the amount (P_2) which if put into an asset yielding a rate of interest r per annum (compounded annually) would be raised to $100 after two years. Since, after one year, P_2 would be increased to $P_2\,(1+r)$ and after two years to $P_2\,(1+r)$ $(1+r)$, we have

$$P_2\,(1+r)^2 = \$100$$

or

$$P_2 = \frac{\$100}{(1+r)^2}$$

---

[1] The illustrations above can be briefly summarized. The equation $P = \$100/(1+r)$ can be interpreted in two ways. If r is known, we can solve for P, which stands for the present discounted value of next year's $100. Or, if r is unknown, and P represents the price of the asset and is known, we can solve for r, the rate of return on the asset. Thus r is the rate which makes the present discounted value of the receipt from the asset equal to the price of the asset.

The present discounted value (P) of the certificate is the sum of the discounted value of the series of receipts. Then

$$P = P_1 + P_2 = \frac{\$100}{(1 + r)} + \frac{\$100}{(1 + r)^2}$$

If r is 0.05, the present discounted value of the certificate is $95.24 + $90.70 or $185.94. Alternatively, we can say that if such a certificate sells for $185.94, it yields a rate of return of 0.05.

In general the present discounted value (P) of an asset which yields a series of returns, $Q_1, Q_2 \ldots Q_n$ in years 1 through n, when the rate of discount is r, is given by

$$P = \frac{Q_1}{1 + r} + \frac{Q_2}{(1 + r)^2} + \cdots \frac{Q_n}{(1 + r)^n}$$

A producer considering an investment which is to be financed by borrowing must compare the rate of interest charged on borrowed funds with the rate of return offered by the asset in question. It will be profitable to undertake all investments which have a rate of return greater than the interest rate.

A similar consideration applies if the investor proposes to use his own funds rather than borrow. He has the alternative of lending those funds at some rate of interest. It will pay him to make only those investments that have a rate of return greater than the rate of interest at which he can lend. If we assume for the moment that the rate at which he can lend is the same as that at which he can borrow, his investment decisions are not affected by whether he finances the purchases with his own or with borrowed funds.

THE MARGINAL EFFICIENCY OF CAPITAL

Having defined the rate of return on an individual capital asset, we can now consider the relation of the rate of return on capital to the aggregate capital stock.

Assume that the supplies of other inputs used with capital (i.e., labor, natural resources) are fixed, and that the state of technological knowledge is fixed. Assume, also, that all the different types of capital goods are accumulated to the point where the rate of return is the same on the marginal unit of each type. The rate of return on capital is then determined by the rate of return on the marginal unit of capital, which depends on the size of the capital stock. As the capital stock is increased, with other inputs and technology being fixed, the marginal rate of return on capital falls because of diminishing returns.

The rate of return on the marginal unit of the capital stock, or the *"marginal efficiency of capital,"* as Keynes called it, is thus a declining function of the capital stock (other things being given). The marginal-efficiency-of-capital function is illustrated in Figure 5–1. The function in this figure is derived on the assumption that

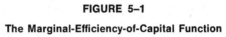

FIGURE 5–1

The Marginal-Efficiency-of-Capital Function

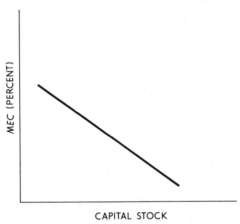

the capital stock works in combination with the existing supply of labor. This function represents, therefore, the expected rate of return on the marginal unit of capital when the economy is expected to be operating at the *full-employment* level of output. The state of the marginal-efficiency-of-capital function when output is expected to be below the full-employment level, will be examined later.

The *MEC* Function and Offsets to Diminishing Returns

The accumulation of capital, when other inputs are constant, causes a fall of the marginal rate of return along the *MEC* function. This declining tendency may, however, be counteracted by certain offsets to diminishing returns. First, technological progress raises the marginal productivity of capital.[2] What this means graphically

---

[2] Some innovations may be of a very capital-saving kind, which lowers the productivity of the marginal unit of capital; but the overall effect of innovation is clearly in the direction of raising the marginal productivity of capital.

is a shift of the *MEC* function to the right. Second, a growing supply of labor raises the marginal product of capital, which has the effect of shifting the *MEC* function to the right.

The *MEC* of capital is, thus, the outcome of a race between the accumulation of capital, which reduces the *MEC*, and technological change and increasing labor supply, which raise the *MEC*. In Figure 5–2 the function is shown shifting to the right in successive time

FIGURE 5–2

Trends of the Marginal Efficiency of Capital

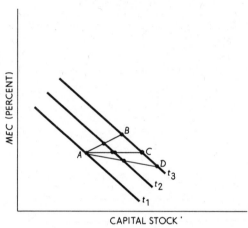

periods t_1, t_2, t_3. Depending on the rate at which the capital stock is growing, the *MEC* may be rising (line *AB*), constant (*AC*), or falling (*AD*). This race between diminishing returns and the offsets of diminishing returns is analyzed in the chapter on growth (Chapter 10).

THE INVESTMENT-DEMAND FUNCTION

Net investment is an addition to the capital stock. If the capital stock is in equilibrium, that is, if producers in the aggregate have exactly the amount of capital that they want, the demand for net investment will be zero. Net investment demand is positive (or negative) when the capital stock is in disequilibrium—when the desired capital stock is greater (or less) than the actual capital stock.

The desired capital stock is determined by the relation between the marginal rate of return on capital and the rate of return on alternative assets (e.g., securities). If the return on capital is greater than the return on securities, it will pay producers to borrow or use their own funds to increase the capital stock. If, for simplification, we speak of "the rate of interest" as a single rate, representing the rate of return on securities, and therefore the rate at which producers can borrow or lend, the desired capital stock can be defined as that stock which equates the rate of return on capital (the *MEC*) with the rate of interest.

This point is illustrated in Figure 5–3. The rate of interest is as-

FIGURE 5–3

The Equilibrium Capital Stock and Investment Demand

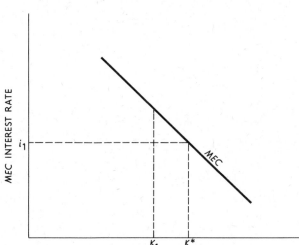

sumed to be i_1 and the capital stock, K_1. The desired (or equilibrium) capital stock is K^*. Investment demand, therefore, will be equal to the difference between K^* and K_1. Investment, however, is a flow, and can hence only be adequately described if it is expressed as an amount *per period of time*. Consequently it is necessary to consider at what rate per period of time the investment $K^* K_1$ will proceed.

The speed with which the investment that adjusts the capital stock to the desired level is carried out will be related to the capacity of the capital goods industries to produce. With the capacity of the capital goods sector given, the cost of capital goods rises as production increases.

A rise of the price of capital goods reduces the rate of return on investment. For instance, in the example on page 95, an asset providing receipts of $100 per year for two years and costing $185.94 yields a rate of return of 5 percent. If the same asset, with the same stream of receipts, cost $188.60, the rate of return would be 4 percent.

The effect of the rising supply price of capital on the rate of return to investment is illustrated in Figure 5–4. The *MEC* is shown

FIGURE 5–4

The Marginal Efficiency of Capital and of Investment

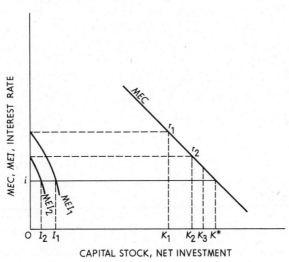

CAPITAL STOCK, NET INVESTMENT

in the right-hand portion of the diagram. At the rate of interest i, which is kept fixed, the desired capital stock K^* exceeds the actual capital stock K_1 at the beginning of period 1. The *MEC*, when the capital stock is K_1, is r_1.

The left-hand portion of the diagram shows the *marginal efficiency of investment* (*MEI*), which is the rate of return to *additions* to the capital stock. On the first small unit of net investment (an addition to K_1), the *MEI* is equal to r_1—the same as the marginal efficiency of K_1. Thereafter the *MEI* falls faster than the *MEC* because of the rising supply price of capital goods as investment increases. The *MEI* function for period 1 is, therefore, MEI_1.

In period 1, producers invest I_1, the amount determined by the intersection of the interest rate and MEI_1. The addition of I_1 to K_1

during period 1 brings the capital stock to K_2 at the beginning of period 2. (The distance $K_1 K_2$ equals the distance OI_1.) With capital stock at K_2, the marginal efficiency of capital becomes r_2, and so the marginal-efficiency-of-investment function shifts to MEI_2, whose first unit of investment has a marginal efficiency equal to r_2. Producers invest in period 2 an amount I_2 (at the intersection of i and MEI_2), which, when added to K_2, brings the capital stock to K_3. This process continues (though without being shown on the diagram) until the capital stock reaches K^* and net investment becomes zero.[3]

The marginal-efficiency-of-investment function can be called the *"investment-demand function,"* showing the quantity of investment demanded as a function of the interest rate. Such a function does not imply that the interest rate is the only, or even the most, important, variable affecting investment demand. It merely divides the variables into two groups. First, there is the interest rate and, by implication, the variables that affect the interest rate. The effect of these on investment will be reflected in the elasticity of the MEI function. Secondly, there are the variables that can shift the MEI function by shifting either the MEC function or the supply curve of capital goods.

The shifting of the MEC function through technological progress and through increase of the labor force has already been mentioned. Such shifts are likely to be gradual. Shifts of a more abrupt nature can be caused by other factors which affect the expected return to capital. The principal case is the shift arising from a change in the expected demand for output.

EXPECTED AGGREGATE DEMAND AND THE *MEC*

The MEC function, as defined in the preceding discussion, showed the expected return to capital when output was expected to be at the

---

[3] A variation of this formulation of the MEI function can be derived by assuming that the supply price of capital goods is constant up to some "capacity" level of output of the capital-goods sector and rises thereafter. In that case, the MEI function will have the same slope as the MEC function up to the point of capacity output of capital goods, while beyond that point, where the supply price of capital goods begins to rise, the MEI will fall faster than the MEC. If the capital goods sector foresees the increase of K^* in each period (as the MEC function shifts outward) and keeps its capacity large enough to provide the desired addition to the capital stock in one period without a rise of the supply price, then net investment in each period will equal the full difference between desired and actual capital stock in that period.

full-employment level. Now we drop the assumption of full-employment expectations and consider what happens to the *MEC* (and, consequently, to the *MEI*) when output is expected to fall below the full-employment level.

Expected Demand and Accelerator Models

The relation between expected demand for output and the investment-demand function is customarily analyzed in terms of a postulated output-investment interaction known as "the accelerator." The simplicity of the accelerator mechanism has made it a popular starting point for building investment-demand models. Despite the many shortcomings of accelerator models, their widespread use as introductory explanatory devices makes it advisable for the student of macroeconomics to become thoroughly acquainted with them.

The accelerator theory, in its basic form, assumes a fixed relation between expected output and the desired capital stock. That is, it assumes:

$$K^*_t = a\overline{Y}_t$$

where K^*_t is the desired capital stock in period t, $\overline{Y}_t$ is the expected output in period t, and a, a constant, is the accelerator relation.

The behavior of the demand for capital will then depend crucially on how expectations of output are formed. The simplest of the accelerator models employs the hypothesis that the expected output is equal to the output of the previous period. Thus,

$$\overline{Y}_t = Y_{t-1}$$

and

$$K^*_t = a\overline{Y}_t = aY_{t-1}$$

At the beginning of period t, the *actual* capital stock, K_t, is given by

$$K_t = aY_{t-2}$$

on the following reasoning: The desired capital stock in period $t-1$ was

$$K^*_{t-1} = a\overline{Y}_{t-1}$$

and, by the assumption that the expected output of each period is equal to the actual output of the previous period,

$$aY^e{}_{t-1} = aY_{t-2}$$

so that

$$K^*{}_{t-1} = aY_{t-2}$$

If, by the end of period $t - 1$, the capital stock has been brought to the desired level, we have

$$K_t = K^*{}_{t-1} = aY_{t-2}$$

Investment demand (I_t) in this simple accelerator model is the difference between the desired and the actual capital stock:

$$I_t = K^*{}_t - K_t = aY_{t-1} - aY_{t-2} = a(Y_{t-1} - Y_{t-2}).$$

(The proposition that investment demand in one period will equal the whole of the difference between the desired and the actual capital stocks implies that the capacity of the capital-goods producers is such as to permit the full adjustment to the desired capital stock to take place in one period without a rise of the supply price of capital goods.)

One important feature of the accelerator equation for investment demand is that it describes investment demand as depending on the *change* of output rather than the *level* of output. (Compare it, for example, with the consumption function, in which consumption depends on the *level* of income.) Thus according to the accelerator hypothesis, a fall of investment demand can be caused simply by a decrease of the rate of increase of output. The implied instability of investment demand and, thereby, of the whole economy is obvious.

By combining this investment equation with a consumption equation, we can obtain an income model which will illustrate the interaction of the accelerator and the multiplier.

For the consumption function, assume

$$C_t = c + bY_{t-1}$$

which is a short-run, or cyclical, consumption function, since that is the type of analysis for which the model is designed. Consumer demand in this equation is subject to a one-period lag, being equal to a constant, c, plus some proportion, b, of the income of the previous period.

For the purpose of a numerical illustration, assume that the accelerator coefficient a in the investment equation is 2, and that the marginal propensity to consume b in the consumption function is 0.5. Government demand is assumed to be autonomous. The capital consumption—the amount of the capital stock which must be replaced in each period just to keep the capital stock constant—will be assumed to be 10 in each period. GNP will be assumed to equal aggregate demand in each period.

In Table 5–1, we begin in period 0 with an economy in which net investment is zero and the capital stock is constant. We will assume that the economy has been in equilibrium in that position, with a constant capital stock and constant income. This assumption is neither realistic nor essential, but it enables us to examine the accelerator-multiplier process under the simplest conditions.

In period 1 an autonomous change is introduced in the form of an increase of government purchases of 2 per period. Thereafter, government demand is assumed to remain constant at this higher level. Because of the assumed lags, consumption and investment demand are unaffected in period 1, and GNP rises by 2, the increase of aggregate demand.

In period 2 consumption demand rises by 1, which is 0.5 of the increase of GNP in the previous period. The desired capital stock rises to 204 ($2 \times Y_{t-1}$) and net investment demand rises to 4—the difference between the desired capital stock (204) and the actual capital stock (200). Gross investment demand is 14—that is, net investment plus 10 for replacement. GNP rises to 107.

In succeeding periods GNP continues to rise, but eventually by diminishing increments, which leads to a fall of investment demand in period 6, and that fall leads in turn to a fall of GNP in period 7. In period 8, net investment becomes negative.[4] A continuation of these calculations will show falling GNP and net disinvestment until the shrinking of the gap between the desired and actual capital stocks reduces disinvestment and GNP turns up.

The behavior of this type of model depends on the size of the accelerator coefficient and the marginal propensity to consume. With a given marginal propensity to consume, the model becomes increasingly unstable as the accelerator coefficient is increased.

---

[4] The excess of the actual capital stock over the desired capital stock in period 8 is 14.92, but net disinvestment cannot exceed the amount of capital consumption, 10. Consequently, a lower limit of −10 is set on net investment.

TABLE 5-1

An Accelerator-Multiplier Model

Period	Demand Govern-ment	Demand Consumption	Demand Gross Investment	GNP	Net Investment	Capital Stock Desired	Capital Stock Actual
0	20	70.00	10.00	100.00	0.00	200.00	200.00
1	22	70.00	10.00	102.00	0.00	200.00	200.00
2	22	71.00	14.00	107.00	4.00	204.00	200.00
3	22	73.50	20.00	115.50	10.00	214.00	204.00
4	22	77.75	27.00	126.75	17.00	231.00	214.00
5	22	83.38	32.50	137.88	22.50	253.50	231.00
6	22	88.94	32.26	144.20	22.26	275.76	253.50
7	22	92.10	22.64	136.74	12.64	288.40	275.76
8	22	88.37	0.00	110.37	−10.00	273.48	288.40
9	22	75.19	0.00	97.19	−10.00	220.74	278.40

Assumptions:

$C_t = 20 + 0.5Y_{t-1}$

Net $I_t = K_t^* - K_t$, Net $I \geqq -10$

$K_t^* = 2Y_{t-1}$

$K_t = K_{t-1} + \text{Net } I_{t-1}$

$Y_t = C_t + G_t + \text{Gross } I_t$

Gross $I_t = \text{Net } I_t + 10$

where: C = consumption; I = investment; K^* = desired capital stock; K = actual capital stock; G = government purchases; Y = GNP.

With very small accelerator coefficients, output, after the autono-mous disturbance, will converge on a new equilibrium level, very much like the period multiplier example in Table 3–1. As the size of the accelerator coefficient is increased, the model passes through phases which yield (1) damped oscillations—fluctuations that be-come successively smaller; (2) antidamped oscillations—fluctua-tions that become successively larger; (3) explosions—output ris-ing or falling, depending on the direction in which it is started, at an increasing rate.[5]

The interest that accelerator-multiplier models have aroused lies chiefly in the possibility that they can provide an explanation for economic fluctuations. In the model just described, a downturn of output occurred simply as a result of a slowdown in the rate of in-crease of output. In other words, the accelerator-multiplier model can describe a process by which fluctuations are generated entirely within the model, without externally caused (i.e., autonomous) shifts of the aggregate demand function.

This simple model is, however, highly unrealistic. It depicts an extremely unstable economy, one which goes into contraction when-ever the rate of expansion decreases and one which fluctuates widely, with substantial disinvestment during the contraction. The actual economy is, by comparison with this model, quite stable. The slowing of expansion has not necessarily been followed by contrac-tion; the fluctuations of output and investment have been small.[6]

The exaggerated instability of the model cannot be attributed to the assumption of an overly large accelerator coefficient. The as-sumed coefficient, 2, is, if anything, an underestimate.[7] If the ac-celerator-multiplier model is to be salvaged, some modification must be introduced which will reduce its instability. Such a modification is considered next.

---

[5] See Paul A. Samuelson, "Interaction between the Multiplier Analysis and the Principle of Acceleration," *Review of Economics and Statistics*, Vol. XXI, No. 2 (May, 1939), pp. 75–87; reprinted in American Economic Association, *Readings in Business Cycle Theory* (Philadelphia: Blakiston Co., 1944), pp. 261–69.

[6] The largest fall of real GNP in any fluctuation in the past 30 years in the United States has been 4.7 percent, and the largest fall of investment, 25 per-cent.

[7] The ratio of capital stock to annual GNP is about 2.5. There is no reason to believe that the ratio of incremental capital to incremental output would be less than the average ratio. Moreover, if the time periods in the model are not years but a shorter period, like quarters, the relevant figure is the ratio of capi-tal stock to *quarterly* GNP, which is about 10.

The Partial-Adjustment Accelerator

In the model above, it was assumed that producers invested in each period an amount which would close the gap between the desired and the actual capital stocks of that period, i.e., net $I_t = K^*_t - K_t$. It is not implausible, however, that producers attempt to carry out only a part of the adjustment between K^*_t and K_t in each period. Partial rather than full adjustment might be explained by producers' caution or by limitations on the speed with which investment plans can be changed or implemented.

Let us assume, therefore, that producers invest only some fraction, q, of the difference between K^*_t and K_t. The investment equation is then

$$\text{Net } I_t = q \ (K^*_t - K_t) = qaY_{t-1} - qK_t$$

This investment equation can now be substituted for the investment equation in the previous model (Table 5–1) to illustrate the operation of the partial-adjustment model. Assume a value of 0.25 for the partial-adjustment coefficient q (a figure low enough to allow for as much entrepreneurial caution and investment delay as seems conceivable under normal circumstances).

In Table 5–2, we observe that the partial-adjustment factor makes the model considerably more stable. Nevertheless, its instability still seems excessive compared to the actual behavior of the economy. The amplitude of the fluctuation is moderate, but net disinvestment occurs;[8] and the length of the contraction phase is unrealistically long.[9]

---

[8] Aggregate net disinvestment is a rare occurrence. The only recorded instance of it that we have is during the worst years of the Great Depression, 1932–33. To avoid net disinvestment and reduce the amplitude of the fluctuations, some accelerator-multiplier models postulate a category of *autonomous* investment, which is independent of expected changes of output, and also a category of induced investment, which is determined by the accelerator mechanism. But, since the desired stock of any kind of capital cannot be unrelated to the expected output, it is difficult to see how there can be any truly autonomous investment in a model in which investment is determined by the relation between the desired and actual capital stocks.

[9] If the time periods be years (implying a one-year lag of investment and consumption adjustments), the nine-year contraction in the model bears no relation to reality. Even if the periods be quarter-years, the nine-quarter contraction is unusually long. Furthermore, if the model is to be based on quarterly lags, it must be recalculated with an accelerator coefficient based on the ratio of capital to *quarterly* output. If the accelerator coefficient, a, is multiplied by four and the partial-adjustment coefficient, q, is divided by four (becoming 0.0625 per quarter, so that the speed of adjustment remains at 0.25 per year), the contraction phase is lengthened to 18 quarters.

TABLE 5-2

A Partial-Adjustment Accelerator Model

Period	Demand Govern-ment	Demand Consumption	Gross Investment	GNP	Net Investment	Capital Stock Desired	Capital Stock Actual
0	20	70.00	10.00	100.00	0.00	200.00	200.00
1	22	70.00	10.00	102.00	0.00	200.00	200.00
2	22	71.00	11.00	104.00	1.00	204.00	200.00
3	22	72.00	11.75	105.75	1.75	208.00	201.00
4	22	72.88	12.19	107.07	2.19	211.50	202.75
5	22	73.54	12.30	107.84	2.30	214.14	204.94
6	22	73.92	12.11	108.03	2.11	215.68	207.24
7	22	74.02	11.68	107.70	1.68	216.06	209.35
8	22	73.85	11.09	106.94	1.09	215.40	211.03
9	22	73.47	10.44	105.91	0.44	213.88	212.12
10	22	72.96	9.81	104.77	−0.19	211.82	212.56
11	22	72.38	9.29	103.67	−0.71	209.54	212.37
12	22	71.84	8.92	102.76	−1.08	207.34	211.66
13	22	71.38	8.73	102.11	−1.27	205.52	210.58
14	22	71.06	8.73	101.79	−1.27	204.22	209.31
15	22	70.90	8.88	101.78	−1.12	203.58	208.04
16	22	70.89	9.16	102.05	−0.84	203.56	206.92

Net $I_t = 0.25 (K_t^* - K_t)$

The other equations are as in Table 5–1, page 104.

The conclusion to be drawn from this examination of the basic accelerator-multiplier models is that with reasonable-looking co-efficients they do not give reasonable-looking results. Statistical tests of the investment functions used in these models have also failed to give them much support.[10]

The Normal-Output Theory of Investment

The inadequacy of the accelerator theories of investment can be traced to a number of oversimplifications and the dubious assumptions which they contain. Among the weak points, a particularly crucial one is the assumption about output expectations. When the desired capital stock is defined as proportional to the output of the previous period, that definition contains the implicit assumption that producers expect the output of the previous period to continue for a number of periods in the future.

The length of the future time period which is relevant to a current investment decision depends on the type of capital good being considered. The longer the life of the capital good, the longer is the relevant output forecast. Investment in capital goods with a short life can be closely related to near-term expected output. But the bulk of investment is in durable goods, which are expected to last many years. An increase of output will not induce an increase of the capital stock unless the increase of output is expected to continue for a substantial portion of the life of the capital goods.

Investment decisions are likely to be geared to long-term expectations for a second reason. When an addition to capital is desired, it cannot be acquired at once. Time is needed for the production and installation of capital goods. The length of time from the decision to invest until the capital goods are ready to be used in production might be called the *"gestation period"* of capital. For a large part of investment, the gestation period can be as long as several years. Consequently, producers must look beyond the expected output of the immediate future and consider the longer term expected increase of output if they are to have their additional capital ready to use when needed.

---

[10] For a review of the chief empirical tests of accelerator hypotheses, see Robert Eisner and Robert H. Strotz, "Determinants of Business Investment," Research Study Number Two in Daniel B. Suits and others, *Impacts of Monetary Policy*, prepared for the Commission on Money and Credit (Englewood Cliffs, N.J.: Prentice-Hall, 1963).

Thus, the longer the life of a capital good, and the longer its gestation period, the longer will be the term of output expectations to which it is geared. While some investments have a short enough life-span that they respond to very short-run expected increases of output, or a short enough gestation period that the investment may be postponed in response to a fall of output which is expected to be temporary, the greatest portion of investment will depend on long-term expectations.

From these considerations, we can derive a "normal-output" theory of investment, analogous to the normal-income theories of consumption. In a normal-output theory, investment depends upon expectations of normal output. Producers' notions of normal output may be derived from the long-term growth experience of the economy, the medium-term behavior of output, and the current state of output, these elements being weighted in some appropriate way.

Some indirect empirical support for the normal-output hypothesis of investment is provided in recent studies by Robert Eisner.[11] These studies of a large number of firms find that the changes of sales in the current and previous six years play a major role in explaining current investment. These changes of sales, extending so far back in time, can be taken as representing (that is, as proxies for) expectations of future long-run sales trends, which are based on the past sales experience. Further tests conclude that firms' investments are more closely related to the changes of sales of the industry to which they belong than to their own sales changes. Since the sales changes of an industry have a smaller transitory component than the sales changes of the individual firms in the industry, the fact that industry sales give a better "explanation" of firms' investments offers support for the hypothesis that firms gear their investments to normal output rather than to actual output.

Inventory Investment

Inventory investment has several characteristics which distinguish it from investment in durable plant and equipment, requiring therefore a separate analysis of the determinants of the demand for inventories.

---

[11] See, for example, Robert Eisner, "A Permanent Income Theory of Investment: Some Empirical Explorations," *American Economic Review*, Vol. LVII, No. 3 (June, 1967), pp. 363–90.

Unlike durable capital goods, inventories do not have a life fixed by the rate of depreciation. Inventory stocks can be reduced simply by producing less than is being sold. Thus, inventories can be regarded as having a very short life, relative to the lives of durables.

Secondly, the gestation period of inventories is typically much shorter than that of durable capital goods. In general, technical production conditions permit a much more rapid increase of stocks of materials and finished consumer goods than stocks of producers' equipment and structures ready to be used.

Given the comparatively more rapid adjustability of inventories, both upward and downward, it is plausible to hypothesize that inventories will be geared to near-term expectations rather than to expectations of longer term or normal output. Such a hypothesis implies that an accelerator model of the simple type (see Table 5–1) will be considerably more successful in explaining inventory investment than it is in explaining investment in plant and equipment.

To illustrate an inventory model, we will assume that producers plan to invest in inventories, in each period, the difference between their desired inventory stock J^* and their actual inventory stock J. Thus:

$$\text{Planned inventory investment } i^*_t = J^*_t - J_t$$

The desired inventory stock will be assumed to be proportional to the expected sales in the current period. As to producers' expectations of sales, we will assume that in each period producers expect the same sales as in the previous period. Then the desired inventory stock will be proportional to the sales S of the previous period:

$$J^*_t = hS_{t-1}$$

A production lag will be assumed in order to illustrate one possible facet of the inventory adjustment problem. That is, we assume that producers set production in each period at the level of sales in the previous period plus planned inventory investment. Thus,

$$Y_t = S_{t-1} + i^*$$

The consumption equation is the same as in the previous accelerator models, except that the lag is eliminated; otherwise the model behaves with unrealistic erraticness. Investment (excluding inventories) is assumed to be autonomous, so as to isolate the effect of the inventory accelerator.

The working of the model is illustrated in Table 5–3. The equi-

TABLE 5-3

An Inventory Investment Model

Period	Sales		Gross Investment (except Inventories)	Planned Inventory Investment	GNP	Total Sales (G + C + I)	Actual Inventory Investment	Inventory Stock	
	Government Purchases	Consumption						Desired	Actual
0	20	70.00	10	0.00	100.00	100.00	0.00	50.00	50.00
1	22	70.00	10	0.00	100.00	102.00	-2.00	50.00	50.00
2	22	72.50	10	3.00	105.00	104.50	0.50	51.00	48.00
3	22	74.13	10	3.75	108.25	106.13	2.12	52.25	48.50
4	22	74.29	10	2.45	108.58	106.29	2.29	53.07	50.62
5	22	73.27	10	0.24	106.53	105.27	1.26	53.15	52.91
6	22	72.40	10	-0.47	104.80	104.40	0.40	52.64	54.17
7	22	71.02	10	-2.37	102.03	103.02	-0.99	52.20	54.57
8	22	70.48	10	-2.07	100.95	102.48	-1.53	51.51	53.58
9	22	70.84	10	-0.81	101.67	102.84	-1.17	51.24	52.05

Assumptions: $C_t = 20 + 0.5Y_t$
$i_t^* = J_t^* - J_t$
$J_t^* = 0.5S_{t-1}$
$Y_t = S_{t-1} + i^*$
G and I are autonomous

Where: C = consumption; Y_t = GNP; i^* = planned inventory investment; J^* = desired inventory stock; J = actual inventory stock; S = sales; G = government purchases; I = gross investment except inventory investment.

librium of period 0 is disturbed by an autonomous increase of government purchases in period 1. Since production lags by one period, this rise of sales in period 1 causes an unintended fall of inventories of two. In period 2, actual inventories are 48 but the desired inventory stock is 51. Producers therefore plan inventory investment of three, which, when added to expected sales (S_{t-1}) of 102, causes them to produce 105 in period 2. However, consumption is induced upward to 72.5 in period 2, so that total sales are larger than expected, and actual inventory investment is therefore only 0.5. By period 4 the actual inventory stock has begun to catch up with the desired inventory stock, so planned inventory investment declines. This decline leads to a fall of GNP in period 5. In period 6, the inventory stock overshoots the desired level and disinvestment in inventories follows, until the actual stock begins to catch up with the desired stock and GNP turns up, at length, in period 9. With the coefficients that have been assumed in this illustration, the model produces a series of damped oscillations until it reaches an equilibrium at a GNP of 104.[12]

PAST PROFITS AND INVESTMENT DEMAND

The variables affecting investment which have been discussed so far are all related to *expected* profit: that is, they determine the marginal efficiency of investment, which is the schedule of the rates of return expected from investment.

The level of investment can also be affected by *past* profits, independently of any influence past profits may have on expectations of future profits. Past profits can affect investment through their effect on the supply of internal funds, which consist of undistributed profits plus capital consumption allowances. These internal funds can be used for expenditure on current investment.

An investor would presumably be indifferent as between internal funds and external funds (funds obtained by borrowing or by selling shares of stock of the company) in a world without risk and

---

[12] This model is, of course, highly simplified and is intended only to give an introductory idea of the nature of inventory fluctuations. For examples of advanced studies of inventory models, see Michael C. Lovell, "Factors Determining Manufacturing Inventory Investment," in U.S. Congress, Joint Economic Committee, *Inventory Fluctuations and Economic Stabilization* (Washington, D.C.: U.S. Government Printing Office, 1961), Part II, pp. 119–57; Paul G. Darling, "Inventory Fluctuations and Economic Instability," *ibid.*, Part III, pp. 1–68.

without the costs of arranging for borrowing or for selling shares. For, in such a world, the rate of interest at which the investor could obtain external funds would be the same as the rate of interest at which he could lend out his internal funds; and therefore the cost of external funds would be the same as the cost of internal funds. (The cost of internal funds is an imputed cost calculated upon the rate of interest that could have been obtained by lending the funds.)

But in actuality, the costs are not the same. The introduction of the borrower-lender relation adds certain costs that are not present when internal funds are used. First, there is the cost of arranging loans or selling securities—the cost of bringing borrower and lender together. Second, there is the "lender's risk," an added element of risk arising from uncertainty felt by the lender about the reliability of the borrower. Third, there is a risk to the borrower arising from the fixed charges on the debt, which make the firm more vulnerable in case of a fall of revenue, heightening the ultimate danger of bankruptcy. (Equity financing—raising funds by selling shares—does not entail the risks associated with fixed-debt charges, but it may involve a cost to the original shareholders from diluting their ownership and the cost to the management of endangering its control of the company.) These risks to the borrower should be viewed as additions to his estimate of the cost of external funds.

For these reasons, the cost of external funds to the borrower will be greater than the cost of using his internal funds. Moreover, the added cost arising from risk will increase as the amount of external funds sought increases. The risks associated with additional debt increase as the amount of indebtedness increases relative to the equity (the owner's investment) in the company. Consequently, the supply curve of funds available to the borrower is shaped something like the curve shown in Figure 5–5.[13] The cost of funds, or "rate of interest" shown in the figure includes the imputed costs as calculated by the borrower.

The segment *IN* of the supply curve represents the amount of internal funds generated by the firm in the current period; and the cost of those funds, or the imputed cost, is in fact the market rate of interest that could be earned on loans of the same degree of risk

---

[13] A supply curve of this shape is often attributed to an "imperfect capital market," but that is a misnomer, as has been pointed out by George J. Stigler, "Imperfections in the Capital Market," *Journal of Political Economy*, Vol. LXXV, No. 3 (June, 1967), pp. 287–92. Rising supply price due to rising cost is not evidence of imperfection in a market.

FIGURE 5–5

The Supply of Funds

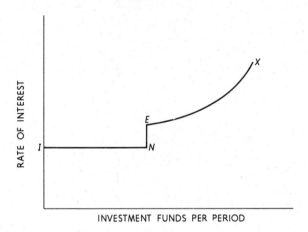

INVESTMENT FUNDS PER PERIOD

as the internal investment. The segment EN represents the added cost attaching to the first increment of external funds. The segment EX shows the rising cost of external funds as the amount obtained increases.

Figure 5–6 illustrates the effect of a change of profits on a firm's investment. Suppose that, as a result of a fall of profits, the firm's internal funds are reduced from N to N', resulting in a shift of the supply-of-funds curve to $IN'E'X'$. If the firm's demand-for-invest-

FIGURE 5–6

Supply of Funds and Investment Demand

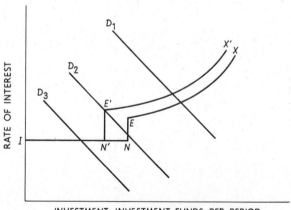

INVESTMENT, INVESTMENT FUNDS, PER PERIOD

ment curve is D_1, its investment expenditure will be reduced because of the increased cost of the marginal unit of external funds. If the firm's demand curve is D_2, so that the firm has been investing only to the extent of its internal funds, the reduction of investment expenditure will be even larger. Only if the demand curve is D_3, where the firm has internal funds in excess of its investment expenditures, will its investment be unaffected by the fall of internal funds.

The Size of the Internal-Funds Effect

How large an effect variations in profits have on investment has been the subject of considerable analysis and disagreement. The largest effect (as we have noted) is on firms whose investment is limited to the amount of their internal funds. But such firms are mainly the smaller firms, which do only a small fraction of the aggregate of investing. The larger firms, which do most of the investing, have readier access to external funds. In their case, the impact of the internal-funds effect on investment depends on the shape of their supply-of-funds curve. If a firm's credit rating is high, the segment EN of its supply curve will be small and the elasticity of the EX segment high, which will limit the internal funds effect.

The effect of fluctuations of profits is further dampened to the extent that firms reduce their dividend payments when profits fall and to the extent that they accumulate liquid assets when profits are above normal in order to sustain their investment programs when profits are below normal.

How important the internal-funds effect is upon investment can only be answered empirically. The conclusions of statistical analyses have ranged from the finding that past profits are the major determinant of investment[14] to the finding that they are of only minor significance.[15] The chief difficulty in estimating the internal-funds effect is that fluctuations of profit are correlated with fluctuations of output. Consequently, what may appear to be the effect of past profits may actually be the effect of past changes of output. Or, in

---

[14] For example, John R. Meyer and Edward Kuh, *The Investment Decision: an Empirical Study* (Cambridge, Mass., Harvard University Press, 1957).

[15] Robert Eisner, "Investment: Fact and Fancy," in *American Economic Review, Papers and Proceedings*, Vol. LIII, No. 2 (May, 1963), pp. 237–46.

other words, what may appear to be an internal-funds effect may actually be an accelerator effect.

In order to estimate these two mechanisms separately, a satisfactory formulation of the relation between changes of output and investment demand must be found. Otherwise, part of the output effect will be attributed to the profits effect.

Eisner's studies find that when the accelerator is formulated as a relation between investment and changes of "normal" output, the role of profits in explaining investment appears small; and the more closely the measure of output change approximates "normality" (i.e., the more it screens out changes which firms consider transitory), the smaller the role of profits appears. These results suggest that in previous studies emphasizing the effect of past profits, the profits variable was serving as a proxy of expected change of output because the output variable included a large transitory element and hence did not correctly represent expected change of output. Though the exact dimensions of the internal-funds effect are still unclear, present indications are that it is among the minor elements in determining investment.

TAXATION ON INCOME FROM INVESTMENT

A full discussion of this complex subject must be left to books on public finance,[16] but some of the major links in the connection between a tax like the corporate income tax and the investment-demand schedule can be examined here. The effect of the tax on the investment-demand function is considered first, and then the effect of the tax on investment through the supply of funds.

Effect on Investment Demand

1. Riskless Investment and Debt Financing   The simplest case to to analyze is that of a corporate income tax under conditions of riskless investment financed by borrowing. Where there is no risk, investors will buy any asset which has a rate of return greater than the rate of interest. If the purchase is financed by borrowing, the rate of interest is treated as a cost in computing income, and the tax falls only on the return in excess of the rate of interest. Any asset

---

[16] See, for example, Richard A. Musgrave, *The Theory of Public Finance* (New York: McGraw-Hill Book Co., Inc., 1959), chap. XIV.

which yields a rate of return greater than the rate of interest when
there is no tax on income will still yield a return greater than the
rate of interest when a tax is imposed on the income (at any tax
rate less than 100 percent). Under conditions of riskless investment
through debt financing, a tax on investment income will have no
effect on the investment-demand function.

2. Riskless Investment and Equity Financing   If investment is
financed by the sale of shares in the firm or by gross business saving, there is, under present tax systems, no interest charge which
is treated as a cost-deduction in computing taxable income. The
whole of the equity income is subject to the tax, and the effect of the
tax is to lower the return on equity financing relative to debt financing. This will cause some shift of financing from equity to debt, but
since investors do not regard them as perfect substitutes, the
decreased rate of return on equity financing can reduce investment
demand.

3. Investment with Risk   Investment typically involves some degree of risk. Investment then takes on the attributes of a gamble
in which the investor bets some amount (the possible loss) on the
chance of winning some return. It may be argued that if a tax reduces the potential winnings, certain "bets" will no longer look attractive. But that conclusion is affected by the possibility of setting
off a loss against other income. Thus, if income on an investment is
taxed at 50 percent but any loss can be used as a deduction from
other income, so that the possible loss is also cut by 50 percent, both
the amount bet and the potential winnings are reduced proportionately. Since there is no change in the "odds," there will be no change
in the willingness to invest.[17]

Full offset of losses may not always be possible. If the investor
has no other income against which to set the loss and does not expect to have any, or if the other income is less than the possible
loss, no offset or only partial offset is open to him. It is true that
a loss which has been recorded by one firm has sale value to another
firm with income, but the price is not likely to be one which gives
the seller the equivalent of full offset. Where losses cannot be fully
offset, the tax on investment income will tend to reduce investment
demand.

---

[17] On the other hand, there are grounds for suggesting that with full loss
offset, an income tax will increase investment demand. The reduction of income
will lead investors to take on riskier investments, which offer higher yields, in
an effort to restore income. It is not known, however, how strong this income
effect is. See Musgrave, *ibid.*

4. Taxation and Accelerated Depreciation　In the absence of a tax on business income, the rate at which a firm chooses to charge off the depreciation of its capital goods is purely a matter of statistical information; the enterprise is generally trying to obtain as realistic a picture of costs and current net income as possible. On the other hand, when business income is taxed, there are certain advantages to the firm in depreciating its capital goods over a shorter period than it would in the interests of "realism." The rate at which depreciation can be charged in computing business income is regulated by the tax statutes. If it can be shown that permitting accelerated depreciation affects investment demand, depreciation policy can be added to the list of determinants of investment.

The key to the relation between accelerated depreciation and investment is simply this: accelerated depreciation reduces the impact of the business income tax and, therefore, it reduces whatever curtailing effect the income tax may have on investment.

Accelerated depreciation limits the impact of the business income tax in three ways:

a) It reduces the effective tax rate by postponing some of the tax payment. Charging off all of the depreciation early in the life of an asset means a reduction of the tax payments in the early years and a greater tax payment in the later years, as compared to tax payments with straight-line depreciation over the life of the asset. The time-path of receipts (net of taxes) is altered, bringing some of the receipts from later periods forward to earlier periods. Since the earlier a given sum is to be received the greater is its present value, accelerated depreciation increases the present discounted value of the net receipts.

The effect of accelerated depreciation is illustrated by an example in Table 5–4. An asset costing $400, with a life of 10 years, is assumed. It yields annually a net revenue of $100, before depreciation allowances and tax liability. The tax on business income is 50 percent. The rate of interest which the firm uses to discount future receipts is 10 percent.

If the asset is depreciated at the rate of $40 per year for 10 years, the net receipts after taxes are $70 each year for 10 years— a stream of returns which has a present discounted value of $430.19. If depreciation is charged at the accelerated rate of $100 for four years, net receipts after taxes are increased to $100 per year for the first four years and reduced to $50 per year in the

TABLE 5–4

Hypothetical Comparison of Standard and Accelerated Depreciation

A. Standard Depreciation

Year	(1) Net Receipts before Taxes	(2) Depreciation Allowance Straight-Line over 10 Years	(3) Tax Payment (50% of Col. 1 Minus Col. 2)	(4) Net Receipts after Taxes	(5) Present Discounted Value of Net Receipts after Taxes*
1	$100	$40	$30	$70	$ 63.64
2	100	40	30	70	57.85
3	100	40	30	70	52.59
4	100	40	30	70	47.81
5	100	40	30	70	43.48
6	100	40	30	70	39.53
7	100	40	30	70	35.93
8	100	40	30	70	32.66
9	100	40	30	70	29.70
10	100	40	30	70	27.00
Total					$430.19

B. Accelerated Depreciation

Year	(1)	(2)	(3)	(4)	(5)
1	$100	$100	$ 0	$100	$ 90.91
2	100	100	0	100	82.64
3	100	100	0	100	75.13
4	100	100	0	100	68.30
5	100	0	50	50	31.06
6	100	0	50	50	28.23
7	100	0	50	50	25.66
8	100	0	50	50	23.33
9	100	0	50	50	21.21
10	100	0	50	50	19.28
Total					$465.75

* Rate of interest, 10 percent.

remaining six years. The present discounted value of the receipts is thereby increased to $465.75.

The increase in the discounted value of the receipts can be viewed as the equivalent of a reduction in the tax rate. In our example it can be shown that the discounted value of the receipts with accelerated depreciation and a 50 percent tax rate is the same as it would be with standard depreciation and a 40 percent tax rate.[18]

[18] Where receipts before taxes are $100 per year, depreciation deduction is $40 per year, t stands for the tax rate and R for the annual receipts after taxes, we have $R = 100 - 60t$. The present discounted value of $1 per year for

b) Accelerated depreciation decreases the investor's uncertainty about having sufficient income in the future from which to deduct his depreciation allowance. The sooner he can charge off the depreciation the more certain he can be that he will be able to utilize his full depreciation allowance as a deduction.

We previously saw that if there is full offset of losses, the business income tax will not change the relationship between the investment risk and the rate of payment for taking the risk. If only partial offset of losses is possible, payment is reduced relative to risk, and investment may be reduced by the tax. Accelerated depreciation can, then, be looked at as a device for reducing the possibility that losses will be only partially offset (by reducing the chances that the depreciation deduction may have to be taken in future years when net receipts are less than the depreciation allowance) and, to that extent, nullifying any discouraging effect of the tax on investment.

c) Accelerated depreciation, by increasing after-tax receipts in early periods at the expense of later receipts, increases the firm's funds for financing investment. Through the supply-of-funds effect, an increase in the internal funds of firms may lead to an increase of investment.

We may conclude that permitting accelerated depreciation is similar to reducing the tax rate on business income and that it will stimulate investment to the same extent as would an equivalent reduction in the tax rate. However, since a cut in the tax rate will apply to all business income while accelerated depreciation can be applied selectively to new investment, accelerated depreciation can achieve a greater increase in investment for a given loss of tax revenue than can a lowering of the tax rate.

Effect on Investment through the Supply of Funds

The profits tax reduces firms' internal funds and tends to reduce investment by the shift of the supply curve illustrated in Figure 5–6. The extent of the impact on investment depends on the size of the internal-funds effect, which, as we have noted, appears to be small.

---

10 years at a 10 percent rate of interest is $6.15. The present discounted value of R dollars per year for 10 years is therefore $6.15R$ or $6.15(\$100 - \$60t)$. Solving for the value of t: $6.15(\$100 - \$60t) = \$465.75$; $t = 0.4$.

THE INTEREST RATE AND INVESTMENT DEMAND

The responsiveness of investment demand to changes of the interest rate has an important bearing on policy issues, for it is the principal determinant of the extent to which aggregate demand can be affected by policies which change the interest rate. The degree of responsiveness—the interest-elasticity of investment demand— is the subject of considerable disagreement.

The elasticity of investment demand depends, first of all, on the elasticity of the demand for capital, i.e., the *MEC* function. The more elastic the *MEC* function, the larger the increase in the desired capital stock that results from a given fall of the interest rate. The elasticity of the *MEC* function depends chiefly on a technological condition—the rate at which the productivity of capital falls as it is increased relative to the quantity of other inputs, or, in other words, the susbtitutability of capital for other inputs. The greater the substitutability, the more slowly the productivity (or rate of return) of capital declines as the capital stock is increased, and, therefore, the more elastic is the *MEC* function.

The elasticity of the *MEC* function is also dependent on the shift in the composition of output that can be induced by a change of the interest rate. A fall of the interest rate lowers the cost of production in proportion to the share of capital cost in total cost. The cost of the more capital-intensive products—those produced with higher ratios of capital to other inputs—falls relative to the cost of the less capital-intensive products, so that production tends to shift toward more capital-intensive products. This shift increases the desired capital stock.

Empirical studies of the interest elasticity of investment demand are inconclusive. Statistical estimation is difficult because of the lack of a satisfactory equation for investment demand. Such an equation is needed in order to isolate the effect of the interest rate from the effect of the other variables that influence investment demand. There has, as yet, been no statistical estimate of the interest-elasticity of investment demand that inspires confidence.

Another approach to gauging the effect of the interest rate has been questionnaire surveys of businessmen. The results in general have indicated that changes of interest rates have little effect on investment. But these studies are subject to serious methodological criticism,[19] so that their evidence is by no means conclusive. For example, these studies have not weighted the results by the amount of investment each firm does. Thus the answers of small firms are overweighted relative to their importance in aggregate investment determination.

Many small firms may be unresponsive to the interest rate because they are in the position shown in Figure 5–7. The firm's

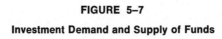

FIGURE 5–7

Investment Demand and Supply of Funds

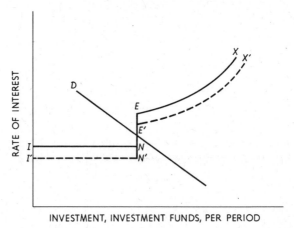

INVESTMENT, INVESTMENT FUNDS, PER PERIOD

demand function intersects the supply function in the vertical segment, *EN*. The firm invests to the full extent of its internal funds *IN*, but no more, because the cost of the first unit of external funds *E* exceeds the expected rate of return on the marginal unit of investment. A fall of the interest rate, lowering the supply function to *I'N'E'X'*, has no effect on the firm's investment because the cost of external funds is still above the marginal rate of return on investment. A sufficiently large change of the interest rate will affect the amount of investment, but for changes which leave the intersection of the demand function in the vertical section of the supply function, investment will not be affected.

Thus, in some firms the unresponsiveness of investment to the interest rate might be explained, not by the inelasticity of the de-

[19] See William H. White, "Interest Inelasticity of Investment Demand— The Case from Business Attitude Surveys Re-examined," *American Economic Review*, Vol. XLVI, No. 4 (September, 1956), pp. 565–87.

mand function, but by an inelasticity in the supply-of-funds function. This explanation, however, would not apply to the larger firms, which do have recourse to external funds and which do most of the investing.

It seems highly probable, therefore, that survey analyses have overstated the degree of inelasticity of investment demand. But we have at present no clear idea of how elastic it is.[20]

Investment in Residential Construction

The determination of investment in residential construction is thought to differ in certain respects from investment in other durables. Since residential construction is a large proportion of private domestic investment (ordinarily over 25 percent), it merits separate examination.

The demand for investment in residential construction depends on the demand for housing services relative to the existing stock of housing. The demand for housing services depends, first, on disposable income. Rising disposable income or expectations of rising disposable income will create expectations of a rise in demand for housing services. Unless there is adequate excess capacity in the existing stock of housing to satisfy the additional demand, investment in residential construction will be induced upward. In its broad outlines, induced investment in housing resembles induced investment in producers' durables, which is brought about by expectations of a rise of demand for output.

The unique feature in housing demand is supposed to be the part played by demographic factors, particularly the rates of population growth and family formation. It is generally presumed that higher rates of growth of population and of number of families increase the proportion of national income devoted to housing services and thus stimulate investment in housing. However, if demographic factors enter into housing investment, they must also enter into the rest of investment demand. If population growth raises the demand for housing services, it diverts demand away from other consumer products. Any demographic stimulus to investment in

---

[20] It is interesting to note that a popular view of investment demand holds it to be interest-inelastic but highly responsive to the internal-funds effect. This view is basically inconsistent, since the internal-funds effect depends on the response of investment to the cost of funds; with a perfectly inelastic demand function, a change of internal funds would have no effect on the amount of investment.

housing is accompanied by a dampening effect from the same source on investment for the production of other consumer products.

Given the demand for housing service, demand for residential construction will depend on the existing stock of housing. The stock of housing refers not only to the quantity but also to the quality and the location of housing. It will be diminished by deterioration and obsolescence. Geographic shifts of population will leave some housing mislocated and will diminish the useful stock. In these respects residential construction is not very different from other types of investment. The demand for producers' durables is related to the existing stock of those capital goods and the stock is affected by depreciation, obsolescence, and location.

Thus, the variables determining the demand for residential construction are not fundamentally different from those determining other kinds of investment. However, there are some significant quantitative differences. If consumer demand shifts to housing services from other consumer products, the result will be a net increase in the desired capital stock. The additional capital wanted to produce the additional housing services will more than offset the reduction of desired capital that follows from the fall of demand for other consumer products. This effect is produced by the fact that the capital-output ratio—the amount of capital needed to produce a unit of output per period—is so much higher for housing services than for other consumer products.

Another quantitative difference between the demand for housing and the demand for other investment is that the demand for housing appears to be considerably more interest-elastic. This difference can also be attributed to the high capital-output ratio of housing services. Because of the high capital-output ratio, interest costs are a relatively high proportion of total costs in the production of housing services and, consequently, the demand for housing tends to be more sensitive to the interest rate.

RECOMMENDED READINGS

American Economic Review, Papers and Proceedings, Vol. LIII, No. 2 (May, 1963), "Topics in Economic Theory":

EISNER, ROBERT. "Investment: Fact and Fancy," pp. 237–46.

JORGENSON, DALE W. "Capital Theory and Investment Behavior," pp. 247–59.

KUH, EDWIN. "Theory and Institutions in the Study of Investment Behavior," pp. 260–68. With discussion by CARL F. CHRIST, EDWIN MANSFIELD, and KARL BORCH, pp. 269–74.

BROWN, E. CARY. "Business-Income Taxation and Investment Incentives," *Income, Employment and Public Policy; Essays in Honor of Alvin H. Hansen,* pp. 300–16. New York: W. W. Norton & Co., Inc., 1948.

DUESENBERRY, JAMES S. *Business Cycles and Economic Growth,* chaps. iv, v. New York: McGraw-Hill Book Co., Inc., 1958.

ECKAUS, R. S. "The Accelerator Principle Reconsidered," *Quarterly Journal of Economics,* Vol. LXVII, No. 2 (May, 1953), pp. 209–30.

EISNER, ROBERT. "A Permanent Income Theory for Investment: Some Empirical Explorations," *American Economic Review,* Vol. LVII, No. 3 (June, 1967), pp. 363–90.

KEYNES, JOHN MAYNARD. *The General Theory of Employment, Interest, and Money,* chaps. xi, xii. New York: Harcourt, Brace & Co., 1936.

WHITE, W. H. "Interest Inelasticity of Investment Demand—The Case from Business Attitude Surveys Re-examined," *American Economic Review,* Vol. XLVI, No. 4 (September, 1956), pp. 565–87.

QUESTIONS

1. What is the formula for computing the present discounted value of a bond which will pay $50 at the end of the first year and $50 at the end of the second year, and will be redeemed for $1000 at the end of the second year? If the price of the bond is $980, what rate of return does it yield?

2. Describe the behavior of net investment demand in an economy in which the capital stock is growing faster than other inputs and technology is constant.

3. Compare, with respect to elasticity, the marginal-efficiency-of-capital function and the marginal-efficiency-of-investment function.

4. What are the limitations of the accelerator-multiplier model as a description of reality?

5. Is the accelerator-multiplier model more applicable to inventory fluctuations than to fluctuations of investment in durables?

6. "Investment outlays depend on expectations of future profits, not on current profits." Discuss.

Chapter
6
PUBLIC
DEMAND

A part of total demand in any economy will consist of purchases made by groups acting through government bodies. We can call such purchases *public* demand, distinguishing them from private demand or purchases made by individuals and nongovernment groups such as families or business units.

Our understanding of the nature of public demand is not aided—in fact, it is probably impeded—by the way the government sector is handled in national income accounting. A brief review of the treatment of the government sector in U.S. accounting and a comparison with the realities of public demand will be useful.

First, we separate out those government agencies which sell their services, such as the Post Office. These agencies, called "government enterprises," are included in the business sector accounts. The remainder of government activity consists of the performance of services which are given away.

The allocations side of the government sector account consists of purchases of goods and services, and transfer payments. The transfer payments are not part of demand for current product (though they affect private demand) and do not concern us here. Government purchases of goods and services comprise the labor services of government employees and the sales to the government by business and abroad. These accounts give the impression that these purchases are consumed by the government, and, indeed, are often referred to as "government consumption."

In actuality, the government sector can best be understood by thinking of it as a *producing* sector. Governments combine the services of labor, capital goods, land, and intermediate goods bought from other producers to produce services that are given away either to consumers or as intermediate products to other producers.

Difficulties in the compilation of statistics have thus far prevented the United States' national income accounts from picturing the government sector as a producing sector. For one thing, the government sector is treated as having no capital goods; all inputs are considered to be bought on current account. For another, all outputs are treated as final products; no attempt is made to measure government output going as intermediate goods to other producers. It is necessary, therefore, to step outside the accounting framework to talk about the determinants of public demand.

PUBLIC CONSUMER DEMAND

Public consumer demand is a component of total consumer demand. Consumers may be imagined to be aiming to divide their expenditures between private and public consumption in such a way as to maximize the satisfaction derived from the total expenditure. Because public consumption requires a collective decision, the problem of reaching an optimum position is much more difficult than it would be if all consumption were private and made by individual decisions; success in achieving an optimum rests upon the adequacy of devices by which the public "signals" its desires and by which conflicting interests are reconciled.[1]

To the extent that an optimum is approached, total consumer demand will be divided between public and private expenditure in accordance with the same principle that the rational consumer applies to a choice among several consumer goods—that the marginal utility of a dollar spent on each shall be the same. Public demand will thus be determined by the size of total consumer demand and by the relative marginal utilities that decide the division of total demand between public and private types. The relative marginal utilities may be affected by changes in national circumstances, as when swings in the state of international relations affect the desirability of national-security expenditures. Or the growth of income may tend to alter the relative marginal utilities—a tendency which will be reflected in unequal income elasticities of demand for private and public consumption. If, for example, the proportion of public consumption to private consumption is kept constant as income grows, the utility of the marginal dollar of private expenditure may fall below that of public expenditure. In this

[1] See Paul A. Samuelson, "The Pure Theory of Public Expenditure," *Review of Economics and Statistics*, Vol. XXXVI, No. 4 (November, 1954), pp. 387–89.

case, public consumption would have to increase faster than private consumption to keep the utilities equated at the margin.

The objective of attaining an optimum proportion of public to private consumption also has important implications for public policy during cyclical fluctuations. In a typical period of depressed economic activity, private investment will have fallen. Public policy will attempt to raise aggregate demand; and while some success may be had in efforts to boost investment, most of the compensatory increase will have to be in consumer demand. The question then arises: Should the additional consumption be entirely private or should public consumption also be increased? If public and private consumption were in the optimum proportions initially, the concentration of the incremental consumption entirely in private consumption would reduce the utility of marginal private expenditure below that of marginal public expenditure. The objective of an optimum proportion of private and public demand calls for an increase of both when pursuing a policy of an antidepression increase of consumption.

PUBLIC INVESTMENT

Public investment consists of the purchase, by both governments and government enterprises, of productive assets lasting longer than the accounting period in which they are bought. Government office buildings, schools, highways, equipment, and inventories would be included.

It is difficult to make any general statements about what determines the level of public investment. Perhaps the principles of the determination of private investment can be applied to investment by government enterprises, with appropriate modifications to allow for the political facets of government-enterprise management and decisions. With further modifications and some stretching of the imagination, some parallels might be drawn between the determination of investment for general government use and private investment. But it is unnecessary to pursue that line of thought here. It is more important to stress that there is such a thing as public investment, though it is not recognized as such in the United States' statistics; awareness of public investment can contribute to clearer thinking about government fiscal policy, as well as to avoiding a source of error in international comparisons of investment rates.

PUBLIC DEMAND AND TAX REVENUES

Taxation is a means of implementing the choice between private and public demand. When public expenditure is to be substituted for private, tax collection is a method by which private expenditure is reduced. However, under certain circumstances, it is possible to increase public expenditure without the necessity of a corresponding reduction in private expenditure. These circumstances arise when the output of the economy remains below the full-potential level. Public expenditure can then be increased without the clear need for an accompanying increase in tax revenues, provided that the government has access to the required funds through borrowing or the creation of new money. A national government will ordinarily have the necessary borrowing or money-creating facilities. State and local governments, on the other hand, have limitations on their borrowing capacity and are not empowered to create money; for them, the link between tax revenues and expenditures cannot be completely severed.

LONG-RUN TRENDS IN PUBLIC DEMAND

Total public purchases of current product have increased more rapidly than gross national product over the past 40 years (see Table 6–1). National defense expenditures account for a large part of the increase, but nondefense purchases have also increased substantially as a proportion of GNP. In the past decade, despite the fall of the proportion of GNP allocated to national defense, the percentage of GNP devoted to government purchases has continued to rise.

This trend suggests that in a growing economy, welfare-maximizing social choice requires a rising proportion of GNP to be devoted to public expenditure.[2] If so, society faces a potential long-run economic difficulty. The difficulty arises from the fact that the proportion of income taken by taxes can eventually rise to a point where the tax adversely affects the supply of productive effort. A

---

[2] We cannot be certain that the actual division of output between public and private purchases represents the welfare-maximizing division. It has been argued by some that voters' ignorance and the process of public decision making lead to overspending by government, and by others that these factors lead to underspending by government.

TABLE 6-1
Government Expenditures, 1929-68
(millions of dollars)

Year	Purchases of Goods and Services					Transfer Payments*			Total Gov't. Expenditures	GNP
	Federal			State & Local	Total	Federal	State & Local	Total		
	National Defense	Other	Total							
1929	$ 700	$ 600	$ 1,300	$ 7,236	$ 8,536	$ 1,251	$ 528	$ 1,779	$ 10,315	$103,095
1939	1,249	3,856	5,105	8,225	13,330	2,837	1,392	4,229	17,559	90,494
1948	10,734	5,781	16,515	15,038	31,553	16,387	2,401	18,788	50,341	257,562
1958	45,902	7,692	53,594	40,564	94,158	29,635	3,413	33,048	127,206	447,334
1968	78,031	21,484	99,515	100,745	200,260	63,700	6,900	70,600	270,820	865,701
Percent of Gross National Product										
1929	0.68	0.58	1.26	7.02	8.28	1.21	0.51	1.72	10.00	
1939	1.38	4.26	5.64	9.08	14.72	3.14	1.54	4.68	19.40	
1948	4.17	2.24	6.41	5.84	12.25	6.36	0.93	7.29	19.54	
1958	10.26	1.72	11.98	9.07	21.05	6.62	0.76	7.35	28.40	
1968	9.01	2.48	11.49	11.63	23.12	7.36	0.80	8.16	31.28	

Source: Survey of Current Business, August, 1965 and July, 1969, except for estimate of national defense expenditure in 1929 which is from Francis M. Bator, The Question of Government Spending (New York: Harper & Bros., 1960), p. 138.
* Transfer payments, net interest paid, and net subsidies to government enterprises.

tax on income or expenditure reduces the rate of payment for economic effort or for giving up leisure, and the reduction of that rate of payment can be carried to the point where the individual chooses to supply less effort and enjoy more leisure.[3]

At what level of taxation this effect would become significant we cannot now estimate, but as a possible long-term problem it cannot be ignored. This is particularly so when we note that public expenditure includes not only government purchases of goods and services, but also transfer payments. As Table 6–1 shows, government expenditures including transfer payments had risen by 1968 to over 30 percent of GNP. While transfer payments are purely redistributive and do not absorb current product, the taxation to cover them has the same effect on effort as taxation to cover government purchases.

RECOMMENDED READINGS

BATOR, FRANCIS M.   *The Question of Government Spending.* New York: Harper & Bros., 1960.

COLM, GERHARD.   "The Theory of Public Expenditures," *Essays in Public Finance and Fiscal Policy*, pp. 27–43. New York: Oxford University Press, 1955.

SAMUELSON, PAUL A.   "Principles and Rules in Modern Fiscal Policy: A Neo-Classical Reformulation," in *Money, Trade, and Economic Growth; Essays in Honor of John Henry Williams*, pp. 157–76. New York: Macmillan Co., 1951.

U.S. Congress, Joint Economic Committee.   *Federal Expenditure Policy for Economic Growth and Stability; Papers Submitted by Panelists.* . . . Washington: U.S. Government Printing Office, 1957:

     LINDBLOM, CHARLES E.   "Historical Change in Demand for Public Expenditure for Community Amenities," pp. 1–6.

     MUSGRAVE, RICHARD A.   "Principles of Budget Determination," pp. 108–15.

     POOLE, KENYON E.   "Some Problems in Optimizing the Level of Public Expenditures," pp. 116–29.

     SOLOWAY, ARNOLD M.   "The Growth of Government over the Past 50 Years: An Analytical Review," pp. 15–59.

---

[3] A tax has a dual effect on effort, a substitution effect and an income effect. The tax reduces the rate of payment for effort and causes a substitution of leisure for effort. It also reduces the individual's net income and induces him to supply more effort in order to raise his income. The net result of these two effects may be no change in supply of effort or even an increase, but as the tax rate rises, the substitution effect must eventually outweigh the income effect and reduce the supply of effort.

QUESTIONS

1. What are the economic characteristics of services that must be publicly consumed? What are the characteristics of investment that must be publicly performed?
2. Under what conditions would the optimum amount of public demand be a rising percentage of total output in a growing economy?

Chapter 7 | MONEY AND AGGREGATE DEMAND

In the determination of aggregate demand, certain assets which we call money or monetary assets play a distinctive role. We touched indirectly but not explicitly on this role in earlier chapters when interest rates and the supply of investment funds were introduced as variables affecting demand. In this chapter, the relation between money and demand will be investigated in more detail. The first part will present the basic Keynesian model of money, interest rates, and income. The second part will discuss some of the post-Keynesian additions to the theory of money and demand.

MONEY, INTEREST RATES, AND INCOME

The model to be presented in this section will be assembled in two stages. The first stage connects the quantity of money and the rate of interest.[1] The second stage connects the rate of interest and the level of income.

---

[1] The economy, of course, does not have a single prevailing interest rate. It has a structure of interest rates. The structure is based chiefly on two characteristics of loans, the credit risk and the term to maturity. The greater the credit risk (risk that the borrower will default), the higher the interest rate. The term to maturity refers to the length of time until the loan must be repaid to the lender. The term-structure of interest rates depends, according to the most generally accepted theory, on expectations about future interest rates.

For an analysis of this subject, see F. A. Lutz, "The Structure of Interest Rates," *Quarterly Journal of Economics*, Vol. LV, No. 1 (November, 1940), pp. 36–63, reprinted in American Economic Association, *Readings in the Theory of Income Distribution* (Philadelphia: Blakiston Co., 1946) ; also David Meiselman, *The Term Structure of Interest Rates* (Englewood Cliffs, N.J.: Prentice-Hall, Inc., 1962).

In this chapter the discussion will be simplified by assuming that the different interest rates maintain their relative positions, all moving up or down together, so that we can speak of "the interest rate" rather than "the structure of interest rates."

THE LIQUIDITY-PREFERENCE THEORY OF INTEREST

The liquidity-preference theory defines the equilibrium interest rate as the rate which equates the demand for holding a stock of money with the supply or stock of money which exists to be held.[2] In all demand and supply analysis, there is a difficulty about defining the thing that is being demanded and supplied. The difficulty is one of deciding how narrowly or broadly to define the item: whether or not to include close substitutes; where, among the substitutes, to draw the line. In the case of money, its unique characteristic is that it is a medium of exchange (i.e., we ordinarily define money as anything that is readily acceptable in payment). But there are certain kinds of property which, while not usable in payment, can be very quickly converted into money with no uncertainty about the rate at which they can be converted. Time (savings) deposits are an example of such property. Government securities can be converted into money with only minor delay and with only slight uncertainty about the price at which they can be converted (particularly for short-term securities). The cash value of life insurance policies also represents an asset that can be fairly quickly exchanged into money. Time deposits, government securities, and the cash value of life insurance policies are, therefore, near to being money because they constitute close substitutes for money. In this chapter, the term "money" will be used in its narrow sense of medium of exchange (in the United States, currency plus demand deposits), but we should keep in mind that there are close substitutes for money and that those substitutes can affect the demand for money.

The Demand for Money

In a modern economy, the owner of wealth has a choice of types of assets in which to hold that wealth. One asset, money, typically earns no interest.[3] It needs to be explained, therefore, why anyone

---

[2] Since interest is a payment for *lending* money, it seems to many people peculiar to explain interest-rate determination in terms of holding or *not lending* money. For those who find this reverse view objectionable, there is an alternative way of stating the equilibrium interest rate: the "loanable-funds" theory. But "liquidity-preference" and "loanable-funds" theories amount to the same thing, as is shown in Appendix A to this chapter.

[3] In some banking systems, interest may be paid on demand deposits. The rate in such cases is low, and well below the rates on other assets.

would hold money when he can hold other assets which do earn interest. Several different reasons for holding money can be offered.

1. Transactions Demand   An individual or business will rarely find that its receipts and expenditures are perfectly synchronized. Some money will be held to pay for transactions in those time intervals during which expenditures exceed receipts. The more closely receipts and expenditures are synchronized, the smaller will be the demand for transactions balances.

It would be possible to get by without holding any money for transactions purposes by putting all receipts into earnings assets and converting them into money as each payment is made. But to curtail transactions balances, certain costs must be incurred—the charges for shifting from money into other assets (such as securities) and returning to cash, and the costs in time and inconvenience of converting nonmoney assets into money for each transaction. At ordinary rates of interest it is unlikely that the decision on the amount of transactions balances to be held will be influenced by consideration of the returns being sacrificed by holding money. But it is certainly possible for the interest rate to be high enough to make it worthwhile to reduce transactions balances. Transactions demand for money may be viewed as completely interest-inelastic at moderate rates of interest but responsive to the interest rate in some higher range.

The institutional arrangements in the economy which determine how closely receipts and expenditures are synchronized can affect transactions demand. Except as a possible very gradual long-run influence, this variable can be ignored.

Transactions demand for money depends chiefly on the volume of transactions to be carried on. Or, if we assume income to be an index of money transactions in the economy, transactions demand for money is a positive function of the level of income.

2. Precautionary Demand   Future receipts and expenditures cannot be known with absolute certainty. There is always the possibility that an unexpected need to increase expenditures or a delay in receipts may place an individual in a difficult position which can be both inconvenient and costly. He may, therefore, hold additional money balances as a precaution against such contingencies.

Precautionary demand is, hence, a variant of transactions demand, arising from uncertainty about future transactions. Its dependence on the interest rate and the income level is similar to that of transactions balances.

3. Speculative Demand   Demand for money of a sort quite different from transactions demand arises from what Keynes called the "speculative motive." The major close substitute for holding money is holding bonds. The prices of marketable bonds are subject to change, rising when interest rates fall and falling when interest rates rise. There is thus the possibility of making a capital gain or incurring a capital loss by holding bonds. This possibility of capital gain or loss affects the choice between holding money and holding bonds. The essence of Keynes's speculative-demand hypothesis is that changes in the current rate of interest will so affect expectations about capital gains and losses in bonds as to cause the demand for money to rise as the interest rate falls. The remainder of this section investigates the connection between the rate of interest and the speculative demand for money.[4]

Suppose an individual has a given amount of wealth, over and above what he holds for transactions and precautionary purposes, which he wants to hold in monetary assets (cash and bonds). We will call this amount his "investment balance." He must decide whether to hold his investment balance in cash or in bonds during the next time period. If he expects bond prices to rise (i.e., expects the interest rate to fall) during the period, he expects the bonds will yield him the current rate of interest plus a capital gain; and he will choose to hold bonds. If he expects bond prices to fall (i.e., expects the interest rate to rise), he expects to earn the current rate of interest minus a capital loss. If that net total is greater than zero, he will buy bonds; if it is less than zero, he will hold cash. There is, then, some critical level of the expected rate of interest relative to the current rate of interest which marks a dividing line. If the expected rate is above the critical level, it will pay the individual to keep his investment balance in cash; if below the critical level, it will pay him to hold it in bonds.

As an illustration of the critical level, take the case of a 5 percent bond with no maturity date (a consol), currently selling at its face value of $100 and yielding 5 percent. Suppose that one year from now the interest rate is expected to be 5.26 percent. The bond is then expected to sell next year at a price which yields 5.26 percent, i.e., $95. Over the year, therefore, the buyer of the bond expects to earn $5 in interest and lose $5 on the value of the bond, an expectation of

---

[4] Much of the discussion that follows is derived from James Tobin, "Liquidity Preference as Behavior towards Risk," *Review of Economic Studies*, Vol. XXV(2), No. 67 (February, 1958), pp. 65–86.

no net gain or loss—an outcome he could have achieved by holding money rather than the bond. We find, then, that when the current interest rate is 5 percent, the critical level of the expected rate is 5.26 percent. With that expected interest rate, the expected return on money and on bonds is the same. At expected rates less than 5.26 percent, a greater return is expected from bonds than from money; at expected rates greater than 5.26 percent, the expected return on bonds is below the return on money.

Why will a rise in the current rate of interest cause a reduction in speculative money balances? To answer this question, the Keynesian analysis links the change in the current rate of interest with the expected rate of interest in a particular way. A current fall in the rate of interest is said to create expectations of a future interest-rate rise, and a current rise is said to create expectations of a future drop in the rate. This view of how expectations will behave is based on the proposition that individuals hold to some notion of a "normal" level to which the rate of interest will tend to return. The further the current rate deviates above or below the "normal," the stronger will grow the expectation that it will reverse its direction and move toward the "normal." It follows that, as the interest rate rises and builds up expectations of an eventual fall of the rate, the point will be reached where the individual will want to shift his investment balance from money to bonds. Thus a rise in the interest rate leads to a fall in the quantity of speculative demand for money.

According to the theory outlined above, we would expect an individual to keep his investment balance either 100 percent in cash or 100 percent in bonds, depending on the relationship between the current rate and his expected rate of interest. However, the aggregate of such assets will be divided between cash and bonds if there is a spread of expected rates among individuals, some above the critical level and some below, so that some individuals hold all cash and the others all bonds.

This Keynesian view of speculative demand for money has the aura of reasonableness about it. Nevertheless, it is somewhat unsatisfactory to base the theory of speculative demand on a pattern of expectational behavior which is not necessarily always in operation. In addition, this traditional theory cannot explain why an individual might hold both speculative money balances and bonds. For these reasons, Tobin[5] has proposed an alternative foundation for the theory of speculative demand.

---

[5] *Ibid.*

Suppose that the asset-holder is uncertain about the future movements of interest rates. He believes there is some chance of making a capital gain and some chance of suffering a capital loss. To distinguish the new approach more clearly from the previous formulation, let us assume that the investor's view of the probabilities of gains and losses on holding bonds is such that the most probable outcome, in his opinion, is zero capital gain or loss, and that he bases his decisions on that expectation. Nevertheless, though he expects no capital gain or loss, he must take on the burden of *risk* if he holds bonds because of his uncertainty about future interest rates. The greater the proportion of bonds to money in his investment balance, the more risk he assumes.

Two attitudes of investors towards risk are possible. Some may be "risk-lovers." To them, risk has positive utility; if necessary, they would give up some interest income from assets in order to take on more risk. Actually, however, they can have more of both interest income and risk by increasing the proportion of bonds to cash. The risk-lovers will, therefore, hold all of their investment balances in bonds and none in cash.

Other investors may be "risk-averters." Risk, to them, has disutility and will be accepted only if compensated for by interest income. The higher the rate of interest, the more risk they will accept (i.e., the larger the proportion of their investment balances they will hold in bonds).[6]

Rising interest rates will not affect risk-lovers, who always hold their investment balances entirely in bonds. But a rise in the rate of interest will induce risk-averters to take on more risk by shifting from cash to bonds. The net effect of a rise in the interest rate is, therefore, to decrease the quantity of money demanded.

This explanation of demand for money is entirely independent of any expectations of capital loss on bonds since it was assumed at the outset that the investor acted on the expectation of zero capital gain or loss. But the responsiveness of demand for money to the interest rate will be increased if, in addition to risk-aversion, the expectational behavior of the orthodox Keynesian liquidity-preference theory is also at work.

---

[6] This type of risk-averter Tobin calls "diversifiers." He also considers the case of risk-averters who are "plungers": at interest rates below some particular level, they will hold their investment balances entirely in cash; at interest rates above that level, entirely in bonds.

Diagrams of Demand for Money

Transactions demand for money has been described as a positive function of the level of income and, to some degree, a negative function of the rate of interest. Figure 7–1 shows transactions demand

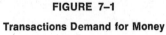

FIGURE 7–1

Transactions Demand for Money

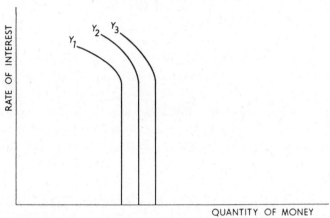

as a function of the rate of interest. Transactions demand here is completely interest-inelastic at low interest rates which would not compensate for the costs of converting money into earning assets and back to money for the interval between the receipt of income and the payment for a transaction. At higher interest rates, the demand is shown as increasingly elastic. The level of income, however, is the principal determinant of transactions demand. Because the diagram has only two dimensions, the effect of the income variable must be shown by separate curves (labeled Y_1, Y_2, Y_3) indicating demand for money at ascending income levels Y_1, Y_2, and Y_3.

For precautionary demand, a set of curves similar to those in Figure 7–1 can be drawn.

Speculative demand for money is a function of the rate of interest but not of income. The general characteristic of such a demand curve is that it slopes downward to the right. The curve in Figure 7–2 is drawn with a special additional feature: increasing elasticity as the interest rate falls, ending in perfect elasticity at some low

FIGURE 7–2

Speculative Demand for Money

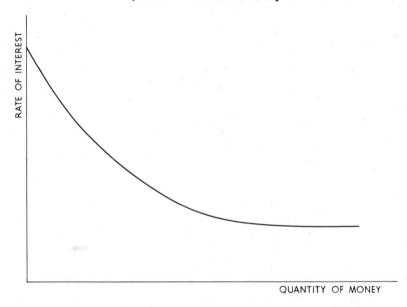

interest rate. The conjecture that the speculative demand function is so shaped is based on the presumption that, as the interest rate falls, expectations of a future rise in the interest rate become increasingly strong until they approach certainty and the demand for holding money becomes infinite.

The aggregate demand for money can now be obtained by summing up the quantity demanded for transactions, precautionary, and speculative reasons at each rate of interest. The summation of curves such as those in Figures 7–1 and 7–2 gives us the total demand-for-money function shown in Figure 7–3.

The Supply of Money

The stock of money (in the United States) consists of certain obligations of the Treasury, the Federal Reserve System, and the commercial banks. The Treasury component of the money supply is Treasury currency. The rest of the currency in circulation is Federal Reserve notes, a liability of the Federal Reserve System. The remainder and bulk of the money supply is made up of demand deposits (the demand-deposit liabilities of the commercial banks plus

FIGURE 7-3

Total Demand for Money

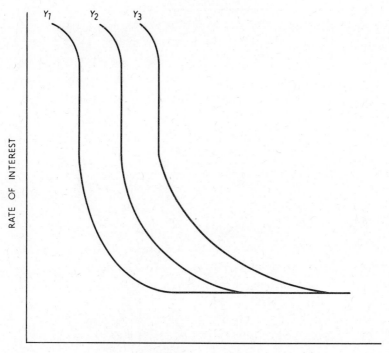

QUANTITY OF MONEY

a small amount of demand deposits held at the Federal Reserve banks by the Treasury and other domestic and foreign government agencies).

The various ways in which the money supply can be affected by government policy and the behavior of the private and foreign sectors need not be discussed here. It is sufficient for the purposes of this chapter to specify that the supply of money is assumed to be determined by public policy and to be independent of either the rate of interest or the level of income. The supply curve in the diagrams is, therefore, a vertical line.

The Equilibrium Rate of Interest

A given stock or supply of money in circulation must be held, in the aggregate, by individuals in the economy. Any person holding more than he wants to can exchange his excess money for other assets, but someone else will then be holding this money. Equilibrium requires that each individual be satisfied with the proportion of his assets which he holds in the form of money and, hence, that the aggregate demand for money equal the aggregate supply.

Assume for the moment that the level of income is fixed. Then, given the supply of money, the demand for money must be equated to the supply by the interest rate. The equilibrium rate of interest is the rate which makes the demand and supply of money equal.

If the stock of money is M and the income level is Y_3, the equilibrium rate of interest in Figure 7–4 is i_3. If the rate is above i_3, the

FIGURE 7–4

The Equilibrium of Demand and Supply of Money

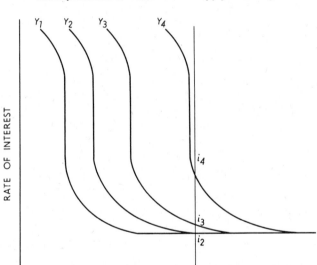

holders of excess amounts of money will attempt to exchange the excess for other assets such as bonds. The increased demand for bonds will tend to raise bond prices and lower bond yields until the interest rate has fallen to the point where the demand for money is equal to M. If the interest rate is below i_3, the demand for money will exceed M, and the sale of bonds to acquire more money will depress bond prices and raise the interest rate until the demand for money is reduced to M.

Stability of the Money-Demand Function

We have just seen that when the money-demand function, the level of income, and the supply of money are given, an equilibrium interest rate is determined. It is obvious from Figure 7–4 that a change in the income level or in the supply of money will change the equilibrium interest rate. We should not overlook the fact that a shift of the demand function can also change the equilibrium interest rate.

The demand function may shift because of (*a*) a change in the proportion of income which spending units feel it desirable to hold in money for transactions purposes; (*b*) a change in the degree of uncertainty about receipts and expenditures, leading to a change in precautionary demand; (*c*) a change in expectations about interest rates; (*d*) a change in the uncertainty about interest rates and, hence, in the risk associated with not holding money; or (*e*) a change in expectations about the general price level.

Causes (*c*) and (*d*) will affect the speculative demand for money. (*e*) will affect the desirability of holding any price-fixed asset, of which money is one. (*a*) and (*b*) are unlikely to cause any significant short-run instability of the aggregate demand function. But widespread changes in expectations or uncertainty about interest rates or expectations about the price level are potential sources of demand shifts.

THE EQUILIBRIUM OF MONEY, INTEREST, AND INCOME

In Chapter 3 a model of income determination was developed, based on the equilibrium condition that intended saving equals intended investment. In its simplest form the model consisted of two parts, a saving function (saving as a function of income) and a constant rate of investment. These two parts of the model in equation form are:

$$S = S(Y)$$
$$I = \bar{I}$$

(where $\bar{I}$ stands for a constant amount).

The income level is determined by solving for the value of Y that makes $S = I$.

This model can now be expanded to include the effects of the quantity of money and the rate of interest.

The savings function stated above can be retained. But investment, instead of being treated as a constant, now becomes a function of the interest rate.

The equilibrium condition, saving equals investment, remains; but a second equilibrium condition must now be added, that the demand for money equals the supply of money.

We have seen that the demand for money can be treated as a function of income and the interest rate. The supply of money will be assumed to be a constant.

There are, then, four equations in the expanded model:

$$S = S(Y)$$
$$I = I(i)$$
$$L = L(Y, i)$$
$$M = \overline{M}$$

where i stands for the interest rate, L the demand for money, and M the supply of money.

The two equilibrium conditions are:

$$S = I$$
$$L = M$$

The equilibrium income and the equilibrium interest rate are given by that combination of income and interest rate that will satisfy the two equilibrium conditions, given the saving function, the investment function, the demand-for-money function, and the supply of money.

The equilibrium solution to the set of equations in this model can most easily be illustrated by a diagram. One line in this diagram shows the various combinations of income and interest rate that will satisfy the first equilibrium condition, $S = I$. The saving function is upward sloping; the higher the level of income, the greater the amount of saving. The investment function is downward sloping; the lower the rate of interest, the greater the amount of investment. It follows that there will be a large number of different combinations of Y and i that will equate saving and investment. For instance, let us assume that in Figure 7–5 the point A designates a particular income–interest rate combination (Y_1 and i_1) that makes saving and investment equal. If income were greater than Y_1—say Y_2—then saving would be greater, and the interest rate would have

FIGURE 7–5

**Interest Rate-Income Combinations Equating
Saving and Investment**

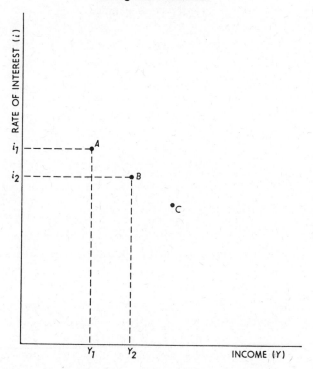

to be lower than i_1—say i_2—to bring investment up to saving. Point
B, then, marks another income–interest rate combination that satisfies the $S = I$ equilibrium condition. The set of such combinations
designated by points A, B, C, etc., will form the negatively sloped
line marked SI in Figure 7–6.

The slope of the SI line depends upon the shape of the underlying
saving and investment functions. The flatter the saving function
(the smaller the marginal propensity to save), the flatter the SI
line. Similarly, the flatter the investment function, the flatter will
be the SI line. If investment is completely interest-inelastic, i.e., if
the investment function is a vertical line, the SI line will also be
vertical.

A method of deriving the SI line from the underlying saving and
investment functions is shown in Figure 7–7. The S and I lines are
the saving and investment functions respectively. A combination of

FIGURE 7–6

Simultaneous Determination of Equilibrium Interest Rate and Income

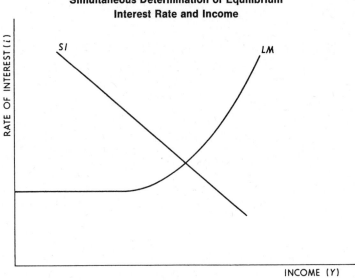

income Y_1 and interest rate i_1 will equate saving and investment $(S_1 = I_1)$. A lower income Y_2 combined with a higher interest rate i_2 will also equate saving and investment $(S_2 = I_2)$. Plotting all the combinations of Y and i obtained in this way produces the SI line. By experimentation with functions of different elasticities, the effect of the elasticity of the functions can be observed. For example, a completely interest-inelastic investment function (in Figure 7–7,

FIGURE 7–7

Derivation of the *SI* Line

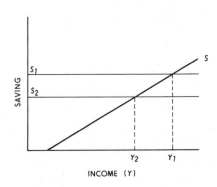
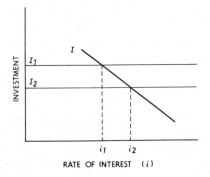

a horizontal line because the labeling of the axes has been reversed from the usual diagram) will show that at any interest rate, the same level of income is required to equate saving and investment, i.e., the *SI* line is vertical.

The second component of the diagram is a line showing all the combinations of income and interest rate that fulfill the equilibrium condition that demand for money equal supply of money. The supply of money is assumed fixed. To keep the demand for money equal to a given supply, any increase of income, which will raise the demand, must be exactly offset by some increase in the interest rate, which reduces the demand. The set of equilibrium combinations forms a positively sloped line, labeled *LM* in Figure 7–6.

The shape of the *LM* curve depends upon the shape of the money demand function. The more interest-elastic the demand for money, the flatter the *LM* line. The extreme flatness at low interest rates and steepness at high interest rates, as the curve is drawn in Figure 7–6, reflects the hypothesis previously put forward that as the interest rate moves toward the extremes, expectations of a reverse movement will strengthen, making demand for money highly elastic at low rates and very inelastic at high rates.

The relationship between the elasticity of the demand for money and the shape of the *LM* curve can be seen in Figure 7–4. When the supply-of-money line intersects the demand curve in its perfectly elastic portion, an increase of income from Y_1 to Y_2 does not change the equilibrium interest rate. In that region, therefore, the *LM* curve is horizontal—the same interest rate (i_2) is combined with various income levels to equate the demand and supply of money. At income level Y_3, a higher interest rate, i_3, is required for equilibrium. As income rises further to Y_4 and the supply curve intersects the demand curve in its inelastic portion, the equilibrium interest rate rises steeply and the *LM* curve becomes perfectly inelastic in that region.

The equilibrium solution can now be easily observed. Income equilibrium requires that $S = I$. Monetary equilibrium requires that $L = M$. The *SI* curve represents income–interest rate combinations that meet one equilibrium condition. The *LM* curve represents combinations that satisfy the second equilibrium condition. The sole combination that satisfies both conditions is given by the only point lying on both curves—the point at which they intersect.

INDUCED MONETARY EFFECTS AND THE MULTIPLIER

One application of the income–interest rate model is to the analysis of the income effects of an autonomous change in aggregate demand. An autonomous increase in consumption, investment, or government expenditure appears in the model diagram (Figure 7–8) as a shift of the SI line to $S'I'$. An autonomous increase in de-

FIGURE 7–8

Effects of an Autonomous Change of Aggregate Demand

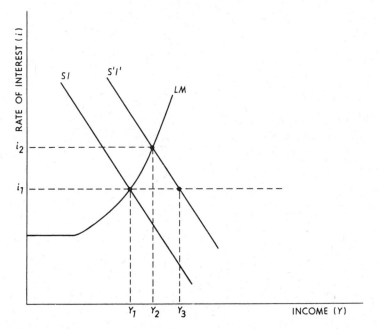

mand for product requires some combination of higher income and higher interest rate to equate saving and investment.

Assume the system initially in equilibrium at income Y_1 and interest rate i_1. In earlier models, where the interest rate was ignored or, in effect, assumed constant, equilibrium was reached by an increase of income from Y_1 to Y_3. In the expanded model, the autonomous rise in demand, by raising income, also increases the demand for money and thereby induces the interest rate upward. The rising interest rate tends to curtail the increase in income. The final solution in Figure 7–8 has the interest rate at i_2 and income raised only to Y_2. The induced monetary effects reduce the size of the income multiplier.[7]

THE QUANTITY OF MONEY AND THE INCOME LEVEL

A second application of the income–interest rate model is to the analysis of the effects of a change in the quantity of money.

An increase in the supply of money necessitates an increase in the

---

[7] The multiplier can be derived as follows.

Assume an autonomous change in expenditure (A), leading to induced changes in consumption $(\triangle C)$ and investment $(\triangle I)$. Then the total change in income is

$$\triangle Y = A + \triangle C + \triangle I \tag{1}$$

Letting b stand for the marginal propensity to consume,

$$\triangle C = b\triangle Y \tag{2}$$

The change in investment is

$$-\triangle I = \frac{\triangle i}{f} \tag{3}$$

where i is the interest rate and f is the slope of the investment function $-\triangle i/\triangle I$. The change in the interest rate, $\triangle i$, is determined by the demand for money function. The increase in transactions balances (L_1) is

$$\triangle L_1 = k\triangle Y$$

where k is the assumed ratio of transactions balances to income.

Speculative money balances (L_2) are a function of the rate of interest. Changes in L_2 are given by

$$-\triangle L_2 = \frac{\triangle i}{l}$$

where l is the slope of the speculative demand function $-\triangle i/\triangle L_2$. Since the supply of money is unchanged, the increased transactions balances must be exactly offset by the decreased speculative balances. That is,

$$\triangle L_1 = -\triangle L_2$$

or

$$k\triangle Y = \frac{-\triangle i}{l}$$

$$\therefore \triangle i = -lk\triangle Y \tag{4}$$

Substituting equations (2), (3), and (4) into (1), we have

$$\triangle Y = A + b\triangle Y + \frac{lk}{f}\triangle Y$$

The multiplier is then

$$\frac{\triangle Y}{A} = \frac{1}{1 - b + \frac{lk}{f}}$$

When compared to the multiplier without induced monetary effects $(1/1 - b)$, the new multiplier is seen to be smaller.

quantity of money demanded to restore equilibrium. The new higher income–lower interest-rate set of combinations that will equate demand to the larger supply of money is shown by a curve such as *L'M'* in Figure 7–9.

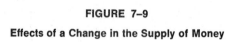

FIGURE 7–9

Effects of a Change in the Supply of Money

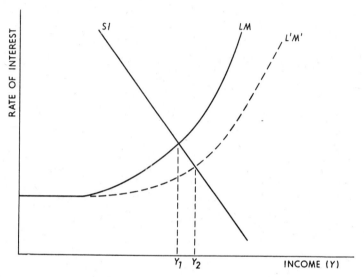

In this model there are two links between the quantity of money and income. To affect income, a change in the money supply must alter the interest rate. The change in the interest rate must then affect aggregate demand. In Figure 7–9, the increase of the money supply, the fall in the interest rate, and the increase in investment demand raise the equilibrium income from Y_1 to Y_2.

The impact of the money supply on income in this analysis depends on (1) the interest-elasticity of demand for money and (2) the interest-elasticity of investment demand. When the supply of money is increased, the willingness of people to hold the additional money will determine the effect on the rate of interest. If they will readily accept an increase in their money balances with little change in the interest rate, i.e., if the demand for money is highly elastic, the supply of money will have little effect on the interest rate. On the other hand, if the demand for money is inelastic, the recipients of additional money balances will exchange them for bonds until the price of bonds has been bid up (the interest rate reduced) by an amount large enough to induce them to hold the total money supply. In that case, changes in the quantity of money will be capable of having a sizable effect on the rate of interest.

The effect of the rate of interest on aggregate demand will depend on the elasticity of the investment-demand function. The more responsive investors are to the interest rate, the greater will be the effect of changes in the money supply on the level of income.

MONETARY VERSUS FISCAL EFFECTS

It often happens that an increase in the quantity of money occurs as a concomitant of a fiscal measure. If the effects of both this monetary change and the fiscal action are attributed solely to the increase in money, as is common in popular thinking, the power of the money supply to affect income will be erroneously exaggerated. The prevalence of the confusion between monetary and fiscal effects justifies a brief digression to draw a clear distinction.

Suppose that the government intends to increase its expenditure on current product by $5 billion per year, financing this additional outlay by selling bonds. This financing can be carried out with no change in the quantity of money in circulation by selling the bonds to the nonbank public. Initially, the sale of bonds by the Treasury results in an increase of $5 billion in the Treasury checking account in the Federal Reserve System. The public has $5 billion more of government bonds which it has paid for (we may assume) with checks. Demand deposits and bank reserves are reduced by $5 billion. This initial position is shown in these balance sheet entries of the Federal Reserve System and the commercial banking system:

INITIAL POSITION

Federal Reserve System		*Commercial Banks*	
ASSETS	LIABILITIES	ASSETS	LIABILITIES
	Member-bank reserves ... —$5 bil. Treasury deposits ... + 5 bil.	Reserves .... —$5 bil.	Demand deposits ... —$5 bil.

The Treasury has borrowed $5 billion in order to spend it. The expenditure of the $5 billion reduces the Treasury deposits and restores $5 billion to demand deposits and reserves in the commercial banking system. The *final position,* therefore, is one of no change in demand deposits. Five billion dollars has passed from the public to the Treasury and back to the public with no change in the total quantity of money in circulation.

Alternatively, the Treasury might sell the bonds to the Federal Reserve banks and the commercial banks. Suppose that $1 billion of bonds is sold to the Federal Reserve. On the Federal Reserve balance sheet, holdings of government securities are increased $1 billion and the Treasury deposit is increased $1 billion. When the Treasury spends the $1 billion, its deposit is decreased and the $1 billion enters the demand deposits of the recipients of Treasury checks. In the commercial banking system, reserves and demand deposits are increased by $1 billion.

The commercial banks now have excess reserves. Assuming a 20 percent reserve requirement against demand deposits, the commercial banks are in a position to buy $4 billion of bonds from the Treasury. When the Treasury has received these funds and spent them, $4 billion has been added to demand deposits. Together with the $1 billion of demand deposits created by the sale of bonds to the Federal Reserve, money in circulation has been increased by $5 billion. This process is summarized in the following balance sheet entries:

(1) FEDERAL RESERVE SYSTEM
Initial Position

ASSETS	LIABILITIES
Government securities .. +$1 bil.	Treasury deposits ... +$1 bil.

(2) FEDERAL RESERVE SYSTEM
Final Position

ASSETS	LIABILITIES
Government securities .. +$1 bil.	Member-bank reserves ... +$1 bil.

COMMERCIAL BANKS
Initial Position

ASSETS	LIABILITIES
Reserves .... +$1 bil.	Demand deposits ... +$1 bil.

(3) COMMERCIAL BANKS
Final Position

ASSETS	LIABILITIES
Reserves .... +$1 bil. Government securities .. +$4 bil.	Demand deposits ... +$5 bil.

The *fiscal* impact on income under either method of financing is the same: government expenditure is increased by $5 billion. But the monetary impact in the two cases is quite different—in the one, the quantity of money is unchanged; in the other, the quantity of money is increased.

The effect of the altered quantity of money on income is measured, not by the change of income in either of the above cases, but by the difference in the income change between the case where the quantity of money was constant and the case where it was increased. By that comparison the fiscal element is eliminated and the purely monetary element is left.

The distinction is shown graphically in Figure 7–10. The shift of

FIGURE 7–10

Fiscal and Monetary Effects Distinguished

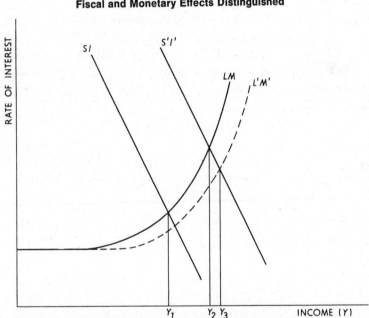

the *SI* curve to *S'I'* is the result of the increase in government expenditure. If the quantity of money is unchanged (and the money-demand function does not shift), the *LM* curve is unchanged, and income is increased from Y_1 to Y_2. If the financing of the additional government expenditure involves an increase in the quantity of money, the *LM* curve shifts to *L'M'*. In that case the income increase is from Y_1 to Y_3.

The increase from Y_1 to Y_2 is a fiscal effect. The increase from Y_2 to Y_3 is a monetary effect.

Note that if government expenditures are reduced to their original level, the fiscal effect is eliminated (the $S'I'$ curve shifts back to SI). That reduction of government expenditures, however, does not eliminate the monetary effect. The additional money remains in circulation and the $L'M'$ curve is not shifted back. The fiscal effect is the result of an increase in a *flow;* and when the flow returns to its original rate, the fiscal effect disappears. The monetary effect is the result of an increase in a *stock,* and the stock continues at its increased level after the flow has been restored to its original level.

The Price Level and the Monetary Model

Another application of the income–interest rate model is to the analysis of the effect of a change of the price level.

Suppose that the price level rises, for whatever reason, and it is now expected to remain at its new level. Assume that the increase is uniform throughout the economy, so that there is no redistribution of income or wealth which might shift the real consumption function or the real investment function. Consequently the IS line in real terms (the combinations of income and interest rate that equate real investment with real saving) will be unaffected by the price level.[8]

In Figure 7–11, the analysis is presented in real terms by dividing all money-valued items by a price index P. The rise of P will not change the IS/P line. The price level (P), however, does affect the LM curve. It is reasonable to suppose that the demand for money is a demand to hold a certain *real* quantity of money and therefore the real demand for money will be unaffected by a change of P. The supply of money, however, is a different matter. A rise of P reduces the real supply of money (M/P). If the nominal supply of money M is kept constant by the monetary authorities, then the real supply of money falls proportionately to the rise of the price level.

With the fall of the real supply of money, the LM/P curve shifts upward, reflecting the fact that some combination of higher interest rate and lower real income is required to equate the real demand for money with the now-reduced real supply of money. The effect of the rise of the price level from P_1 to P_2 is to shift $(LM/P)_1$ upward to $(LM/P)_2$, raising the equilibrium interest rate from i_1 to i_2 and

---

[8] The mechanisms by which a rise of the price level might shift the IS line downward are discussed in Chapter 10.

FIGURE 7–11

Effects of a Change of the Price Level

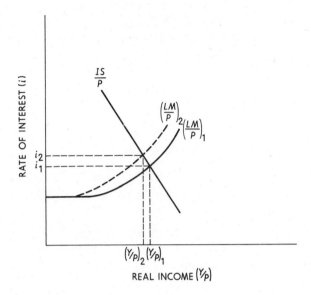

lowering the equilibrium level of real income from $(Y/P)_1$ to $(Y/P)_2$.

Price Expectations and the Monetary Model

The preceding analysis dealt with the effects of a price increase that had already occurred. It did not deal with the effects of price expectations, since it was assumed that no further price changes were expected. Now let us consider the case of expectations of a price increase.

When a price increase is expected, the real rate of interest is approximately the nominal rate of interest minus the expected rate of price increase. To the investor, it is the real rate of interest, not the nominal rate, that matters.

In the demand for money, however, it is the nominal rate of interest that matters. The expected rate of price change affects equally the real value of money and the real value of interest-bearing assets, so that it has no effect on the choice between holding money and holding interest-bearing assets. The nominal rate of interest, not the real rate, measures the cost of holding money (as against holding interest-bearing assets) and it is therefore the relevant rate in the demand for money.

The effect of price expectations is illustrated in Figure 7–12. An

FIGURE 7–12

Effects of Price Expectations

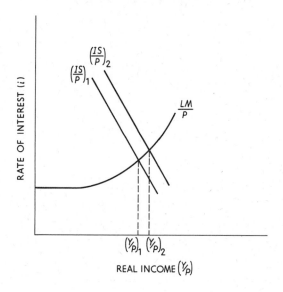

REAL INCOME $\left(\frac{Y}{P}\right)$

initial position, when no price change is expected, is represented by the curves $(IS/N)_1$ and $(LM/P)_1$. When the expectation of a price increase is introduced, the real interest rate falls by an amount equal to the expected rate of price increase, and since investment depends upon the real interest rate, the IS/P curve shifts upward to $(IS/P)_2$. The LM curve, which depends on the nominal rate of interest i, is unaffected. Equilibrium income rises from $(Y/P)_1$ to $(Y/P)_2$.

This analysis of the effects of price expectations can now be combined with the preceding analysis of the effects of actual price changes. We start from a position of income at full employment, since it is in the neighborhood of full employment that expectations of a price increase ordinarily develop.

In Figure 7–13, where no price change is expected, the IS/P curve is at $(IS/P)_1$, the LM/P curve is at $(LM/P)_1$, and income is in equilibrium at the full-employment level $(Y/P)_f$. When expectation of a price increase is introduced, the IS/P curve shifts to $(IS/P)_2$

FIGURE 7–13

Effects of Price Expectations and Price Changes

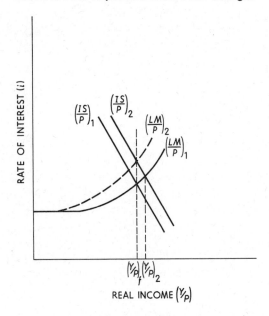

and the equilibrium income is raised to $(Y/P)_2$, which means that an inflationary gap has been created. Prices then rise, reducing the real supply of money and thus shifting the LM/P curve until it reaches the position $(LM/P)_2$, where the equilibrium level of income is again at $(Y/P)_f$ and the inflationary gap has been eliminated.

At this point, real investment and saving have been restored to their initial level, from which we can conclude that the nominal interest rate has risen by the amount of the expected price increase, restoring the real interest rate to its initial level.

If prices are now expected to stabilize, the IS/P curve will return to $(IS/P)_1$, lowering the equilibrium income below the full-employment level. If, instead of stabilizing, prices are expected to increase at the same rate as was previously expected, the IS/P curve will remain at $(IS/P)_2$ and equilibrium income will remain at $(Y/P)_f$. Prices cannot actually increase, however, without shifting the LM/P curve upward further, which will reduce the equilibrium income below the full-employment level.

It is difficult, therefore, for price expectations to create a sustained increase of real aggregate demand. For if those expectations are fulfilled (and the supply of money is not increased), the money rate of interest will rise and the real rate of interest will return to the level that prevailed when no price change was expected. Only if the expected rate of price increase were continuously to increase at a rate equal to or greater than the rate of increase of the money interest rate, could the real interest rate be kept from rising toward its initial level.

CREDIT RATIONING

The effectiveness of monetary policy, in the theoretical system outlined in this chapter thus far, depends on the interest-elasticity of effective demand and on the interest-elasticity of the demand for money. Those who believe effective demand to be interest-elastic and demand for money interest-inelastic have confidence in the capacity of monetary policy to affect income. Those who believe that effective demand is highly unresponsive to interest rates regard monetary policy as a weak device for affecting income and consider that even a modest monetary effect requires an extreme change of the interest rate.

There is still another group of economists who believe that the effects of monetary policy include one effect which is independent of the elasticity of investment demand and which thereby enables the supply of money to affect income appreciably even if demand is highly interest-inelastic. Their approach depends upon "credit rationing," the alleged propensity of lenders to curtail their lending and ration the credit that they extend to borrowers when money becomes tighter, rather than raise their interest rates sufficiently to equate the demand for and supply of credit. If the rationing of credit is tightened or loosened by lenders as the money supply is tightened or loosened, then monetary policy can affect investment without extreme changes of the interest rate, even if investment demand is extremely interest-inelastic.

A satisfactory theory of credit rationing would have to explain why interest rates do not rise to clear the market when money is tightened. The most common explanation is that the practices of lending institutions make interest rates rather sticky.[9] The interest rates charged by banks and other lending organizations are "ad-

---

[9] See R. V. Roosa, "Interest Rates and the Central Bank," in *Money, Trade and Economic Growth: Essays in Honor of John Henry Williams* (New York: Macmillan Co., 1951) ; James Tobin, "Monetary Policy and the Management of the Public Debt," *Review of Economics and Statistics*, Vol. XXXV, No. 2 (May, 1953) ; John H. Kareken, "Lenders' Preferences, Credit Rationing, and the Effectiveness of Monetary Policy," *Review of Economics and Statistics*, Vol. XXXIX, No. 3 (August, 1957).

ministered" prices rather than prices determined by the free play of market forces, and administered prices ordinarily lag in adjusting to changed market conditions. This sticky interest-rate argument can explain some short-term credit rationing by lending institutions. But it cannot account for any persistent rationing effect, nor does it cover the flow of credit through the bond market, where interest rates are not sticky. An additional explanation for credit rationing, which can account for a persistent effect and which does cover the bond market, is offered in Appendix B.

APPENDIX A

The "Loanable-Funds" Theory of the Interest Rate

An alternative to the liquidity-preference theory of interest rate determination is the "loanable-funds" theory. This approach defines the equilibrium interest rate as that rate which equates the supply of funds to borrowers with the demand of borrowers for such funds. It is a perfectly reasonable proposition that equilibrium requires the equating of the supply and demand of loanable funds, that the supply and demand are functions of the rate of interest. and that the equilibrium interest rate must be one which equates loanable-funds demand and supply. But it is also a reasonable proposition, in the liquidity-preference explanation, that equilibrium requires the equating of the demand and supply of money, that demand and supply of money are functions of the rate of interest, and that the equilibrium rate of interest must be the one which equates the demand and supply of money.

The interest rate must, apparently, satisfy two equilibrium conditions. To have an equilibrium interest rate, it must be shown that a rate which satisfies one condition necessarily satisfies the other. In other words, it must be shown that the liquidity-preference theory and the loanable-funds theory amount to the same thing. Much effort has been devoted to that proof.[10]

---

[10] See Don Patinkin, "Liquidity Preference and Loanable Funds: Stock and Flow Analysis," *Economica*, N.S. Vol. XXV, No. 100 (November, 1958), pp. 300–318. See also S. C. Tsiang, "Liquidity Preference and Loanable Funds Theories, Multiplier and Velocity Analysis: A Synthesis," *American Economic Review*, Vol. XLVI, No. 4 (September, 1956), pp. 539–64; "Comment" on Tsiang by Gardner Ackley and "Reply" by Tsiang, *American Economic Review*, Vol. XLVII, No. 5 (September, 1957), pp. 662–78; Warren L. Smith, "Monetary Theories of the Rate of Interest: A Dynamic Analysis," *Review of Economics and Statistics*, Vol. XL, No. 1, Part 1 (February, 1958), pp. 15–21; also the literature cited in these articles.

The stumbling block to an integration of the two theories is that the loanable-funds theory is about *flows*—the flow of funds between borrowers and lenders during some period of time—while the liquidity-preference theory is about stocks—the demand for and supply of a stock of money. The difficulty is one of relating a statement with a time dimension to a statement apparently without a time dimension. The key to the difficulty is that while a stock has no time dimension, the *excess* demand for a stock—the difference between the stock being held and the desired stock—does have a time dimension. The difference between the stock of money being held (the supply of money) and the desired stock (the demand for money) represents the *planned adjustment* of stocks. This planned adjustment is to be carried out over some period of time; the excess demand is the gap between the supply of money at the beginning of the planning period and the demand for money, which is the planned holding of money at the end of the period. The time dimension of excess demand is the planning period.

The determination of the equilibrium interest rate can be put entirely in terms of excess demand. When excess demand is zero, the interest rate is in equilibrium.

If, now, the statement about the excess demand for a stock (the liquidity-preference theory) pertains to the same time period as the statement about flows, the two theories can be compared.

Let M_d and M_s be, respectively, the demand for and supply of money; S, the supply of goods and services; D, the demand for goods and services; B, the demand for borrowing; L, the supply of lending.

Anyone with an excess demand for money can add to his stock of money by selling goods and services or by borrowing. Anyone with an excess supply of money can reduce his stock of money by buying goods and services or by lending. In the aggregate, an excess demand for money $M_d - M_s$ is equivalent to the sum of an excess supply of goods and services $S - D$ plus an excess demand for borrowing $B - L$. Thus:

$$M_d - M_s = (S - D) + (B - L)$$

where all items pertain to the same time period.

If we now set income at an equilibrium level, where $S = D$, the term $S - D$ drops out and we have

$$M_d - M_s = B - L$$

Now, if we ask what the equilibrium interest rate will be, we find that any interest rate which equates the demand for and supply of money will also equate the demand for borrowing with the supply of lending. In other words, when the commodity market is in equilibrium $(S = D)$, then the interest rate that equilibrates the money market $(M_d = M_s)$, must also equilibrate the loanable funds market, $(B = L)$, because an excess demand for money is equal to an excess demand for borrowing.

Hence we conclude that the liquidity-preference theory of interest (equilibrium of the money market) and the loanable-funds theory of interest (equilibrium of the loanable-funds market) are the same theory, being merely two ways of looking at the same equilibrium solution.

APPENDIX B

Credit Rationing

The difficulty with the credit rationing argument has always been to explain why lenders would ration credit rather than raise the rate of interest that they charge. One type of explanation has been in terms of the stickiness or lagging adjustment of administered prices in an imperfectly competitive credit market. Even if the proposition of stickiness of interest rates in parts of the credit market were valid, this explanation could only account for temporary rationing among certain types of lenders, and it could not explain rationing in securities markets, where price stickiness is not a characteristic. It is possible, however, to put the theory of credit rationing on a firmer footing, basing it on the special character of credit risk.[11]

We will consider the case of a firm seeking to borrow a specific amount of money for a specific project. The maximum rate of interest the borrower will be willing to pay is the expected rate of return on his project minus some percentage for risk allowance, which is a positive function of the degree of risk that the borrower associates with the project.

The minimum rate of interest which the lender will accept is the

---

[11] For an extended analysis, see Donald R. Hodgman, "Credit Risk and Credit Rationing," *Quarterly Journal of Economics*, Vol. LXXIV, No. 2 (May, 1960), pp. 258–78.

going market rate for riskless loans (pure interest) plus a risk premium, which is a positive function of the degree of risk which the lender associates with the loan.

The special character of credit risk on which this argument rests is: *The degree of risk, to both borrower and lender, increases with the interest rate.* The higher the fixed interest charges, the greater the risk of default on the loan.

These relations are illustrated in Figure 7–14. The curve labeled

FIGURE 7–14

Interest Rates and Default Risk

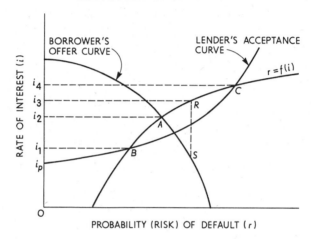

"borrower's offer curve" shows the upper boundary of interest rates that the borrower is willing to pay. It decreases as the risk of default increases. The "lender's acceptance curve" shows the lower boundary of interest rates that the lender will accept, starting from the pure (riskless) interest rate (i_p) at zero risk of default and rising as the risk of default rises. The default-risk function, labeled "$r = f(i)$," shows how the risk of default is believed to increase as the interest rate increases. We assume for simplicity that both borrower and lender have the same estimates of default risk, so that the default-risk function in the diagram applies to the calculations of both. This assumption is not essential to the analysis.

Putting together the borrower's offer curve with the default-risk function, we find that the highest rate the borrower will be willing to pay is i_2, marked by the intersection of the two functions at A. At any interest rate higher than i_2, the default risk would be such that the maximum rate the borrower would be willing to pay would be lower than i_2. For example, at interest rate i_3, the default risk (point R on the default-risk function) is such that the highest interest rate the borrower will offer is shown by point S on the borrower's offer curve.

The lowest rate the lender will accept is i_1, and the highest rate he will charge is i_4, marked by the intersections B and C respectively. Rates below i_1 do not cover the lender's requirements for pure interest plus risk premium, while for rates above i_4, the default risk rises to a point where the interest rate again cannot cover the lender's requirements.

The borrower is willing to pay an interest rate that falls within the range of rates acceptable to the lender (i_2 to i_4) and so the loan can be made.

Now assume that money becomes tighter and that the pure interest rate rises from i_{p1} to i_{p2}. In Figure 7–15, the lender's ac-

FIGURE 7–15

Interest Rates, Default Risk, and Credit Rationing

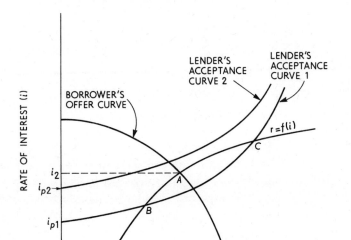

ceptance curve shifts upward from position 1 to position 2. The borrower is still willing to pay an interest rate as high as i_2, but the lender is unwilling to lend to him at any interest rate. There is no interest rate that will cover the pure interest rate plus the lender's risk premium. Consequently, this borrower will be subject to rationing. No increase in the interest rate offered by him will get him this loan.

APPENDIX C

The Velocity of Money

An alternative approach to the relation between the quantity of money and income is through the concept of the velocity of money. If money income per period, specifically defined, is divided by the quantity of money, specifically defined, the quotient can be described as the average number of times during the period that a unit of money was exchanged in carrying out the transactions that generate money income. That rate of turnover of money is called the "income velocity of money."

If M stands for the quantity of money and Y for income, velocity (V) is defined as

$$V = \frac{Y}{M}$$

or, alternatively, income is defined as

$$Y = MV$$

If V is assumed to be constant, it provides a very simple link between money and income: Y is always proportional to M.

The velocity approach can be readily translated into the demand-for-money approach. The demand for money, as previously discussed, depends on the level of income and the rate of interest. Assume that the transactions demand for money is some constant proportion, k, of income. In addition, there is some speculative demand for money, L_L. In equilibrium, the supply of money, M, is equal to the demand for money, L:

$$M = L = kY + L_L$$

The velocity of money, Y/M, is then

$$\frac{Y}{M} = \frac{1}{k}\left(1 - \frac{L_L}{M}\right)$$

If money were held only for transactions purposes, L_L being zero, velocity would equal $1/k$ and would be constant if k is a constant.

With those assumptions, consider the effect of an increase of M on an economy in an equilibrium position. The additional supply of money will be in excess of demand. Holders of the excess supply will attempt to buy earning assets, driving down the interest rate. The interest rate must fall (even become negative) until it has stimulated spending on current product, raised the level of income, and thereby raised the demand for money to equal the enlarged supply. Income rises proportionately to the increase in the quantity of money, to restore equilibrium. This conclusion follows from the assumption that the income level is the *only* equilibrator of the demand and supply of money.

If, however, money is also held for speculative reasons and speculative demand is a function of the interest rate, the demand and supply of money can be equated by the rate of interest. An increase of M may lead only to a fall of the interest rate, equating demand and supply of money with no change of income; or income may rise but not proportionately to M. Velocity need not be constant if L_L balances are not zero.

RECOMMENDED READINGS

Hansen, Alvin H. *Monetary Theory and Fiscal Policy.* New York: McGraw-Hill Book Co., Inc., 1949.

Hart, Albert Gailord, and Kenen, Peter B. *Money, Debt, and Economic Activity.* 3d ed. New York: Prentice-Hall, Inc., 1961.

Johnson, Harry G. "Monetary Theory and Policy," *American Economic Review,* Vol. LII, No. 3 (June, 1962), pp. 335–84.

Kareken, John H. "Lenders' Preferences, Credit Rationing, and the Effectiveness of Monetary Policy," *Review of Economics and Statistics,* Vol. XXXIX, No. 3 (August, 1957), pp. 292–302.

Tobin, James. "Monetary Policy and the Management of the Public Debt: The Patman Inquiry," *Review of Economics and Statistics,* Vol. XXXV, No. 2 (May, 1953), pp. 118–27.

QUESTIONS

1. Explain how the existence of close substitutes for money affects the elasticity of demand for money.
2. What can cause a shift of the demand curve for speculative money balances?
3. Assume the following functional relationships:
   - (1) $I = 60 - 600i$
   - (2) $S = 0.2Y - 20$
   - (3) $L_T = 0.25Y$

(4) $L_L = \dfrac{100}{(100i)^2}$ for i greater than 0.01; $L_L = \infty$ for i equal to 0.01

(5) $M = 110$

where I is investment per year, S is total saving per year, Y is income per year, i is the rate of interest, M is the quantity of money, L_T is the transactions demand for money, L_L is the speculative demand for money.

a) Construct a diagram on the basis of these data to show the equilibrium level of income.

b) What would be the effect of increasing M to 130?

c) If the full-potential level of income is 400, can it be reached in this model by increasing the quantity of money? Explain briefly.

d) Assume a shift of the investment function so that $I = 70 - 600i$. What is the effect on the level of income?

4. Can expectations of a rise of the price level lead to a rise of the price level? Explain, illustrating diagrammatically.

   If a price rise creates expectations of the same rate of increase in the next period, can this process generate a continuous upward price trend when the quantity of money is kept constant?

5. Is the effect of the price level on aggregate demand through its effect on the real supply of money, the same as the Pigou effect?

6. Explain why a constant velocity of money implies a perfectly interest-inelastic demand for money.

PART III

Problems and Policies

INCOME
FLUCTUATIONS

The many and varied theories of income fluctuations, or business cycles, which have been developed over a long period bear witness to the difficulty of providing a satisfactory explanation of the observed phenomena. Some light may be thrown on the puzzle of fluctuations by applying the macroeconomic analysis of the preceding chapters.

THE THEORIES OF FLUCTUATIONS: TWO TYPES

Theories of fluctuations can be divided into two broad categories. *Endogenous* theories attempt to explain fluctuations by some process inherent in the economic mechanism. An income model of this type could show how fluctuations are generated entirely by forces within the model. *Exogenous* theories require some autonomous change or shock external to the model, coming from the outside into the income model, to start the fluctuation. For example, a fall of government spending or an increase of tax rates or a reduction in the quantity of money are autonomous changes which could start a fall of aggregate income. The income model could then show how the cycle, once it has been started by a force external to the model, is carried on by the induced relations within the model.

According to endogeneous theory, the economy is inherently unstable and fluctuations therefore are inevitable unless prevented by some autonomous change of demand. According to exogenous theory, the economy is inherently stable and will not fluctuate unless it is disturbed by an autonomous change of demand.

Endogenous Theories

Endogenous theories depend, fundamentally, on the accelerator.
The Ceiling and Floor Theory   In one major type of endogenous

theory, the economy rises until it hits a ceiling. The ceiling may be set by the full-potential level of output. Or it may be a monetary ceiling, resulting from the induced tightening of money as income rises relative to the quantity of money. In either case, the rate of increase of output slows down when the ceiling is reached and the fall in the rate of increase causes, through the accelerator mechanism, a fall of output.

The subsequent course of the fluctuation in this type of theory depends on the size of the accelerator coefficient and the marginal propensity to consume.[1] If they are large enough to make the system highly unstable, output will continue to fall until it hits a floor set by the autonomous components of aggregate demand. When the floor is reached and output stops falling, the accelerator mechanism produces a rise of gross investment and output turns upward.[2]

The Damped Accelerator Theory   If the accelerator coefficient and marginal propensity to consume are sufficiently small that the oscillations of the system are damped and eventually die out, a different sort of theory follows. An initial exogenous shock is required to start the fluctuation process. Thereafter a series of endogenously produced fluctuations occur, diminishing in size until they die out. Periodic exogenous shocks are needed, in this model, to continue the fluctuations.

The Overshooting Theory   Another type of endogenous theory is based on the hypothesis of a systematic form of miscalculation by investors. According to this hypothesis, in an upswing investors overestimate their expected rate of increase of sales and so over-invest. Upon realizing that they have overinvested, they cut back investment demand and output falls. The downswing and then the upturn proceed as in an accelerator-multiplier model, with possible overdisinvestment of inventories at the bottom of the cycle. Thus, fluctuations can be generated by a propensity of investors, in the aggregate, to overshoot and then undershoot their optimum capital stock.

Conclusion   The ceiling and floor, the damped accelerator, and the overshooting theories are the chief contenders for an endogenous explanation of cycles.[3] It should be noted that in all of these

---

[1] See pp. 104–5 above.

[2] See J. R. Hicks, *A Contribution to the Theory of the Trade Cycle* (Oxford: Clarendon Press, 1950) for an extended discussion of this type of model.

[3] Another endogenous explanation, once highly regarded but now fading, is based on the hypothesis of an inherent irregularity in either the rate of inven-

endogenous theories, some initial exogenous disturbance of the rate
of growth of output is needed to start the machinery which generates the subsequent fluctuations.

Exogenous Theories

Exogenous explanations of fluctuations are easier to formulate
than endogenous. They hypothesize an economy which grows stead-
ily unless aggregate demand is subjected to an exogenous shock.
The size of the fluctuation following from such a shock depends
upon the size of the shock and upon the extent to which its impact
on demand is magnified by the multiplier and induced changes in
investment.

THE EVIDENCE: FLUCTUATIONS OF THE U.S. ECONOMY, 1870–1961

Before attempting an evaluation of the various theories of fluctuations, we can usefully review the cyclical experience which these
theories are supposed to explain.

Data on early fluctuations of real output is limited, but a reasonably accurate impression of the length and amplitude of U.S. fluctuations since 1870 is presented in Chart 8–1. The chart shows a
monthly index of the physical volume of business, composed chiefly
of production series in manufacturing, mining, construction, and
railway freight. The shaded portions of the chart show periods of
cyclical contraction, according to the dates arrived at by the National Bureau of Economic Research.

The Minor Cycles

One notable feature of this cyclical history, which tends to be
forgotten, is that most of the fluctuations have been quite small.

---

tion or the rate of innovation (the introduction of inventions into the production process). In the case of invention, a study using patent data concludes
that it is demand which determines the rate of invention, rather than the reverse. See Jacob Schmookler, *Invention and Economic Growth* (Cambridge,
Mass.: Harvard University Press, 1966), chap. vi. In the case of innovation
and aggregate demand, it is difficult to separate cause and effect, but it is at
least as probable that demand causes innovation as that innovation causes
demand. In any event, the hypothesis of irregularity in the rate of innovation
is based on an exaggeration of the importance of a few major innovations.
Technological change actually proceeds by a stream of many innovations, and
even the so-called major innovations are composed of a series of innovations.

Even though the chart shows industrial production, which fluctuates much more widely than GNP, most of the contractions look mild. Two of them, 1887–88 and 1890–91, do not show up in the production data at all; they were essentially periods of price decline rather than contraction of real output. Three others, 1910–12, 1923–24, and 1926–27, were barely perceptible declines. Four— 1899–1900, 1902–1904, 1913–14, and 1918–19—were brief, small dips.

The Major Cycles

The remaining eight fluctuations in Chart 8–1 are listed in cycle histories as major cycles.[4] Even among these eight, however, we find that the prevailing notion of their severity is exaggerated.

The 1873–79 Recession

The contraction traditionally dated 1873 to 1879 lasted only, in terms of real output, to 1876, and the fall of industrial production

CHART 8–1

Index of Physical Volume of Business Activity, 1870–1939

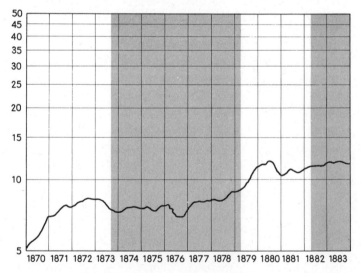

---

[4] As dated by the National Bureau of Economic Research: 1873–79, 1882–85, 1893–94, 1895–97, 1907–08, 1920–21, 1929–33, 1937–38.

CHART 8–1 (Continued)

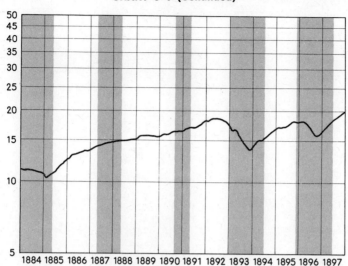

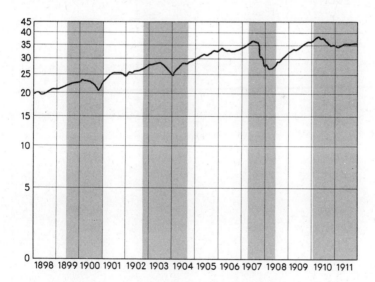

from peak to trough was about 15 percent. The prevalent notion
that the contraction was deep and protracted arose from the heavy
reliance placed on price series and series measured in money values
in studies of the period. Prices declined sharply until 1879 under a
monetary policy aimed at reducing U.S. prices sufficiently, relative
to British prices, to permit the return to the gold standard at the

CHART 8–1 (Continued)

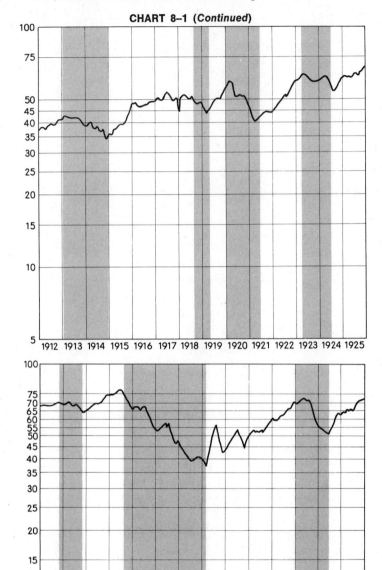

Source: Babson Statistical Organization. See U.S. Bureau of the Census, *Historical Statistics of the United States* (Washington, D.C., 1949), pp. 322–23, for description.

pre–Civil War dollar–pound sterling exchange rate. That this pro-longed deflationary pressure did not produce a great decline of out-put is an indication of the resiliency and stability of the economy. In 1879, at the supposed end of the contraction, real output was substantially above its level at the beginning of the contraction in 1873.

1879–1914: Monetary Disturbances

The period from 1879 to 1914 was marked by a series of mone-tary disturbances. The supply of money was subject to sharp changes originating in shifts of the flow of capital and gold into and out of the country. The shifts of these flows arose partly from changes in the prices of the United States relative to those of other countries, partly from economic disturbances abroad, and partly (until 1897) from capital flights incited by periodic losses of confi-dence in the United States' ability to adhere to the gold standard and the fixed exchange rate. The fluctuations in the monetary base arising from these international flows were magnified by the bank-ing system. The pressure on banks in times of tightening money weakened depositors' confidence in the banks and led to a drain of deposits into currency, which further contracted the money supply. In extreme cases, a banking panic developed, with runs on banks, bank failures, and a sharp drop of the money supply. The major contractions of 1882–85, 1893–94, 1895–97, and 1907–1908 are all associated with outflows of gold, followed by (except for 1895–97) serious banking panics.

The establishment of the Federal Reserve System in 1913 changed the monetary rules of the game but it did not prevent three more major fluctuations.

The 1920–21 Recession

The contraction of 1920–21 was short but deep. Primarily, it was a product of the disequilibrium conditions left by World War I —a backlog of unsatisfied demand, excess liquidity, and rising prices. These conditions, creating overestimates of future sales and price increases, led in 1919 to excessive accumulation of inventories. The excess aggregate demand and, in particular, the overinvest-ment in inventories were further stimulated by the Federal Re-serve's easy-money policy. When, in 1920, the backlog of demand was disappearing and liquidity had fallen, the government reduced its spending and the Federal Reserve shifted rapidly to a tight-money policy, and the boom collapsed. Heavy disinvestment in inventories brought a sharp drop of aggregate demand and output.

The Great Depression

The great contraction of 1929–33 was unique. No other contraction in cyclical history approaches it in length or depth. Being unique, it needs some special explanation, a need which economists have had great difficulty in filling. The events preceding the downturn—the speculative atmosphere of 1928–29 which led to the stock market boom and some overinvestment in capital goods—can explain only a moderate recession. The stock market crash cannot explain more than a short and moderate slump. Foreign economic disorders, frequently offered as an explanation, appear to be more a result than a cause of the severe depression in the United States. Many other efforts to account for the great contraction—a wage-price squeeze on profits, a change in the distribution of income, and so on—are unsupported by empirical evidence or theory.

The one analysis which does appear capable of accounting for the great contraction is that of Friedman and Schwartz in their *Monetary History*.[5] A distinctive feature of the 1929–33 contraction was the drastic fall in the quantity of money. From peak to trough the money stock fell by over one third, more than three times the largest previous fall in any contraction going back to 1870. This plunge of the money stock was largely due to the extraordinary number of bank failures and bank closings, which occurred at an abnormal rate throughout the period but particularly in four great waves: in late 1930, mid-1931, early 1932, and early 1933.

The effect of the banking crises on the economy was not only through the losses suffered by the depositors, creditors, and stockholders of the failed banks. Of much greater consequence was the loss of confidence in the banking system, which led depositors to withdraw currency from the banks and led the banks to increase their excess reserves (by curtailing loans and deposits) as a precautionary measure. The loss of bank reserves through the currency

---

[5] Milton Friedman and Anna Jacobson Schwartz, *A Monetary History of the United States, 1867–1960* (Princeton, N.J.: Princeton University Press for National Bureau of Economic Research, 1963), chap. 7.

drain and the banks' reduction of their deposit-reserve ratios brought about the fall of the money stock.

An explanation is still needed for the prolonged series of bank failures in 1929–33, when in all bank panics of the previous 60 years the crises had died out quickly. The answer provided by Friedman and Schwartz lies in the change that occurred under the Federal Reserve System in the procedure for dealing with bank panics. Before the Federal Reserve, bank panics were countered by the "restriction of payment." That is, the banks stopped converting demand deposits into currency, though the depositors could still use their deposits as a means of payment by check. In areas where runs on banks became a serious threat, restriction was made general, with the assistance and approval of state officials. Restriction enabled banks to remain open and in operation until confidence in them was restored. As a result, bank failures were limited, confidence returned quickly, and the panics were brief. Under the Federal Reserve System, however, no government action was taken to introduce restriction during the banking crises of 1929–33, because the Federal Reserve had been established to back up the banking system with emergency reserves and make restriction unnecessary. But the Federal Reserve did not provide the banks with the needed reserves, so that bank failures bred more bank failures for over three years.

The 1937–38 Contraction

The last of the major contractions was short—May, 1937, to June, 1938—but fairly deep. It was touched off by several contractionary public policies which were introduced despite the fact that the recovery from the Great Depression was still far from complete. The federal government budget, which, before the 1930's, had been a significant factor in economic stability only in wartime, had by now grown large enough that a fiscal shock to the economy became a possibility at any time. Beginning in late 1936, government expenditures were cut, for the purpose of reducing the budget deficit. At the same time the tax receipts of the new social security program increased sharply. In the latter part of 1936 and in early 1937 the Federal Reserve undertook a precautionary reduction of excess bank reserves by raising reserve requirements. In the atmosphere of caution and unoptimistic expectations then prevailing, these measures provoked a more severe contraction than might have been expected in more normal circumstances.

The Postwar Recessions

The four recessions since 1947 have all been small and brief. The fall of real GNP from peak quarter to trough quarter, and the length of each contraction, were:

Contraction	Fall of Real GNP	Length of Contraction
1948–49	2.4%	11 months
1953–54	3.7	13 months
1957–58	4.7	9 months
1960–61	1.8	10 months

The broad outlines of the recessions can be observed in Chart 8–2. Disposable income fluctuated less than GNP and consumption fluctuated less than disposable income. Consumption of nondurables and services was particularly stable and most of the consumption fluctuation was in consumer durables, which behaved very much like fixed investment (gross private domestic investment excluding inventories). Fixed investment fell only moderately in contractions; its largest decline was 10 percent, during the 1957–58 recession. The most unstable element of demand was investment in inventories, which, on the average, fell more than twice as much (in absolute amount) as fixed investment.

The 1948–49 Recession

At the end of the war, the economy was left with pent-up demand for investment goods and consumer durables, and with businesses and households holding an abnormally large proportion of their wealth in highly liquid form. For several years the combination of pent-up demand and high liquidity created excess demand and rapidly rising prices, until, by mid-1948, much of the backlog of demand had been satisfied and most of the excess liquidity was gone. Demand for consumer goods leveled off, demand for fixed investment and exports declined slightly, and demand for inventories fell sharply.

As the boom was tapering off in 1948, the Federal Reserve took steps to tighten money and credit, a policy which it did not reverse

CHART 8–2

Real GNP and Components, 1947–69
(seasonally adjusted quarterly totals at annual rates, in billions of 1958 dollars)

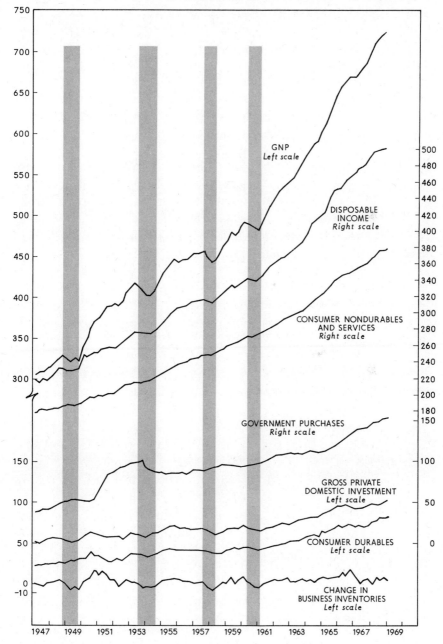

Source: *Survey of Current Business,* August, 1965; July, 1967; July, 1969.

until after the recession had passed its trough. Fiscal policy was more helpful. The Revenue Act of 1948, which became effective early in the recession, cut taxes, despite the opposition of the President and the Council of Economic Advisors.[6]

The 1953–54 Recession

The contraction that began in July, 1953, originated in the readjustment of the economy to the termination of the Korean War. Though government expenditures did not begin to fall until after the contraction had started, defense orders had begun to fall much earlier. The fall of orders led to a fall of inventory investment. Unlike the situation at the end of World War II, there was no backlog of unsatisfied demand when the Korean War ended. On the contrary, producers and consumers may have been slightly overstocked with goods which they had bought anticipating shortages that never materialized. Consequently, the transition from war to peace, with no compensatory government policies to smooth the adjustment, produced a contraction. On January 1, 1954, scheduled tax cuts, which had been legislated before the contraction began, took effect and contributed to the recovery.

The 1957–58 Recession

During 1955 the federal government, concerned over inflation, reduced its expenditures. In 1956, it reduced them a bit more. Meanwhile, tax receipts were being induced upward as the economy grew, and the federal budget surplus was rising. The Federal Reserve also pursued a tightening policy and interest rates rose sharply.

These policies had their intended braking effect and the rate of increase of GNP fell. The drastic slowing of economic expansion that had begun in late 1955 eventually produced a fall of investment demand which turned GNP down beginning in the third quarter of 1957. Monetary policy was eased during the end of 1957 and early 1958. Though too late to account for the upturn in April, 1958, it

---

[6] Inflation was still considered the problem to be dealt with. Congress did not pass the tax cut as a stabilizing measure but as a political maneuver. That it turned out to be a correct antirecession policy was fortunate but fortuitous. See Wilfred Lewis, Jr., *Federal Fiscal Policy in the Postwar Recessions* (Washington, D.C.: Brookings Institution, 1962), pp. 92–96.

was helpful in the recovery, as was a modest increase in federal spending that occurred after the upturn.

The 1960–61 Recession

Before the economy had reached full employment following the 1957–58 recession, the federal policy makers, still concerned about inflation, resumed their tightening operations. Federal government purchases were reduced in every quarter from the first quarter of 1959 until the second quarter of 1960, when the contraction began. The Federal Reserve tightened money during 1959 and interest rates climbed. As in the case of the 1957–58 recession, the rate of economic expansion was severely reduced, leading to a sharp drop of inventory investment and some decline of fixed investment.[7]

THEORY AND EVIDENCE

The historical evidence on fluctuations summarized in the preceding section can now be applied to the theoretical questions raised in the first section of this chapter. Are cycles endogenous or exogenous? Is the economy best described by a model which is prone to oscillation or one which tends to be stable and resistant to oscillation?

The weight of the evidence favors a model in which fluctuations are produced by exogenous shocks and the economy tends to stability. It appears that past fluctuations can be explained best by exogenous shocks, that large shocks produce only minor contractions, and that a very large shock is required to produce a major contraction.

Since 1870, all the major contractions can be traced to a major exogenous disturbance, either a monetary contraction and banking crisis (1873–76, 1882–85, 1893–94, 1895–97, 1907–1908, 1929–33), or a postwar disequilibrium complicated by destabilizing monetary policy (1920–21), or a destabilizing fiscal policy with some assistance from unwise monetary policy (1937–38).

---

[7] These trends were somewhat obscured by a long steel strike from July to November, 1959. In anticipation of the strike, inventory investment increased heavily during the second quarter of 1959 and GNP jumped. During the strike, steel inventories were used up and GNP fell. After the strike, inventories of steel were restored, raising inventory investment and boosting GNP, until inventory stocks approached the desired level in the second quarter of 1960, when inventory investment began to fall.

Most of the minor contractions are also traceable to exogenous disturbances: monetary disturbances (1887–88, 1902–1904), readjustments following a war (1899–1900, 1918–19, 1945, 1948–49, 1953–54), and destabilizing fiscal policy (1957–58, 1960–61).[8]

The long, cumulative decline associated with a highly unstable model of the accelerator-multiplier type does not appear, except for 1929–33, when a series of banking crises kept the contraction going. In general, the models of an unstable economy generating its own downturns or rocking at a light tap receive no support from the evidence.

THE GREAT STAGNATION, 1956–64

From the end of World War II until 1956, except for the short recession periods, output was at or very close to the full-potential level. But from 1956 to 1964, output remained substantially below the full-potential level, even in the peak years. This period of persistent tendency toward stagnation was considerably more costly in terms of lost output than all of the small postwar recessions together.

In Chart 8–3 real GNP is compared to an estimate of potential GNP.[9] The continuous gap between potential and actual output

---

[8] The four remaining very mild contractions, 1910–12, 1913–14, 1923–24, 1926–27, have no very conspicuous cause. Friedman and Schwartz attribute them to small monetary disturbances: 1910–12 to a retardation in the growth of the money supply due to international capital flows; 1913–14 to a retardation of the growth of the money stock followed by the uncertainty and disorganization at the outbreak of war in Europe; 1923–24 and 1926–27 to monetary tightening by the Federal Reserve quickly followed by a reversal of policy after the start of the contraction. (Milton Friedman and Anna Jacobson Schwartz, *op. cit.*, pp. 173–74, 288–89.)

[9] Various methods have been used to estimate potential GNP. One, developed by Arthur M. Okun, is based on a calculation of the relation between changes in the unemployment rate and changes of real GNP. Okun's results are summed up in the estimate that a 1 percent reduction of the unemployment rate will be accompanied by a 3.2 percent increase of GNP. If 4 percent is taken as the unemployment rate signifying full-potential GNP, the Okun formula becomes:

$$Y_p = Y_a \, (1 + 0.032 \, [u - 4])$$

where Y_p, Y_a, and u stand for full-potential GNP, actual GNP, and the unemployment rate respectively. Thus, if the unemployment rate were 5 percent, full-potential GNP would be estimated to be 3.2 percent above actual GNP. (See Okun, "Potential GNP: Its Measurement and Significance," *Cowles Foundation Paper No. 190* (New Haven, Conn.: Cowles Foundation for Research in Economics at Yale University, 1963). This paper was reprinted from

CHART 8–3

Actual and Potential Gross National Product, 1947–68
(billions of 1958 dollars)

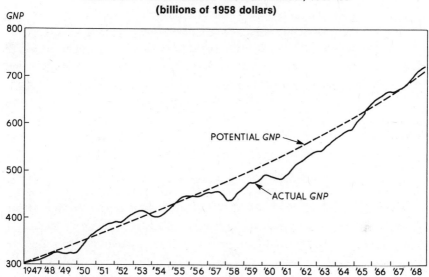

For the method of estimating potential GNP, see footnote 9.

from 1956 to 1964 stands out as a remarkable feature of the post-war economy.

An explanation for this chronic underproduction can be found in the budget of the federal government. Federal government expenditures were held under tight restraint and allowed to rise only slowly during most of this period. Meanwhile, the tax rates were not reduced, potential output was growing, and the amount of tax receipts that would be collected at the full-potential level of output was rising. The budget thus had built into it a growing "full-potential budget surplus"—the surplus that would have existed if output had been at the full-potential level.

The position as it would appear at one point in time is illustrated in Figure 8–1. In the upper diagram (a) are shown tax receipts

American Statistical Association, *1962 Proceedings of the Business and Economic Statistics Section.*

The potential GNP in Chart 8–3 is estimated by the Okun method. For a comparison of several methods of estimating potential output, see Michael E. Levy, *Fiscal Policy, Cycles and Growth* (New York: National Industrial Conference Board, 1963).

(with fixed tax rates) as a function of GNP, and government expenditures as fixed in the budget. The difference between expenditures and receipts gives the budget surplus or government saving curve. At full-potential output, Y_f, the budget yields a surplus.

In the lower diagram (b), the private saving function is added to the government saving function to give the total saving function. An investment function is introduced to determine the equilibrium level of GNP. The intersection of the investment function and the total saving function at A sets the equilibrium GNP at the underemployment level Y_e. Note that though the budget has a full-potential surplus, the actual budget condition at Y_e is a deficit.

If the government saving function were shifted down so that government saving were zero at Y_f, the investment and total saving functions would intersect at B. Equilibrium output would then be at the full-potential level Y_f and the budget would be in balance.

Figure 8–1 represents the condition of "fiscal drag" as it was observed by the President's Council of Economic Advisers in the early 1960's. Their analysis indicated that the full-potential budget surplus was acting as a drag on the economy, creating the persistent

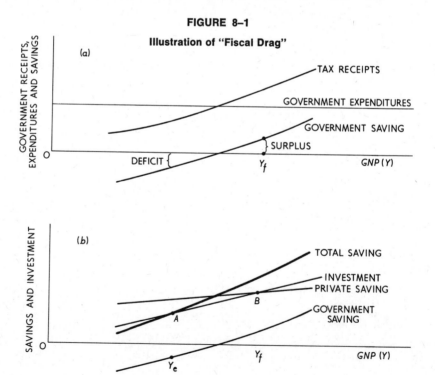

FIGURE 8–1

Illustration of "Fiscal Drag"

high unemployment, and that if the budget were adjusted to eliminate the potential surplus, consumer and investment demand would rise, raising output to the full-potential level.[10] This analysis gained belated acceptance[11] and, by the Revenue Act of 1964, taxes were cut, part of the cut taking effect in March of that year and part in the following year. Output began to rise at an accelerated rate in 1965 and was approaching the full-potential level when military expenditures for the Vietnam War were stepped up, pushing the economy into the zone of excess demand.

CODA

Since the last recession, there has been an expansion of unprecedented length—more than eight years thus far. This experience supports the conclusion drawn from the earlier evidence, that the economy is inherently stable and prone to steady expansion unless it is disturbed by destabilizing fiscal or monetary policy. A thorough overhaul of the orthodox theory and history of fluctuations is past due.

RECOMMENDED READINGS

FRIEDMAN, MILTON, and SCHWARTZ, ANNA J. "Money and Business Cycles," *Review of Economics and Statistics*, Vol. XLV, No. 1, Part 2 (February, 1963), pp. 32–64 and "Comments," pp. 64–78.

GORDON, ROBERT AARON. *Business Fluctuations*. New York: Harper & Bros., 1951.

HANSEN, ALVIN H. *Business Cycles and National Income*. New York: W. W. Norton & Co., Inc., 1951.

HICKS, J. R. *A Contribution to the Theory of the Trade Cycle*. Oxford: Clarendon Press, 1950.

LEWIS, WILFRED, JR. *Federal Fiscal Policy in the Postwar Recessions*. Washington, D.C.: Brookings Institution, 1962.

---

[10] An alternative to lowering saving by fiscal means would have been some measure to raise investment demand, but that did not appear feasible. An effort in that direction was made with an investment tax credit in 1962. An easier monetary policy might have helped somewhat, but monetary policy during the period was pursuing a middle course between ease to raise output and tightness to discourage the outflow of capital abroad (in order to reduce the balance of payments deficit).

[11] Its acceptance was impeded by the resurgence of a popular old explanation for persistent unemployment, job-destroying technological change, which was called in this reincarnation, "automation." Since the return to full employment, the automation bugaboo has been laid quietly to rest.

LUNDBERG, ERIK (ed.). *The Business Cycle in the Post-War World; Proceedings of a Conference Held by the International Economic Association.* London: Macmillan & Co., Ltd., 1955.

MATTHEWS, R. C. O. *The Business Cycle.* Chicago: University of Chicago Press, 1959.

QUESTIONS

1. Assess the accelerator models for fixed investment and inventory investment in the light of U.S. cyclical experience.
2. Describe and evaluate an example of an endogenous theory of fluctuations.
3. "Since 1948 fiscal policy has been more prominent in initiating recessions than in promoting recovery." Discuss.
4. What accounts for the persistent unemployment in the U.S. economy from 1956 to 1964?

Chapter 9 | INFLATION

By "inflation" we ordinarily mean a condition of the economy which produces a rising trend in the general price level of current output. However, it is also possible to have inflation without rising prices, if various controls are imposed to prevent price rises that would otherwise occur; a condition of that sort is called "suppressed inflation." A simple definition of inflation in terms of a rising price level is, therefore, inadequate. To arrive at a more complete definition, we must first distinguish the several types of inflation.

TYPES OF INFLATION

"Excess-Demand" Inflation

The simplest kind of inflation to describe is the one that arises from excess demand for current output. In an earlier chapter, we referred to excess demand as an "inflationary gap." In Figure 9–1, where Y_f is the full-potential level of real gross national product and Y_e is the equilibrium gross national product, output will be at full potential, and aggregate demand (AY_f) will exceed output (BY_f) by the inflationary gap, AB. The excess demand for output which implies also excess demand for inputs, will, through the competitive bidding of buyers, raise the prices of outputs and inputs, provided prices are free to rise. The system must continue in disequilibrium until either (a) some autonomous change lowers the aggregate demand function in real terms, bringing Y_e down to the level of Y_f, or (b) the process of rising prices, through certain induced effects, lowers the aggregate demand function and reduces Y_e to equality with Y_f.

If prices are prevented from rising by governmental controls, "open" inflation may be prevented, but "suppressed" inflation is

FIGURE 9–1

An Inflationary Gap

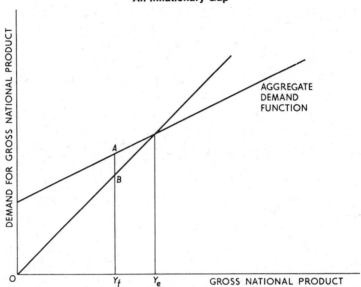

present. The symptoms are altered, rising prices being replaced by queuing and other forms of nonprice rationing, but the economy continues to be afflicted with an inflationary problem. Indeed, the affliction may be even greater under suppressed than under open inflation since (*a*) the equilibrating effects of rising prices (to be described below) are prevented in suppressed inflation and (*b*) excess demand is more likely to be increased by expectations of future shortages and nonprice rationing than by expectations of rising prices.[1]

Wage-Push or Profit-Push Inflation

Economic analysts have become increasingly aware, in recent years, of the possibility of a generally rising price level even in the absence of excess demand. A number of different mechanisms which might cause this seeming contradiction have been suggested. Of these, the most frequently mentioned is the wage-push process, in

---

[1] See p. 74.

which wage increases obtained through the bargaining power of labor unions raise the costs of production, thereby causing producers to raise prices.

The question has been raised as to whether wage-push inflation without excess demand is possible. The argument that it is not possible rests on the proposition that an increase of the wage level will cause a fall of employment unless there is excess demand, and that the threat of a fall of employment will deter unions from pushing up wages.

The answer to this argument is that the threat of unemployment does not appear to be an absolute deterrent to the unions' pursuit of wage increases. Getting wage increases is the unions' primary function, and in the pursuit of that function they are usually prepared to trade off some loss of jobs for higher wages. In addition, union leaders may not always recognize that their wage demands can result in a reduction of employment; but even when they do, they are under pressure to seek wage increases large enough to justify their union's existence or to match the increases obtained by other unions. At some point the unemployment problem can be severe enough to deter further wage demands; but below that point, it need not be a bar to an inflationary wage-push.

Another type of "push" inflation whose existence has been suggested is "profit-push," in which producers seek to increase profits by increasing their markups over cost. For firms to engage in profit-push inflationary behavior, they must hold to the persistent belief that, with no change of demand or cost conditions, their prices are below the profit-maximizing level. For firms to sustain that belief, they must have a persistently exaggerated idea of the inelasticity of demand for their products, or else have only a very crude method of calculating the profit-maximizing price. It should be noted that, unlike unions, businesses are under no pressure to initiate price increases or imitate other firms that have raised prices.

It is difficult, perhaps impossible, to tell by statistical test whether a particular inflationary episode is due to wage push or profit push, if either. The final statistical results of the two cases will look alike. If wages are the aggressor, prices of products will rise defensively to maintain profits. If product prices are the aggressor, wages will rise defensively to maintain real wages. In the end, aggressive wages and defensive prices or aggressive prices and defensive wages look very much alike. Searching for cause and effect in time sequences is unlikely to help, since, when wage and price increases alternate, the determination of which came first will depend, as in the chicken-versus-egg question, on what point in the series is chosen as the starting point. With the present state of our empirical tests, our evaluation of the relative probabilities of wage-push and profit-push depends on our evaluation of the likely behavior of unions and producers.

For much the same reason—because the final outcomes look alike —it is difficult to distinguish by statistical tests a push inflation from a demand-pull inflation. Whether excess demand raises prices and wages or whether wage-push raises wages which then cause prices to rise, the final pattern of increases looks the same. Distinguishing between the two types of inflation depends primarily on an examination of the state of aggregate demand. Prices rising when there is a deflationary gap (as shown by unemployment rates or other indicators) may be taken as evidence of push inflation provided that the possibility is eliminated that the price increases are a lagged effect from some previous period of excess demand. In periods when the existence of an inflationary gap is obvious, the diagnosis of demand-pull inflation can be made with considerable confidence. In the border area, where demand is in the neighborhood of the full-potential output, the comparative roles of pull and push in the inflation process remain obscure.

DEFINITION OF INFLATION

From the preceding discussion of types of inflation, we can see that we need not one but two definitions of inflation. By inflation we mean *either* a condition of aggregate excess demand in which price rises may be open or suppressed *or* a condition of rising prices without excess demand. In the former, the excess demand is the illness and the rising prices only a symptom; in the latter, the rising price level is the illness.

THE EQUILIBRATING PROCESS IN INFLATION

The economy has a built-in equilibrating process which can bring an inflationary condition to an end. This equilibrating process works through the contractionary effect of price rises on real aggregate demand.

Aggregate Demand and the Price Level

The way in which a rise of the price level tends to contract real aggregate demand needs careful explaining. One should not leap from the proposition about the negative slope of the demand curve for a single product to the conclusion that aggregate product has a similarly shaped demand curve. The demand curve for the single product is drawn on the assumption that all other prices are constant; it tells us nothing about what happens to aggregate demand when the general price level changes. The substitution and income effects that explain the price-elasticity of demand for a single product have no counterparts in aggregate demand. Nevertheless, we can list a number of ways in which the price level affects aggregate demand.

1. The Induced Monetary Effect   In the analysis on pages 154–55 and in Figure 7–11, we saw how a rise of the price level reduces the real supply of money while leaving the real demand for money unchanged. As a result, the money market becomes tighter, interest rates rise, and real aggregate demand is reduced. This effect depends, of course, on there being no increase in the nominal supply of money that would offset a contraction of the real supply of money as the price level rises.

2. The Pigou Effect   Rising prices will decrease the real value of the net indebtedness of the public sector to the private sector. This reduction in the real assets of the private sector will lower aggregate demand.[2]

3. The Progressive Income Tax Effect   With a given real income and rising prices, money income increases proportionately to the price level. If taxes are proportional to money income, tax receipts rise proportionately with the price level, and there is no change in real tax receipts. But, if the tax structure is progressive, money tax receipts rise more than proportionately to the price level and real tax receipts increase. Corresponding to the increase in real tax receipts there is a decrease in real disposable income, which will reduce consumer demand. This effect, of course, depends on there being no offsetting reduction in tax rates nor any tendency for real government expenditures to keep pace with real tax receipts.

---

[2] See pp. 77–78.

4. The Net-Foreign-Investment Effect   An increase in the price level relative to foreign prices will tend to increase the volume of imports and to decrease the volume of exports. The net foreign investment component of aggregate demand will be reduced. If inflation abroad is raising foreign prices proportionately with domestic prices, or if a relative increase of domestic prices is balanced by exchange-rate devaluation or foreign-trade restrictions, this effect will be canceled out.

5. Redistributive Effects   There was, at one time, a widely held belief that rising prices redistribute income from low- to high-income households and that such a redistribution reduces total consumer demand. The redistribution was attributed to a tendency for wages to lag behind prices (thus transferring real income from wages to profits) and to the reduction in the real value of certain fixed incomes (pensions, annuities, interest) which affects lower more than upper incomes. However, recent careful studies of the redistributive effects of inflation suggest that the extent of the redistribution is very small; and such transfers as there are, are not clearly in the low- to high-income direction.[3] In any event, it is doubtful that a nonextreme redistribution of personal income by size has a significant effect on aggregate consumer demand.[4] As for the redistribution of net worth from creditors to debtors, there is no persuasive reason to expect it to affect aggregate demand, except for the redistribution from the private to the public sector, via the public debt, which has already been discussed as the Pigou effect.

The redistributive effect, then, is dubious, but the other four effects will operate in an equilibrating direction if not counteracted by public policies. Against these equilibrating effects, we must weigh the possible disequilibrating effect of expectations of further price rises. Our earlier discussion of price expectations (pp. 155–56) has shown that expectations of a price increase lower the real interest rate and thereby tend to increase real demand. But Figure 7–12 shows how price increases raise the money rate of interest and cancel out the tendency of expectations to lower the real rate of interest. Consequently, with the induced monetary effect in operation, the possible disequilibrating effects of price expectations would be limited and temporary.

---

[3] See G. L. Bach and Albert Ando, "The Redistributional Effects of Inflation," *Review of Economics and Statistics*, Vol. XXXIX, No. 1 (February, 1957), pp. 1–13.

[4] See pp. 78–81.

Demand, Supply, and the Price Level

The preceding analysis of the price-demand relation permits the introduction of the negatively sloped curve in Figure 9–2 showing

FIGURE 9–2

Demand, Supply, and the Price Level

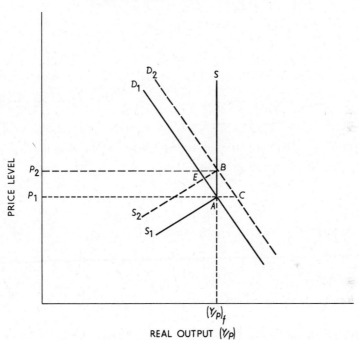

REAL OUTPUT (Y/P)

aggregate demand as a function of the price level. This demand function, combined with the aggregate supply function developed in Chapter 3, can be used to illustrate the equilibrating process in inflation.

The first illustration is a case of excess demand. We begin with demand curve D_1 and the supply curve S_1S. The equilibrium position is at the intersection A, at full-employment output $(Y/P)_f$ and price level P_1. We assume an autonomous increase of demand, shifting the demand curve upward from D_1 to D_2. Excess demand has now been created. At price level P_1, equilibrium output is marked by point C, which is above the full-employment level and therefore unattainable. The system continues in disequilibrium until the price level rises to P_2, eliminating the excess demand and returning the equilibrium position of output to $(Y/P)_f$.

At the same time that the price level is rising and approaching an equilibrium at intersection B, the supply curve is shifting upward from S_1S to S_2S. The reason for this shift of the supply curve is the rise of the money wage rate, as shown in Figure 9–3 (which

FIGURE 9–3

Effect of the Money Wage Rate on the Aggregate Supply Function

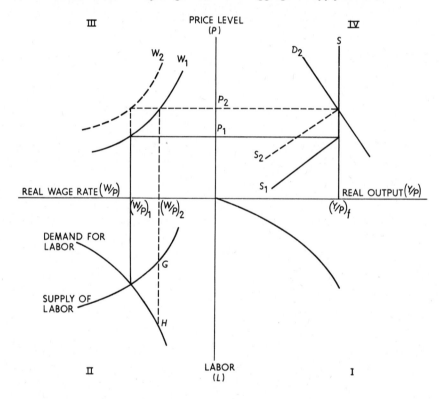

reproduces the derivation of the aggregate supply function presented above in Figure 3–13).

The initial position is at output $(Y/P)_f$, price level P_1, money wage rate W_1, and real wage rate $(W/P)_1$. As the price level rises toward P_2, the real wage rate moving along the W_1 curve in quadrant III falls toward $(W/P)_2$. A fall of the real wage rate, however, causes excess demand for labor [e.g., at $(W/P)_2$ the excess demand for labor in quadrant II is GH]. The excess demand for labor leads to a rise of the money wage rate, which shifts upward the W curve in quadrant III. Equilibrium is reached when the money wage rate reaches W_2 and the price level reaches P_2; the real wage rate is then at its original level $(W/P)_1$, and the demand for and supply of labor are equated in quadrant II. With the rise of the money wage rate from W_1 to W_2, the aggregate supply function in quadrant IV has shifted upward from S_1S to S_2S.

The case of cost-push inflation can also be illustrated with Figures 9-2 and 9-3, by simply reversing the order of events. Start in Figure 9-2 with demand and supply curves D_1 and S_1S. Then assume that as a result of union pressure the money wage rate is raised from W_1 to W_2 (Figure 9-3, quadrant III). In Figure 9-3, we observe that the increase of the wage rate to W_2 shifts the aggregate supply curve up to S_2S. Returning to Figure 9-2, observe that the shift of the supply curve S_1S to S_2S leads to a rise of the price level P_1 to P_2. However, at this point we note a major difference between the cost-push case and the previous case of excess demand. At the equilibrium position marked by the intersection of D_1 and S_2S (point E in Figure 9-2), the equilibrium output is below the full-employment level.

A rise of the wage rate and of the price level, when there has been no upward shift of the demand curve, lowers real output and creates unemployment. This fact raises the question of whether continuous wage-push inflation is possible.

Continuous Wage-Push Inflation?

It is possible for wages and prices to be continuously pushed up while unemployment is continuously increasing, but it is highly improbable. Union wage demands weaken as unemployment or fears of unemployment develop. Employer resistance to wage demands increases as the demand for output falls. There is every likelihood that the process of wage-push inflation will be stifled by rising unemployment. This likelihood is the basis for the commonly held view that continuous wage-push inflation is impossible.

However, a change in one of our underlying assumptions will permit the wage-push mechanism to operate as a continuous inflationary force. The automatic demand-depressing effect of rising prices functions only on the assumption that public policy does not nullify it. In actuality, the spread of unemployment creates strong pressures upon the government to take expansionary measures, such as increasing the quantity of money, reducing tax rates, increasing government expenditures, or intervening in the international market in various ways which will limit imports or increase exports. If the pressures on the government to reduce unemployment are powerful enough, as they are likely to be in a modern democratic society, a continuous wage-push inflation becomes a possibility.

INFLATION EXPERIENCE IN THE UNITED STATES

A brief glance at the broad outlines of American inflation experience will help to put the theoretical discussion into perspective. From 1947 to 1968, the price level, as measured by the implicit price deflator for gross national product,[5] increased at an average rate of 2.3 percent per year.[6]

The year-to-year percentage changes of the price index are shown in Chart 9–1. Except for the sharp increases in 1948 and 1951, the first an aftereffect of World War II and the second an effect of the Korean War, the annual increases are not far from the average for the period, most of them being in the 1 to 3 percent range.

A rough relation between the rate of price change and the state of aggregate demand, as reflected in the unemployment rate, can be discerned in Chart 9–1. The rate of price increase rises sharply when the unemployment rate falls below 4 percent, which suggests the presence of significant excess demand. Note, however, that in the period 1953 to 1965, when the unemployment rate was always above 4 percent, the price index increased at rates between 1 and 3.7 percent. It is this persistence of inflation during a period without excess demand that supports the argument for the existence of a push type of inflation.

---

[5] The implicit price deflator is obtained by dividing the figure for gross national product in current prices by the figure of gross national product in constant prices. Gross national product in constant prices is obtained by subdividing current-price GNP into many components and deflating each such component by its own price index. The implicit deflator is, then, a weighted average of the price indexes employed in estimating gross national product in constant prices. An implicit deflator is also available for certain of the broad subgroups of gross national product.

[6] The price index overstates the rate of inflation to some small extent. Index numbers cannot be adequately adjusted for improvement in the quality of products. Also, in the case of the product of government employees (services) and certain consumer services, the change of the price of the output is measured by the change of the rate of pay for the labor. This calculation does not adjust for any increase in the productivity of the labor and therefore overestimates the rise of the price of the output.

CHART 9–1

Price Change and Unemployment Rate, 1948–68

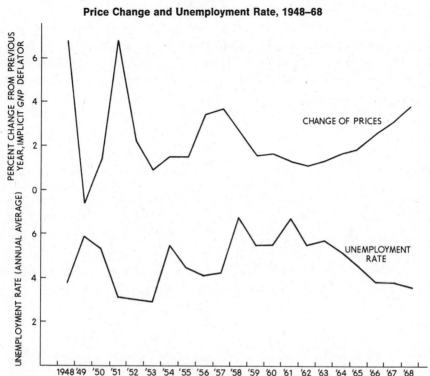

Source: *Economic Report of the President,* January, 1969.

THE INFLATION-UNEMPLOYMENT "TRADE-OFF"

It seems reasonable to expect that the rate of wage increase will be inversely related to the rate of unemployment. At very low rates of unemployment, general excess demand will exist, resulting in a demand pull on wages. At higher rates of unemployment, excess demand will disappear from some markets, but exist in others, so that the average wage level will still rise though at a slower rate. Also wages may rise through a wage-push process even in markets without excess demand. At still higher rates of unemployment, excess demand becomes negligible and the demand pull on wages disappears, but the wage push can continue. Finally, as the rate of unemployment rises further, union demands become weaker and employer resistance becomes stronger and the rate of wage increase becomes still smaller.

Expectations of this sort are supported by studies of the past relationship between the rate of wage increase and the rate of unemployment. A careful study of the relationship has been made for the British economy by A. W. Phillips[7] and the idea has been applied to find that the relationship is expressed by a curve shaped like the one in Chart 9–2. In Chart 9–2 the combination of the unemployment the U.S. economy by Samuelson and Solow.[8] Both of these studies find that the relationship is expressed by a curve shaped like the one in Chart 9–2. In Chart 9–2 the combination of the unemployment

CHART 9–2

The Unemployment Rate and Percentage Change of Employee Compensation, 1947–62

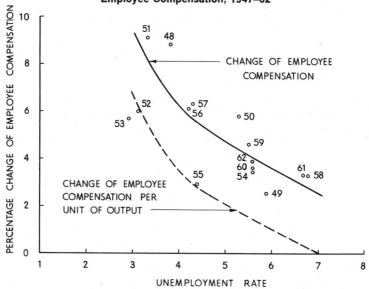

Source: U.S. Department of Labor, Bureau of Labor Statistics, "Comparison of Indexes of Labor and Nonlabor Payments, Prices and Output per Manhour, 1947–1962," December 23, 1963.

rate and the percentage increase of employee compensation from the previous year is plotted for each year and a line is fitted to these points.

Given a relationship between wage rates and the unemployment

[7] "The Relation between Unemployment and the Rate of Change of Money Wage Rates in the United Kingdom, 1861–1957," *Economica*, N.S., Vol. XXV, No. 100 (November, 1958), pp. 283–99.

[8] Paul A. Samuelson and Robert M. Solow, "Analytical Aspects of Anti-Inflation Policy," *American Economic Review*, Vol. L, No. 2 (May, 1960), pp. 177–94.

rate, it should be possible to derive a relationship between changes in the price level and the unemployment rate. The price level is not directly related to wage rates, but it is closely related to wage costs per unit of output.[9] The effect of wages on the price level, therefore, depends not only on the percentage of wage increases but also on the change in labor productivity, i.e., output per man-hour. Over the period 1947 to 1962, the year-to-year increase of output per man-hour was highly irregular. It averaged 2.5 percent per year but it ranged from −0.2 to 5.1 percent. Consequently, the rate of wage increase and the rate of increase of wage cost per unit of output are not closely related and, hence, a simple relationship between the increase of wages and the increase of the price level, or between the increase of prices and the rate of unemployment, will not be found. However, it is possible to suggest an "average" relationship between the rate of unemployment and the rate of price increase by the expedient of discounting the employee compensation-unemployment curve in Chart 9–2 by the *average* rate of increase of labor productivity.

The broken line in Chart 9–2 represents the employee-compensation curve adjusted by a rate of productivity increase of 2.5 percent to give a curve indicating the rate of increase of employee compensation per unit of output to be expected at various rates of unemployment. On the assumption that the price level will increase at the same rate as labor cost per unit of output, this curve also represents the rate of price increase to be expected at various rates of unemployment. In effect, the broken line is a "trade-off" curve between inflation and unemployment; the lower the rate of inflation you want, the higher the rate of unemployment you must accept.

The trade-off curve as derived in Chart 9–2 is obviously a very rough approximation to reality. The observed points are widely scattered about the curve describing the relation between the rate of unemployment and the percentage change of wages. Recent studies have attempted to refine the analysis by introducing additional variables.

One of the more thorough reexaminations of the wage-unemployment relation[10] arrives at the following preferred equation:

---

[9] From 1947 to 1962, employee compensation per unit of output increased 42 percent (U.S. Department of Labor, Bureau of Labor Statistics, "Comparison of Indexes of Labor and Nonlabor Payments, Prices and Output per Manhour, 1947–1962," December 23, 1963). The GNP implicit deflator increased 41 percent.

[10] George L. Perry, *Unemployment, Money Wage Rates, and Inflation* (Cambridge, Mass.: The M.I.T. Press, 1966).

$$\dot{W}_t = -4.313 + 0.367\dot{C}_{t-1} + 14.711 \frac{1}{U_t} + 0.424\, R_{t-1} + 0.796\, \triangle R_t$$

where

$\dot{W}$ is the percentage change in straight-time hourly earnings over the past year.

$\dot{C}$ is the percentage change in the consumer price index over the year.

U is the average unemployment rate during the year.

R is the average rate of aftertax profits in manufacturing during the year.

$\triangle R$ is the quarterly change of R.

That wage increases sought and obtained would be positively related to the consumer price index and to the profit rate, is plausible. The change of the profit rate ($\triangle R$) is an indicator of the direction in which the economy is moving; one would expect, other things equal, that wages would increase more when the economy is expanding and the demand for labor is rising than when the economy and the demand for labor are contracting. Adding these variables to the unemployment rate considerably improves the fit of the equation.[11]

Some of the implications of this wage equation can be seen in Chart 9–3, which shows the wage-price-unemployment relation under "steady-state" conditions ($\dot{C} = 0$, $\triangle R = 0$) and with a profit rate (R) of 11 percent—approximately the long-run average. The left scale shows the annual percentage wage increase associated with various rates of unemployment. For example, with a 4 percent unemployment rate, the expected rate of wage increase would be

---

[11] A later study by Gail Pierson, "The Effect of Union Strength on the U.S. Phillips Curve," *American Economic Review*, Vol. LVIII, No. 3, Part 1 (June, 1968), pp. 456–67, fits the same type of equation to data from 1953 to the middle of 1966. In the resulting equation, the profit variable R was no longer significant and was dropped, but it was necessary to add a new term, S, a dummy variable representing the wage-price guidelines (a government program of exhortation-*cum*-arm-twisting to persuade unions and employers to hold wage increases to a noninflationary level) introduced in 1962. Miss Pierson's equation is:

$$\dot{W}_t = -0.0598 + 0.2836\,\dot{C}_{t-1} + 17.6576\,\frac{1}{U_t} + 0.6762\triangle R_t - 1.0164\, S$$

Her finding that the guidelines appear to have been rather effective is particularly interesting if not a little surprising. (For further discussion of the guidelines, see Chapter 12 below.)

CHART 9–3

Wage-Price-Unemployment Relation, Steady State

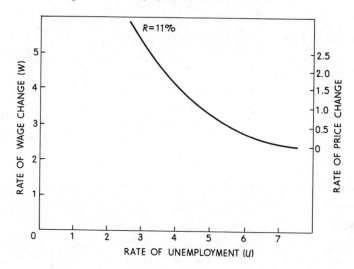

4.03 percent per year. The right scale shows the corresponding expected rate of price increase. The price scale is derived by assuming an average increase of labor productivity of 2.5 percent per year. Labor cost per unit of product would then rise at the rate of wage increase minus 2.5 percent, and prices are assumed to rise at the same rate as unit labor cost. Thus, at 4 percent unemployment, the expected rate of price increase is $4.03\% - 2.5\%$, or 1.53% per year.

If, now, we drop the steady-state assumption and allow the rise of the price index in each period to add to the wage increase of the next period, we find that the rate of wage increase converges on a somewhat higher level.[12] For example, keeping the unemployment rate at 4 percent, and beginning in period 1 with $\dot{C}_0 = 0$, $\dot{C}_1$ (as we saw above) will be 1.53 percent. In period 2, $\dot{W}_2 = 0.367 \ (.0153) +$

---

[12] The convergence occurs because the coefficient of $\dot{C}$ is less than 1. The smaller this coefficient, the more damped is the wage-price spiral. The equilibrium rate of $\dot{C}$ is given by $a(1 + b + b^2 + \ldots b^n) = a \left(\dfrac{1}{1-b} \right)$, where a is the rate of price increase when $\dot{C} = 0$, and b is the coefficient of $\dot{C}$. In the example above, $a = 1.53\%$, $b = 0.367$, and the equilibrium rate of $\dot{C} = 1.53 \left(\dfrac{1}{1 - 0.367} \right) = 2.42\%$.

.0403 = .0459; and $\dot{C}_2$ = .0459 − .025 = .0209. Calculated in this way through succeeding periods, $\dot{W}$ approaches 4.92 percent and $\dot{C}$ approaches 2.42 percent. At these levels, the rates of wage increase and price increase would be in equilibrium.

The equilibrium rates of wage and price increase at various rates of unemployment are shown in Chart 9–4. According to the trade-

CHART 9–4

Equilibrium Trade-Off Curve

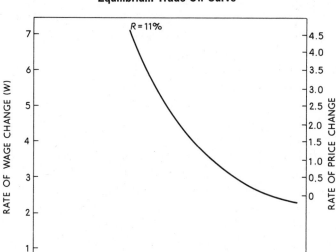

off curve in this chart, an unemployment rate of nearly 7 percent is needed for price stability. At 5 percent unemployment, the curve predicts a small rate of price increase, 1.25 percent. For lower rates of unemployment, the predicted rate of inflation rises to 2.42 percent at 4 percent unemployment, and to 3.24 percent at 3.5 percent unemployment.

Full employment in the United States is generally estimated to be, in terms of the unemployment statistics, between 3.5 and 4 percent unemployment.[13] According to the trade-off curve, a moderate

---

[13] At full employment, which is the point at which no appreciable increase of output and employment can be procured by an increase of aggregate demand, there will still be some frictional and structural unemployment.

rate of inflation must be anticipated at full employment.[14] Unless
the trade-off curve can somehow be shifted downward, the goals of
full employment and stable prices cannot be reconciled.

THE "PROS" AND "CONS" OF INFLATION

Unlike income fluctuations, which are objectionable on the
grounds of the unemployment and loss of income they impose on the
economy, and for which few can find a good word to say, inflation
may involve no loss of total income or employment, and may even,
it has been argued, contribute to the increase of real aggregate income. The case for and against inflation must be examined with
some care.[15]

1. The most frequently voiced objection to inflation is that it effects an unjust redistribution of income and wealth. The income
losers are alleged to be the recipients of incomes fixed in money
terms: interest, social security payments, pensions, and annuities.[16]
The decision to hold interest-bearing assets or to enter into pension
or annuity plans that do not adjust to the price level is largely voluntary; and the losses of income from those assets through inflation
are avoidable, *provided the inflation is foreseen.* If the inflation is
foreseen, the fall of demand for interest-bearing assets will raise
the rate of interest until it compensates for the expected rate of
price increase. Those who are free to choose in the matter of pension and annuity plans can choose plans which protect them against
inflation or they can buy assets (e.g., common stocks) which provide a hedge against inflation. The social security program is not
voluntary, but its payments are subject to adjustment by the government—a feature which has adequately protected participants

---

[14] It should be kept in mind that, because the increase of productivity of
labor in government service and in certain consumer services is omitted from
our statistics and because adequate allowance is not made for product improvement, the data understate the increase of labor productivity and overstate
the rate of price increase. Some low rate of statistical price increase is equivalent to actual price stability, but it is difficult even to guess at what that rate
might be.

[15] Consideration of the implications of inflation for international economic
relations will be postponed to Chapter 11.

[16] Temporary losses of real income, in either absolute terms or relative to
other income groups, may be incurred by persons whose wages lag in the adjustment to inflation, particularly the employees of governments and nonprofit
institutions. It is difficult to know what portion of these income shifts would
have occurred because of the changes in the underlying demand and supply
conditions even if the aggregate price level had been stable.

against inflation in the post-war period. In general, therefore, it would be more precise to say that unjust redistribution of income results, not from inflation, but from *unforeseen* inflation.

With respect to wealth, inflation will inflict losses on the holders of assets with fixed prices, such as bonds, time deposits, and life insurance policies, and on the holders of money. If the inflation is foreseen, the returns on income-yielding assets will rise to compensate for the expected increase of the price level, provided no artificial restrictions are placed on interest rates. If interest rates are not permitted to rise sufficiently, the flow of credit through debt instruments will be disrupted. But, assuming freedom of interest rates to adjust, there need be no interference with credit nor loss of wealth by creditors in the case of an inflation that is foreseen.

To the holders of money, inflation adds to the cost of holding money. If this additional cost is foreseen, money holders can reduce their money balances to amounts they find it desirable to hold at the higher cost, but they cannot escape some of the cost of inflation. The burden of a foreseen inflation on owners of wealth, therefore, falls mainly on holders of money. The cost to the holders of money depends on their ability to shift from money to other assets—i.e., on their elasticity of demand for money.

2. A second charge often made against inflation is that it discourages saving, i.e., expectations of inflation cause an increase of consumption. However, as was previously pointed out,[17] expectations of price increases will increase consumption only if the rate of interest fails to adjust to the expected rate of price rise.

3. A more substantial objection to inflation is that it leads to misallocation of resources. When excess demand exists, the existing price level is not equating the demand and supply of output. Consumers and investors are frustrated in their attempts to buy the quantities they want at current prices. Prices do not ration the supply; substitute rationing mechanisms develop which are likely to allocate output in a way inferior to price allocation. Note that this proposition constitutes an objection, not to *rising prices*, but to *excess demand*. It applies to both suppressed inflation and open inflation, if they reflect excess demand. It does not apply to inflations, such as cost-push types, without excess demand.

4. Certain of the preceding propositions would have to be qualified in the case of a very high rate of price increase, generally

---

[17] See pp. 72–73.

known as "hyperinflation." Under hyperinflation, the cost of holding money becomes extreme; and the efficient device of using money for purposes of exchange is, to some extent, replaced by the cumbersome and wasteful techniques of barter. The cost of avoiding the use of money must be reckoned as one of the costs of hyperinflation.

Another difficulty that may be encountered in hyperinflation is a lag of the interest rate behind the rate of inflation. If the rate of interest falls behind the rate of price increase, lending becomes increasingly unattractive to creditors and funds are diverted to equity financing, to direct investment, or to consumption. This dislocation of the normal channels of credit will cut funds off from some types of investment and lead to overinvestment in other types. If consumption is stimulated, there is some validity to the claim that inflation reduces saving, and, hence, investment. Under conditions of hyperinflation and a lagging interest rate, therefore, the allocation of investment will be made less efficient and the total volume of investment may be reduced.

The utility of a distinction between small or "creeping" inflation and hyperinflation has sometimes been denied on the grounds that a persistent creeping inflation must eventually become a hyperinflation. If a small rate of price increase builds up expectations of a continuation of price increases, and if those expectations heighten current demand, the rate of price increase will be accelerated to the point of hyperinflation. However, we have seen that an adjustment of the interest rate to the expected rate of price increase will cancel the effect of expectations on current demand, so that a small rate of inflation can persist without acceleration.

5. Insofar as arguments have been offered in favor of inflation, they rest on the notion that inflation stimulates or makes possible more rapid economic growth. One line of this argument runs as follows. Investment, and therefore growth, is limited by the amount of saving in the economy. Excess demand and inflation will increase saving in either of two ways: (1) consumers will be unable to fulfill their spending plans and will be forced to save more than they intend, and (2) rising prices will redistribute income in a manner that increases the aggregate propensity to save. Neither of these supposed paths to greater saving inspires confidence. Where demand is excessive, investment as well as consumption can be frustrated; it is at least possible that the disappointments will fall more heavily on investment plans, and that consumption, rather than being constrained, will increase. The income redistribution result-

ing from inflation, as has previously been suggested, is likely to have negligible effects on the propensity to save.

A second approach emphasizes the dependence of growth, through investment and innovations, on the level of demand for output. When demand is expected to be high relative to potential output, the demand for investment goods and innovations for the purpose of increasing capacity will be stimulated. If demand is expected to be below potential output, investment demand and the search for new techniques for expansion will slacken. The surest way to sustain expectations of future high levels of demand is to maintain current demand at a high level.

Strictly speaking, the preceding is not an argument in favor of inflation and rising prices. It is an argument for a high level of demand, which may verge on the excessive. Rising prices are only an undesired by-product of the desired policy. The plea is not for inflation but for accepting inflation with resignation in the interest of economic growth.

SUMMARY AND CONCLUSIONS

Two sources of inflation have been distinguished: (1) excess demand, and (2) wage push.

The broad outlines of the corrective policy to be applied to an excess-demand inflation are generally agreed upon. Dispute may arise over which kinds of demand shall be reduced and what methods shall be used to reduce them, but that the elimination of excessive demand is the basic policy requirement is clear enough. Policies to deal with inflations not attributable to excess demand are more difficult to propose. Reform of fundamental economic institutions is a slow and painful process which may create problems more serious than the one that is being attacked. Policy-makers may be attracted to the easier solution of curbing the inflationary forces by depressing aggregate demand. Wage-push inflation can be halted by a sufficiently high level of unemployment and excess productive capacity. But there is a strong probability that such a policy will fall between the two stools of price stability and growth. Political realities will prevent a continued restriction of demand to a level that will stop inflation, but demand may be depressed enough to retard growth.

If an anti-inflationary policy does involve holding demand below the full-potential level, one may well ask whether the cure is not worse than the disease. In surveying the harmful effects of inflation, we saw that most of the complaints apply to excess-demand inflation rather than to push inflations. It is true that hyperinflation of either kind would have objectionable consequences, but it is most difficult to imagine a pattern of union, business, and government behavior that would produce hyperinflation without excess demand. The objectionable consequences of creeping inflation without excess demand lie entirely in the area of the redistributive effects on creditors and fixed-income groups—effects which can largely be prevented by interest rate adjustments, rearrangements by individuals of the composition of their assets, and by increases by governments of the payments under their pension and social security programs.

The prevention of creeping push inflation is undoubtedly worth something. But, if the prevention requires a depressed level of demand, is it worth the price? The most costly example of inflation may be the inflated price paid for price stability.

RECOMMENDED READINGS

LERNER, ABBA P. "The Inflationary Process—Some Theoretical Aspects," *Review of Economics and Statistics,* Vol. XXXI, No. 3 (August, 1949), pp. 193–99. Reprinted in Abba P. Lerner, *Essays in Economic Analysis,* pp. 328–46. London: Macmillan & Co., Ltd., 1953.

BRONFENBRENNER, MARTIN, and HOLZMAN, F. D. "Survey of Inflation Theory," *American Economic Review,* Vol. LIII, No. 4 (September, 1963), pp. 593–661.

MACHLUP, FRITZ. "Another View of Cost-Push and Demand-Pull Inflation," *Review of Economics and Statistics,* Vol. XLII, No. 2 (May, 1960), pp. 125–39.

U.S. Congress, Joint Economic Committee. *The Relationship of Prices to Economic Stability and Growth; Compendium of Papers Submitted by Panelists Appearing before the Joint Economic Committee,* 85th Cong., 2d Sess. Washington, D.C.: U.S. Government Printing Office, 1958:

HICKMAN, BERT G. "An Interpretation of Price Movements Since the End of World War II," pp. 143–209.

LERNER, ABBA P. "Inflationary Depression and the Regulation of Administered Prices," pp. 257–68.

RUGGLES, RICHARD and NANCY D. "Prices, Costs, Demand, and Output in the United States, 1947–57," pp. 297–308.

LANZILLOTTI, ROBERT K. "Some Characteristics and Economic Effects of Pricing Objectives in Large Corporations," pp. 441–59.

REES, ALBERT E. "Price Level Stability and Economic Policy," pp. 651–63.

208 · *Introduction to Macroeconomic Theory*

U.S. Congress, Joint Economic Committee. *Study of Employment, Growth, and Price Levels.* Washington, D.C.: U.S. Government Printing Office, 1959:

HARRIS, SEYMOUR E. *Study Paper No. 7; The Incidence of Inflation: or Who Gets Hurt?*

QUESTIONS

1. Is an excess-demand inflation self-correcting?
2. Is a wage-push inflation self-correcting? If so, is a continuous wage-push inflation impossible?
3. What is the difference in the cost to society between an excess-demand inflation and a wage-push inflation?
4. If, during an inflationary period, wage rates rise faster than labor productivity, does that fact help to identify the inflation as a wage-push type?
5. What determines the elasticity of the aggregate demand function (i.e., demand as a function of the price level)? What variables are assumed constant in drawing such a function?

Chapter　GROWTH IN
10　AN ADVANCED ECONOMY

In an economy dedicated to the promotion of the welfare of its members, growth should be defined as the increase of welfare. Since no direct measure of welfare nor any prospect of obtaining one exists, discussions of growth are conducted in terms of the increase of economic product. As an indicator of welfare, national product is crude,[1] but it is the best index we have. Some simple improvements can be made. Per capita product is doubtless a better gauge of welfare than total product. A factor can be added to count the part of growing product which the society takes in the form of additional leisure. However the measure is improved, output cannot be equated with welfare; but it can serve as a rough register of changes in welfare.

Much of the current interest in growth analysis is focused on the problems of the "underdeveloped" areas—areas where per capita income is very low and has shown little or no long-run tendency to rise. In most cases, the underdeveloped areas are characterized by institutions, customs, attitudes, motivations, education, and skills which, whatever their virtues in other respects, are ill-adapted and inhibiting to economic growth. Growth in those economies depends so crucially on extensive social renovation that the growth factors discussed in this chapter are, by comparison, of minor significance. The analysis that follows, therefore, is primarily relevant to advanced countries, the term "advanced" being used in the sense of having the social prerequisites for sustained economic growth.

GROWTH AS A SUPPLY CONCEPT

Much misunderstanding can be prevented if, at the outset, the difference is clearly drawn between the subject of growth and the subject of the determination of aggregate product that occupied

[1] See p. 24.

the preceding chapters. Aggregate product is dependent on aggregate demand, within the upper limit set by the potential output of the economy. The analysis of the determination of product, therefore, is the analysis of demand. The analysis of growth is concerned with the upper limit of potential output. Specifically, it studies the determination of the rate at which the upper limit—the potential output of the economy—rises through time. Growth, in other words, is concerned with the supply capacity of the economy, and not with the actual output or aggregate demand.

The failure to keep clear the distinction between the behavior of actual output and potential output has frequently muddled economic discussion. For example, in recent years there has been much talk of a slowdown in the rate of growth in the United States since 1957. The slowdown, as we saw in Chapter 8, was in actual output; the potential output continued to grow, according to our estimates, at a rate that compares favorably with the past. The correct question to have asked was not, "What has gone wrong with the determinants of supply?" but "What has gone wrong with aggregate demand?"

By keeping the two concepts distinct we do not imply that there is no interaction between them. Fluctuations of output may affect the rate of growth of potential output, or growth may affect fluctuations. The interrelation will be examined at a later point.

THE SOURCES OF GROWTH

For the purposes of analyzing growth, the economy will be treated as a single production process, with inputs being fed in at one end and product coming out the other. The quantity of output that can be obtained from the various possible quantities and proportions of inputs defines the *production function*. This procedure of combining the many different production processes in the economy into an aggregate production function is a great simplification but one which is highly useful in gaining an insight into the growth mechanism. We have no reason to think it a seriously misleading procedure.

The inputs are labor and capital.[2] With a given production func-

---

[2] Natural resources might be listed as another factor of production but it is simpler to lump them in with capital, as the statistical studies in the field have done. Another question which arises with regard to the concept of capital concerns the proper treatment of outlays for education and the development of

tion, growth depends upon increases in the quantity of inputs. The production function, however, can be changed by technological advances. Technological progress provides a second possible source of economic growth.

If the economy is making optimum use of its available supply of inputs within the framework of the existing production function, then growth of inputs and technological change are the only sources of growth. However, should the economy be misallocating resources because of immobility of inputs, restrictions on the movement of inputs, lack of information, or poor management, potential output can be increased by overcoming these obstacles to efficient operation. As a source of growth, the correction of misallocation is different in kind from the sources previously mentioned; the movement from a suboptimum to an optimum position is a once-for-all change, not one which can be repeated continuously like the increase of inputs or technological progress. The possibility for growth through improved allocation obviously depends on how badly mismanaged the economy is: in the United States it is likely to be very small relative to other sources of growth, but not necessarily insignificant.[3]

A MODEL OF GROWTH

A theoretical analysis of the growth process, based on an aggregate production function, will reach conclusions which depend on the characteristics of the production function assumed. The model presented here utilizes a specific type of function, known as the Cobb-Douglas production function. This choice can be justified on the grounds that the function embodies economic characteristics which seem reasonable and that a number of empirical studies, though not all, have found it fairly consistent with production data. It is, moreover, a highly convenient type of function with which to begin the construction of a growth model.

The Cobb-Douglas function takes the form

$$Y = vK^aL^{1-a}$$

---

labor skills. Conceptually, these should be treated as investment in human capital, an addition to the capital stock. In statistical studies, they are ordinarily omitted from the capital stock.

[3] See Edward F. Denison, *The Sources of Economic Growth in the United States* (New York: Committee for Economic Development, 1962), for some learned guesses at the possible magnitudes.

where

Y is total product.
K is capital input.
L is labor input.
v is a constant.
a is a fraction.

One characteristic of this function is that if K is increased by any percentage r, Y will increase by the percentage ar. Similarly, if L is increased by r, Y will increase by $(1 - a)r$.[4]

Since the two exponents a and $1 - a$ are fractions which add up to one, an increase of both K and L by the same percentage r will increase Y by the percentage r. In other words, the function specifies constant returns to scale.

Production requires some of both inputs. The inputs are substitutable but are not perfect substitutes, i.e., the function obeys the principle of diminishing returns.

A model of growth can now be derived.[5] Growth depends upon the growth of capital, the growth of labor, and technological progress.

1. The Growth of Capital

Assume a constant long-run ratio of net saving to net output. Let s stand for this ratio. Saving in any period when output is Y will equal sY.

Since saving equals investment, net investment equals sY. Net investment is the addition to the capital stock, K. The percentage increase of the capital stock is $I/K = sY/K$.

---

[4] Differentiating $Y = vK^aL^{1-a}$ with respect to K gives the marginal product of K,

$$\frac{\partial Y}{\partial K} = vaK^{a-1}L^{1-a}.$$

If capital is increased by rK, the increase of output,

$$\triangle Y = rKvaK^{a-1}L^{1-a} = rvaK^aL^{1-a}.$$

The percentage increase of output,

$$\frac{\triangle Y}{Y} = \frac{rvaK^aL^{1-a}}{vK^aL^{1-a}} = ar.$$

A similar proof can be applied to an increase of L.

[5] The following analysis is based on T. W. Swan, "Economic Growth and Capital Accumulation," *Economic Record*, Vol. XXXII, No. 63 (November, 1956), pp. 334–61.

From the production function, we know that if capital grows at the rate sY/K, it will contribute asY/K to the rate of growth of output.

2. The Growth of Labor

The growth of the labor supply depends on the growth of population, the proportion of the population that participates in the labor force, and the number of hours supplied per worker. We will adopt the assumption that the labor supply is independent of the other variables in the model and grows at a constant percentage rate, n, per period.

According to the production function, L growing at the rate n will contribute $(1 - a)n$ to the rate of growth of output. To shorten the notation,[6] we will substitute the symbol b for $(1 - a)$. Thus, the growth of labor contributes bn to the rate of growth of output.

3. Technological Change

We assume, first of all, that technological change is "neutral," meaning that technological change with given factor inputs increases the marginal productivity of capital and labor in the same proportion. Particular innovations may be labor-saving (may increase the marginal product of capital by a larger proportion than the marginal product of labor) or capital-saving (the contrary case), but in the aggregate the effect of innovations is assumed to be neutral.

The effect of neutral technological progress is to leave the exponents in the production function, a and b, unchanged. Instead, the scale factor v, by which $K^a L^b$ is multiplied in the production function, is increased.

For the moment we will assume that technological change occurs at a rate which increases v by a constant percentage m per period. Thus technological change contributes the percentage m to the growth rate of output.

4. The Growth Rate of Output

Output grows at a rate which is the sum of the contributions of capital, labor, and technology. Letting g represent the rate of growth of Y per period, we have

---

[6] The production function becomes $Y = vK^a L^b$, where $a + b = 1$.

$$g = as\,\frac{Y}{K} + bn + m.$$

5. The Equilibrium Growth Rate

The growth-rate equation shows that, in this model, g will tend toward an equilibrium rate. This equilibrium can be demonstrated diagrammatically. In the equation for g, there are five constants—s, a, b, n, and m—and only one variable, Y/K, or the output-capital ratio. We can diagram g as a function of Y/K. In Figure 10–1, Y/K

FIGURE 10–1

The Equilibrium Growth Rate

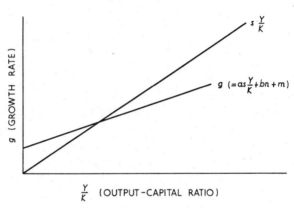

is measured on the horizontal axis, g on the vertical. The g line shows how the growth rate rises as Y/K rises. With a given saving rate, s, the higher the output-capital ratio, Y/K, the faster the rate of growth of capital, sY/K; and the faster the rate of growth of capital, the faster output grows. However, with capital stock, K, and output, Y, growing, the variable Y/K will change, unless K and Y grow at the same rate.

To see what is happening to K, we put in the line sY/K. Since sY/K is the growth rate of K, a line with the slope s shows the rate of growth of K as a function of Y/K. Thus, the two lines in Figure 10–1 show, respectively, the growth rates of capital and output.

It can now be seen that the point E marks the equilibrium growth rate and the equilibrium output-capital ratio. Suppose that Y/K is at d, in Figure 10–2. At that Y/K ratio, Y grows at the rate F while K grows at a lower rate, H. With Y growing faster than K, Y/K

FIGURE 10–2

Equilibrating the Growth Rate

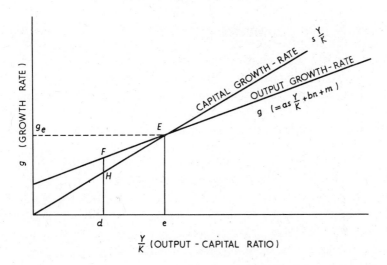

rises, and the rate of growth of K rises and catches up with the rate of growth of Y, until at E, both are growing at the same rate. When Y and K are growing at the same rate, Y/K is in equilibrium at e and the growth rate of output, g_e, is an equilibrium rate. If Y/K were to the right of e, K would be growing faster than Y, causing Y/K to fall to e.

The essence of the growth model is simply this: if saving is a fixed proportion of output, then the higher the ratio of output to the capital stock, the faster the capital stock grows. If capital grows faster, output grows faster, but the increase in the rate of growth of output is only a fraction, a, of the increase in the growth rate of capital. Thus, any difference between the growth rates of output and capital results in a change in the output-capital ratio, which in turn adjusts the growth rates until output and capital are growing at the same rate.

THE SAVING RATE AND GROWTH

This growth model contains some highly interesting and important implications about the effect of changes in the saving rate on the rate of growth of output. Suppose that, through fiscal policy or other means, the proportion of output saved, s, can be increased. What will be the effect on the growth rate?

An increase of the saving rate from s to s' will increase the rate of growth of capital from sY/K to $s'Y/K$. The growth rate of output will be increased by the difference between $as'Y/K$ and asY/K. This increase, however, will not be permanent. Since a is a fraction, the growth rate of output rises less than the growth rate of capital. The system is now in disequilibrium, with capital growing faster than output. The Y/K ratio falls and the growth rate falls back toward equilibrium. The equilibrium position can be easily calculated.

In equilibrium, the growth rates of output and of capital must be equal. Therefore, in equilibrium

$$s \frac{Y}{K} = as \frac{Y}{K} + bn + m.$$

Then

$$s \frac{Y}{K} (1 - a) = bn + m$$

and

$$s \frac{Y}{K} = \frac{bn + m}{1 - a}.$$

Thus, in equilibrium, capital and output are growing at the rate $(bn + m)/(1 - a)$. Since s does not appear in that expression, the equilibrium growth rate is independent of the saving rate. A change in the saving rate does not change the equilibrium growth rate. It only changes the equilibrium output-capital ratio. From the equilibrium expression,

$$s \frac{Y}{K} = \frac{bn + m}{1 - a}$$

we find that in equilibrium,

$$\frac{Y}{K} = \frac{bn + m}{s(1 - a)} = \frac{g_e}{s}.$$

An increase of s reduces the equilibrium Y/K proportionately.

The effects of a change in the saving rate are shown diagrammatically in Figure 10–3. The increase of the saving rate from s to s' raises the capital-growth line from sY/K to $s'Y/K$. The increase of s raises the $s'Y/K$ output-growth line from g to g'. From the previous analysis we know that the shift of the g line must be such as to intersect $s'Y/K$ at a level which leaves the equilibrium

FIGURE 10–3

Effect of the Saving Rate on the Equilibrium Growth Rate

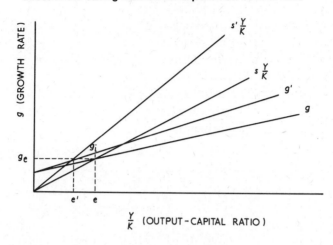

$\frac{Y}{K}$ (OUTPUT-CAPITAL RATIO)

growth rate, g_e, unchanged. The output-capital ratio is reduced from e to e'.

The Transitional Effects of the Saving Rate

Though the saving rate has no effect on the equilibrium rate of growth in this model, it does affect the rate of growth during the transitional period from the time s is changed until equilibrium is restored. The initial effect is to raise the growth rate to g_i in Figure 10–3. Then, as Y/K falls, the growth rate slides down along g', approaching g_e. Consequently, even though the equilibrium growth rate is unchanged, the *level* of output is higher because of the transitional acceleration of growth. The result of the increase of s is illustrated in Figure 10–4. The curves y_1 and y_2 represent two paths of income through time, both growing at the same rate. Starting with an increase of s at time t_1, income follows the broken line until at some time, t_2, the growth rate is restored to the original equilibrium rate, and income grows along y_2.

Besides being temporary, the increase in the growth rate through increasing s is likely to be rather small relative to the equilibrium growth rate. This can be illustrated with some plausible figures. The contribution of capital growth to output growth is asY/K. In equilibrium, Y/K was shown to be equal to g_e/s. Capital's contribution is then

FIGURE 10–4

Illustration of the Effect of an Increase of s

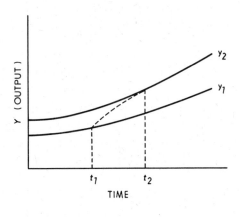

$$as \frac{g_e}{s} = ag_e .$$

If s is increased to s', capital's contribution is initially raised to

$$as' \frac{g_e}{s} = \frac{s'}{s} ag_e .$$

The initial increase in capital's contribution is proportionate to the increase in the saving rate. Assuming an equilibrium growth rate of 4 percent, an original saving rate of 12 percent, and $a = \frac{1}{3}$ (which is approximately the figure found for Cobb-Douglas functions fitted to U.S. data), $ag_e = 1\frac{1}{3}\%$. If the saving rate is now increased to 15 percent,

$$\frac{s'}{s} ag_e = 1.25\ ag_e = 1\frac{2}{3}\%$$

Capital's contribution to the growth rate has been raised by one third of 1 percent and the growth rate has been increased to $4\frac{1}{3}$ percent. An increase of 25 percent in the saving rate was required for an initial addition of one third of 1 percent to the rate of growth.

A word should be said about the length of the transitional period. Strictly speaking, the return of the growth rate to equilibrium is an infinite process; the fall of Y/K reduces the growth rate which reduces the rate of fall of Y/K which reduces the rate of fall of the growth rate, so that equilibrium is approached by ever-diminishing steps. In Figure 10–4, the path from y_1 to y_2 approaches y_2 asymptotically. In practical terms, the growth rate gets very close to equilibrium within some finite time period.

AN "OPTIMUM" RATE OF SAVING

In the previous section we noted the conclusion that, given the other parameters of the model, changing the saving rate cannot affect the equilibrium rate of growth, but that an increase of the saving rate will produce an increase of the growth rate during the subsequent disequilibrium period. When the system returns to the equilibrium growth rate, income is on a higher plane than it would have been, and the output-capital ratio is lower than it would have been, had the saving rate not been raised.

There is another side to this coin: though income is higher, the higher saving rate means that a smaller proportion can be enjoyed as current consumption. Is there some one rate of saving (and, correspondingly, some unique output-capital ratio) which results in the highest consumption-path as the economy grows at its equilibrium rate? An ingenious answer has recently been provided,[7] the gist of which can be explained with the aid of Figure 10–5. Output per period is measured on the vertical axis, the capital stock on the horizontal. On the assumption of a constant amount of labor in-

FIGURE 10–5

The Optimum Saving Rate

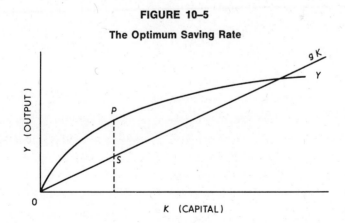

[7] Edmund Phelps, "The Golden Rule of Accumulation," *American Economic Review*, Vol. LI, No. 4 (September, 1961), pp. 638–43; Joan Robinson, "A Neo-Classical Theorem," *Review of Economic Studies*, Vol. XXIX (3), No. 80 (June, 1962), pp. 219–26.

The diagrammatic presentation of this proposition is derived from Alvin L. Marty, "The Neoclassical Theorem," *American Economic Review*, Vol. LIV, No. 6 (December, 1964), pp. 1026–29.

220 · *Introduction to Macroeconomic Theory*

put and a given technology, the line OY showing total output as a
function of the capital stock is obtained from the production function. In equilibrium growth, with output growing at the equilibrium
rate g, capital is also growing at the rate g. The addition to the
capital stock in each period is gK. The addition to the capital stock
is investment, which is equal to saving. Therefore gK measures total
saving per period. The distance between the Y and the gK lines
(such as PS) measures output minus saving, which is consumption.
Consumption is maximized when the distance between the two lines
is maximized, and that will be at the point where the lines have the
same slope. (If P is the point at which the lines are parallel, then to
the left of P, Y is drawing away from gK, and to the right of P, Y
is drawing closer to gK, so that P is the point where they are
furthest apart.)

The proposition that consumption is maximized when the Y and
gK lines are parallel is equivalent to the proposition that consumption is maximized when the marginal product of capital is equal to
the equilibrium growth rate. The slope of the Y line is the marginal
product of capital (the increment of output due to a small increment of capital), and the slope of the gK line is the equilibrium
growth rate (g).

Figure 10–5 shows maximum consumption for one time period
out of all the periods in long-run equilibrium growth. In Figure
10–6, the same demonstration is carried out for succeeding periods.
In period t_1, Y as a function of K is shown by Y_{t1}. P is the point at
which Y_{t1} and gK are parallel, and consumption is maximized.
Growth continues at the rate g because labor is growing at a con-

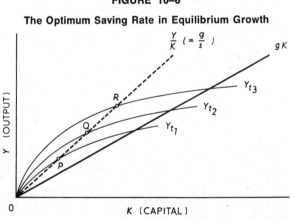

FIGURE 10–6

The Optimum Saving Rate in Equilibrium Growth

stant rate and technological progress is neutral and occurring at a constant rate. The effects of labor increase and technological progress are shown by the upward shifting of the Y line to Y_{t2}, Y_{t3}, etc.

Let P, Q, and R mark the points where the gK line is parallel to Y_{t1}, Y_{t2}, Y_{t3} respectively. It can now be shown that P, Q, R, etc., will all lie on the same straight line (labeled Y/K). The slope of this line measures the output-capital ratio. In other words, it will be shown that as equilibrium growth proceeds through time, the same output-capital ratio is required to maximize consumption in all periods.

The marginal product of capital, in the type of production function used here, can be shown to be equal to aY/K.[8] If innovation is neutral, a does not change. Since, in order to maximize consumption, the marginal product of capital must be kept constant (equal to a constant equilibrium growth rate, g), then Y/K must be kept constant. Hence, the points P, Q, R must all lie on the same Y/K line.

Once the Y/K that will maximize consumption is known, the saving ratio that will maximize consumption is known. From the fact that in equilibrium $Y/K = g/s$, we can select the s that will give the desired Y/K.

The conclusion reached by this analysis, therefore, is that once the economy is on its equilibrium growth path, there is one saving rate for all time periods that will maximize consumption. This saving rate turns out to be the one which makes the marginal product of capital equal to the equilibrium growth rate. In a competitive economy, where the rate of return to capital is equal to the marginal product of capital, this saving rate can be described as the one that equates the rate of return to capital and the equilibrium growth rate.

There is one question with which this analysis does not deal. If the economy does not have the Y/K required for the maximum consumption path, how fast should it adjust Y/K to the desired level? Suppose, for example, that the saving rate has been less

---

[8] The marginal product of capital, in the function $Y = vK^aL^b$, is

$$\frac{\partial Y}{\partial K} = vaK^{a-1}L^b.$$

Multiplying by K, we have

$$\frac{\partial Y}{\partial K}K = vaK^aL^b = aY$$

$$\frac{\partial Y}{\partial K} = a\frac{Y}{K}$$

than the "optimum" as defined above, and Y/K is in equilibrium at a higher level than the optimum. The saving rate can be raised very high so as to bring Y/K to the optimum level quickly and then the saving rate can be reduced to the rate that will keep Y/K at the optimum level. Or the saving rate can be raised less drastically, causing the optimum Y/K to be approached more gradually. The problem is essentially one of deciding what sacrifices the present generation ought to make on behalf of future generations. Once the economy is on the optimum path, the conflict between generations disappears, in the sense that if one saving rate is to be chosen for all generations, the same rate is the best for all generations. But, until the economy is on the optimum path, the speed of adjustment to the optimum is a difficult question, involving the rights and obligations of the present generation vis-à-vis future generations.[9]

A QUALIFICATION OF THE GROWTH MODEL

The growth model under discussion contains one crucial assumption which, in some circumstances, may have to be modified. The model assumes that the rate of technological progress, m, is independent of the rate of growth of sY/K. To the extent that m is a function of sY/K, the conclusion of the model will have to be qualified.

One connection between m and sY/K is this: some technological change can only be introduced when it is embodied in new capital. This type of change is known as "embodied" technological progress. Technological change which can be applied to both old and new capital is known as "disembodied" technological progress. The rate of embodied technological progress depends upon the rate that new capital (for replacement or net addition to the capital stock) is being created. To the extent that technological progress is of the embodied, rather than the disembodied, type, the rate of technological progress depends upon the rate of growth of the capital stock.

It is probable that the embodiment effect is rather small in most countries.[10] The effect can be estimated by putting it in terms of the reduction in the average age of the capital stock achieved by in-

---

[9] For a discussion of some of the pertinent considerations, see James Tobin, "Economic Growth as an Objective of Government Policy," *American Economic Review*, Vol. LIV, No. 3 (May, 1964), pp. 1–20, with discussion by Harry G. Johnson and Herbert Stein, *ibid.*, pp. 21–27.

[10] See Edward F. Denison, "The Unimportance of the Embodied Question," *American Economic Review*, Vol. LIV, No. 2 (March, 1964), pp. 90–94.

creasing the rate of growth of capital. The younger the capital stock, the more technological progress it embodies. However, the average age of the capital stock changes very little and very slowly in response to an increase of sY/K.[11] Hence, even if all technological progress is of the embodied type, an increase of sY/K will produce a trivial increase of m. If part of technological progress is disembodied, the impact obviously will be even smaller.

While changes in the saving rate will have little effect on the average age of capital in most economies, special notice should be taken of the case of economies in which the capital stock embodies abnormally antiquated technology. The more antiquated the technology contained in the capital stock, the greater the embodiment effect of an increase in the saving rate. If the technology is sufficiently behind the current state of knowledge, the rate of technological improvement can be significantly affected by an increase in the growth rate of capital.

A moderate example of this situation is provided by France, where prewar stagnation and the wartime limitations on investment left the French economy at the end of World War II with an abnormally overaged and outdated capital stock. In the postwar period, France's high rate of investment has permitted a rapid embodiment of the accumlated technical knowledge in the capital stock, with the result that the growth rate has been comparatively high. This phase is temporary—as the capital stock becomes modernized, the rate of technological advance declines—but while it lasts, a high saving rate contributes to a high growth rate.

A more extreme example is the case of an underdeveloped country which is advanced with respect to the institutions and social conditions required for development, and which has brought its skills, motivations, and organization to the point where they impose no serious limitation on the economy's capacity to absorb capital and modern technology. Its capital stock, however, is small and old

---

11 Moreover, the reduction in the average age of capital achieved by an increase in the rate of growth of capital will not be permanent. An increase in the rate of investment means more new capital now, but it also means more old capital in the capital stock in the future. It has been shown that the average age of capital, when the economy is growing at its equilibrium rate, depends on the rate of depreciation of capital and on the equilibrium growth rate, and that both of these rates are independent of the saving rate. An increase of the saving rate will temporarily reduce the average age of the capital stock, but the average age will then rise again to its equilibrium level. See Edmund S. Phelps, "The New View of Investment: A Neoclassical Analysis," *Quarterly Journal of Economics*, Vol. LXXVI, No. 4 (November, 1962), pp. 548–67.

in terms of the kind of technology it embodies. Examples are Japan and Russia at the end of the 19th century. High saving rates and high rates of growth of capital will enable such an economy to increase its rate of technological improvement and to experience a rapid rate of growth. As long as the reservoir of unemployed technical knowledge lasts, a higher saving rate will mean faster technical progress. When the reservoir is exhausted, i.e., when further improvements in technology depend on the rate at which new knowledge is discovered rather than on the rate at which existing knowledge can be employed, the economy approaches an equilibrium growth rate which will be lower than the rate during the developing phase.

EMPIRICAL INVESTIGATIONS

A number of empirical studies have been made which quantify the type of growth model we have been discussing.[12] Despite the shortcomings of the available data and of the methods that must be employed to circumvent the inadequacies of the data, the general conclusions of these studies seem well supported.

The techniques of these studies are broadly similar. An index of labor input, an index of capital input, and an index of output are prepared for a long span of years. The indexes of capital and labor are combined by a weighted average to obtain an index of total factor input. From these indexes the portion of the growth of output which can be attributed to the increase of input and the portion that can be attributed to other causes, including technological progress, are computed.

The findings of the Kendrick study will serve to illustrate the results of this type of investigation. From 1889 to 1957, according to Kendrick's data, the real gross product of the private domestic economy increased at the rate of 3.5 percent per year. The index of total factor input increased at the rate of 1.7 percent per year. On

---

[12] John W. Kendrick, *Productivity Trends in the United States* (Princeton, N.J.: Princeton University Press, 1961); Jacob Schmookler, "The Changing Efficiency of the American Economy, 1869–1938," *Review of Economics and Statistics*, Vol. XXXIV, No. 3 (August, 1952), pp. 214–31; Robert M. Solow, "Technical Change and the Aggregate Production Function," *ibid.*, Vol. XXXIX, No. 3 (August, 1957), pp. 312–20; Moses Abramovitz, "Resources and Output Trends in the United States Since 1870," *American Economic Review*, Vol. LXVI, No. 2 (May, 1956), pp. 5–23; Denison, *The Sources of Economic Growth in the United States, op. cit.*

the assumption of constant returns to scale, an increase of output of 1.7 percent per year can be attributed to the increase of input. The remaining 1.8 percent per year in the growth of output can then be attributed to technical progress and the increase of knowledge. Thus, one half of the growth rate is attributed to the growth of input and one half to technical progress. These proportions are about the same as those found in the studies by Schmookler and Abramovitz.

With the data in Table 10–1, we can carry the attribution of growth a step further. For the period 1889 to 1957, output growth of 1.7 percent per year has been attributed to the growth of input. Labor input increased at 1.47 percent per year. If capital input had increased at the same rate, then, on the assumption of constant returns to scale, the growth of input would have contributed 1.4 percent per year to the growth of output. There remains, therefore, 0.3 percent of the output-growth rate which can be attributed to the 1.1 percent growth of capital in excess of the growth of labor. That is, the increase of capital per unit of labor by 1.1 percent per year added 0.3 percent to the growth rate of output.[13]

The rather small part of the growth rate which empirical studies assign to the increase of capital has been something of a surprise. Several points have been raised which suggest that capital's contribution has been underestimated.

If, instead of the constant returns to scale that have been assumed in the empirical investigations, the economy is actually subject to increasing returns, more of the growth of output should be credited to the increase of input and less to the increase of factor productivity. However, in view of the lack of evidence that returns to scale differ significantly in the aggregate from constancy,[14] this criticism

---

[13] This result can be compared with the finding of Solow, *op. cit.* (after correction by Warren P. Hogan of a computational error, "Technical Progress and Production Functions," *Review of Economics and Statistics*, Vol. XL, No. 4 [November, 1958], pp. 407–11). Solow's analysis found that the growth of capital per unit of labor had contributed 10 percent of the growth of output per unit of labor. From Kendrick's data we compute that over the period 1889–1957, output per unit of labor input increased 2.1 percent per year, i.e., 1.035/1.014. The growth of output attributed to the growth of capital per unit of labor was 0.3 percent, which is 14 percent of the growth of output per unit of labor (2.1 percent). It should be kept in mind that both of these calculations depend on the assumption of constant returns to scale.

[14] See Murray Brown and Joel Popkin, "A Measure of Technological Change and Returns to Scale," *Review of Economics and Statistics*, Vol. XLIV, No. 4 (November, 1962), pp. 402–11, which finds evidence of increasing returns for the period 1890–1918, but approximately constant returns for the period 1919–58.

of the productivity studies seems to be a minor one. A more substantial criticism concerns the fact that part of the increase of factor productivity is due to expenditures on education, training, and research. If the resources put in to increase knowledge and skills were counted as investment and the capital stock were redefined so as to include that type of investment, more of the growth rate would be attributed to the increase of the capital stock and less would be left in the residual category of increases of factor productivity. Consequently, the findings of the empirical studies with respect to the small contribution of the capital stock should be qualified by the clause, "where the capital stock is defined to include only tangible assets."

A number of interesting questions are raised by Kendrick's data, a part of which is summarized in Table 10–1. The data indicate that

TABLE 10–1

Annual Percentage Increases in the Private Domestic Economy, 1889–1957

	Real Gross Product	Labor Input	Capital Input	Total Factor Input	Total Factor Productivity
1889–1919	3.9	2.2	3.4	2.6	1.3
1919–1957	3.1	0.8	1.8	1.0	2.1
1889–1957	3.5	1.4	2.5	1.7	1.8

Source: John W. Kendrick, *Productivity Trends in the United States* (Princeton, N.J.: Princeton University Press, 1961), Table A-XXII, pp. 333–35.

around 1919 a significant change in trends occurred. The rate of growth of inputs slowed down, while the rate of rise of factor productivity increased. Despite the sharp drop in the rate of growth of labor (due to the declines of immigration, the natural growth of population, and hours per worker) and the lesser but still very large fall in the growth rate of capital, the fall in the growth rate of output from 1919 to 1957 was kept to modest proportions by the acceleration in the rise of factor productivity. The rise in the rate of increase of factor productivity has not been explained. Perhaps necessity, in the form of a tighter labor supply, was the mother of innovation.

Another curious feature of the data is that after 1919, the growth rate appears to have moved away from rather than toward equilibrium. The excess of the output growth rate over the capital

growth rate increased. However, 1919 to 1957 includes a long inter-
lude of depression and war, from 1929 to 1945, when the rate of
capital growth was subnormal. Since 1945, capital has been growing
faster than output (3.5 percent per year for output, 4.1 percent per
year for capital, in Kendrick's data), and the system is presumably
approaching an equilibrium.

A tentative attempt to show the experience since 1919 in terms of
our growth-model diagram is presented in Figure 10–7. Initially

FIGURE 10–7

The Growth Model Applied to the U.S. Economy Since 1919

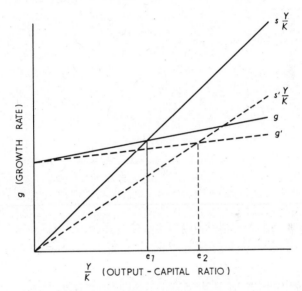

the saving rate is s, the output-growth line is g, and Y/K is rising
toward equilibrium at e_1. During the depression and World War II,
the proportion of output saved falls to s', the growth line shifts to g',
and Y/K rises toward equilibrium at e_2. After the war, the saving
ratio returns to s, the growth line returns to g, and Y/K falls back
toward equilibrium at e_1. The diagram is intended only to illustrate
the direction of movements. The equilibrium level of Y/K may not
actually be the same (e_1) at the end of the period as it was in the
beginning, since the growth rates of labor and technological progress may have changed. But it seems probable that Y/K rose above
its long-run equilibrium level before 1945 and has since been in the
process of falling toward equilibrium.

GROWTH WITH A FIXED OUTPUT-CAPITAL RATIO

Extensive consideration has been given in growth theory to models based on a fixed output-capital ratio. Growth analyses of this type are generally known as Harrod-Domar models.[15] It will be helpful, both for understanding the discussion centering around the Harrod-Domar approach and for exploring the implications of the previous model with a variable output-capital ratio, to compare the two models.

In a growing economy, a fixed output-capital ratio means that output and capital must grow at the same rate. If output and capital grow at the same rate, we can say that a g percent increase of K, together with the given rates of increase of labor input and technological progress, generates a g percent increase in the output capacity of the economy. Or, to put the matter in reverse, output must grow at the rate g in order to use the additional productive capacity created when capital grows at the rate g. Harrod calls this rate the "warranted rate of growth," the rate of growth of output which will utilize the additions to the capital stock and leave entrepreneurs satisfied with the rate of increase of the capital stock.

The warranted rate of growth, g_w, is derived in this way:

Let c stand for the ratio of the increase of output capacity ($\triangle Y$) to the increase of the capital stock ($\triangle K$). The ratio $\triangle Y/\triangle K$ is known as the marginal output-capital ratio. Under conditions of a constant output-capital ratio, the marginal output-capital ratio is equal to the average output-capital ratio. Thus

$$c = \frac{\triangle Y}{\triangle K} = \frac{Y}{K}.$$

From $c = \triangle Y/\triangle K$ we obtain $\triangle Y = c\triangle K$.

Dividing by Y to obtain the percentage growth of Y, we have

$$\frac{\triangle Y}{Y} = \frac{c\triangle K}{Y} = g_w$$

---

[15] See R. F. Harrod, "An Essay in Dynamic Theory," *Economic Journal*, Vol. XLIX, No. 193 (March, 1939), and *Towards a Dynamic Economics* (London: Macmillan & Co. Ltd., 1949); Evsey D. Domar, "Expansion and Employment," *American Economic Review*, Vol. XXXVII, No. 1 (March, 1947), pp. 34–55, and "The Problem of Capital Accumulation," *American Economic Review*, Vol. XXXVIII, No. 5 (December, 1948), pp. 777–94.

The increase of the capital stock ($\triangle K$) is net investment. Net investment equals net saving. Assuming a constant net saving rate, s, then $\triangle K = I = sY$. Substituting sY for $\triangle K$ we have

$$g_w = \frac{sYc}{Y} = sc.$$

The warranted rate of growth is equal to the product of the saving rate and the output-capital ratio. If Y grows at the warranted rate, the capital stock will be fully utilized and entrepreneurs will be willing to continue to invest sY, the amount of saving generated at full-potential income. g_w is therefore a self-sustaining rate of growth.

To relate the Harrod-Domar analysis to our previous model, we note that $c = Y/K$ and, therefore, $g_w = sc = sY/K$. sY/K, as we saw earlier, is the growth rate of capital. The warranted rate of growth of output is therefore the growth rate of capital. This result is not unexpected, since we have already noted that if the output-capital ratio must be constant, output and capital must grow at the same rate.

The warranted rate of growth is represented by the sY/K line in Figure 10–8. The line shows an infinite number of warranted

FIGURE 10–8

Warranted and Natural Rates of Growth

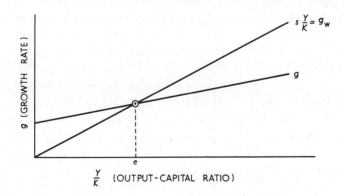

growth rates, one for every possible output-capital ratio. The distinguishing feature of the Harrod-Domar analysis is that only one output-capital ratio is assumed possible, and, therefore, only one warranted rate of growth.

The equilibrium growth rate of output, which is determined by the growth of labor and technical progress, is called by Harrod the "natural rate of growth."

If the output-capital ratio that must be maintained happens to be e, the natural rate of growth equals the warranted rate of growth. The equilibrium rate of growth is equal to the self-sustaining rate of growth, and output can grow along the full-potential equilibrium path.

If, however, the output-capital ratio is fixed to the right of e, the warranted rate of growth exceeds the natural rate. The economy cannot maintain a level of investment so high as sY (full-potential saving) and output falls below the full-potential level. If the output-capital ratio is fixed to the left of e, the natural rate exceeds the warranted rate and investment demand is chronically in excess of full-potential saving.

The chief difficulty in understanding the Harrod-Domar analysis is to see why the output-capital ratio must remain constant. Actually, if the output-capital ratio is to the left of e, there is nothing to prevent a rise of the output-capital ratio, so that eventually the natural and warranted growth rates are brought into equality. The real problem arises when the output-capital ratio is to the right of e and must fall in order to equate the natural and warranted rates.

As the output-capital ratio falls, the rate of return to capital falls.[16] Investment depends upon the relationship between the rate of return to capital and the minimum rate of return to capital acceptable to entrepreneurs. The minimum acceptable rate is the rate of interest on riskless loans (the pure rate of interest) plus a risk allowance (the return entrepreneurs consider necessary for assuming the risk of investment).[17] Unless either the rate of interest or the risk allowance is reduced in step with the falling rate of return to capital, investment will be depressed. Reducing the risk allowance is a difficult matter, for which we have as yet no simple or promising policies. For the moment, we will concentrate on the

---

[16] One way to demonstrate the falling rate of profit is to return to the discussion which follows Figure 10–6. We note there that along a constant output-capital line, the marginal product of capital is constant, and that the lower the output-capital line, the smaller the marginal product of capital. Hence, as the output-capital ratio falls, the marginal product of capital and the rate of return to capital, which depends upon the marginal product of capital—under competitive conditions, it is equal to the marginal product of capital—falls.

[17] The same proposition can be put this way: Investment depends on the relationship between the pure rate of interest and the rate of return to capital minus risk allowance.

policy of reducing the rate of interest. As the output-capital ratio falls, a continuous reduction of the rate of interest can keep investment equal to sY, the amount that will be saved at a full-potential level of output. The limit is reached when the rate of interest has been reduced to its minimum.[18] The output-capital ratio cannot fall further, since any further fall would reduce the rate of return to capital relative to the rate of interest, reduce investment, and thus reduce the rate of growth of capital. If the minimum output-capital ratio is to the right of e, i.e., the warranted rate of growth is larger than the natural rate, capital must grow at the natural rate, which is less than the warranted rate, sY/K. On the assumption that s is constant, the amount saved at full-potential income will exceed investment demand and income must fall below full-potential.[19]

SECULAR STAGNATION

The position just described, in which the output-capital ratio has been reduced to a minimum and the warranted rate of growth still exceeds the natural rate, is the same as the economic condition known as "secular stagnation."[20] In the late thirties, Hansen argued that the mature economies had reached a state of stagnation because of (1) a tendency for the saving rate to rise as household incomes grow; (2) a decline in the rate of population increase, which reduces the rate of growth of labor input; (3) a decline in the rate of technical progress. In terms of our growth model, the hypothesis is that s tends to rise, and n and m to fall. The situation is illustrated in Figure 10–9. Initially, the warranted and natural growth rates are given by the lines g_w and g_n. The equilibrium Y/K ratio is e_1. The fall of n and m lowers the natural growth line to g'_n and the rise of s raises the warranted growth line to g'_w. The equilibrium Y/K ratio is reduced to e_2. Assume that the minimum attainable Y/K ratio is d, which is greater than e_2. When Y/K has fallen to d, secular stagnation appears.

Actual events have not borne out the pessimistic forecast of the thirties. The saving rate, for the reasons discussed in Chapter 4,

---

[18] See Chapter 7, pp. 139–40.

[19] If Y/K cannot fall, K must fall proportionately with Y. The warranted rate remains above the natural rate, and Y and K must fall to zero, if s is constant. If the assumption of a constant s is dropped and s is allowed to fall when income declines, equilibrium can be reached with a more limited fall of income.

[20] See Alvin H. Hansen, *Full Recovery or Stagnation?* (New York: W. W. Norton & Co., Inc., 1938), chap. xix.

FIGURE 10–9

Secular Stagnation

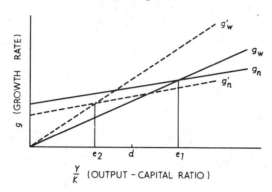

does not tend to rise as the economy grows. The steep decline in the rate of population growth experienced in the thirties has been reversed. There is no evidence that the rate of technological progress has declined. There are no signs of secular stagnation in any of the mature economies at present. Nevertheless, secular stagnation remains a theoretical possibility, and it is not totally irrelevant to think about policy solutions to the problem.

Three points of attack on stagnation are obvious from the growth model. We can attempt to raise the rate of technical progress, raise the rate of growth of labor, or decrease the saving rate. Accelerated technical progress is desirable, not only as a corrective for stagnation, but also as a method of increasing the growth rate of the economy. Unfortunately, it is difficult to improve the rate of progress significantly, for reasons which are discussed below. The rate of growth of labor, which can only be permanently increased by increasing the rate of growth of population, is also difficult to influence by policy, and, aside from counteracting stagnation, has nothing to recommend it by the criterion of economic welfare; on the contrary, it has the drawbacks associated with increased congestion. The third antistagnation policy—a reduction of the saving rate—is comparatively easy to implement and has no drawbacks worth mentioning.

It is quite possible that in any economy approaching secular stagnation, the saving rate will tend to fall without policy intervention. The fall of the rate of return to capital may reduce the propensity to save of entrepreneurs. A second reason is suggested by the life-cycle hypothesis of consumption, which concludes that the saving rate depends on the rate of growth of aggregate output.[21] If this hypothesis is correct, the saving rate will fall as the rate of growth of output falls.

If the saving rate does not fall sufficiently to prevent stagnation, fiscal policy can be used to accomplish that end. Government dissaving can be adjusted to offset private saving and keep the overall saving rate at the desired level.

OPTIMUM SAVING VERSUS SECULAR STAGNATION

In the preceding analysis we noted the existence of a saving rate which, in equilibrium growth, maximizes the consumption-path through time. Subject to the various assumptions in the analysis, that saving rate was found to be the one which, given the other growth parameters, establishes an equilibrium output-capital ratio such that the rate of return to capital equals the equilibrium rate of growth.

We have also noted that as the output-capital ratio declines, and with it the rate of return to capital, a point may be reached where the rate of return to capital falls below the minimum acceptable rate of return. At that point, investment demand falls below the level of full-potential saving. The economy faces secular stagnation. In a sense, secular stagnation is a purely frictional problem— how to reduce a particular price, the minimum acceptable rate of return—but it could be a real problem nonetheless.

The possibility that secular stagnation may prevent the establishment of the optimum output-capital ratio arises if the optimum output-capital ratio entails a rate of return to capital which is below the point to which the minimum acceptable rate of return can be pushed.

The rate of return to capital associated with the optimum output-capital ratio, being equal to the equilibrium rate of growth, is positive in an economy with growth of labor and technological progress. In that sort of an economy, secular stagnation poses less of a problem than it would in the "stationary" state where labor supply and technology are constant, the equilibrium rate of growth is zero, and, therefore, the rate of return to capital, when the output-capital ratio is optimal, is zero. Nevertheless, even in a dynamic economy,

---

[21] See pp. 87–88.

the mechanism of lowering the minimum acceptable rate of return to the level of the equilibrium growth rate or of devising satisfactory alternative methods of sustaining investment (e.g., subsidizing private investment or increasing public investment) presents a genuine difficulty. While, in principle, the optimum output-capital ratio and the optimum saving rate can be identified, practical considerations may impede their attainment.

GROWTH, AGGREGATE DEMAND, AND FLUCTUATIONS

Barring any problem of secular stagnation, we can say that the output-capital ratio will adjust so that output and capital grow at the same rate, i.e., that the warranted and natural rates of growth are brought into equality by the movement of the output-capital ratio to an equilibrium position. Output can then grow at an equilibrium rate. However, nothing has been said thus far about the fact that growth at the equilibrium rate requires that aggregate demand grow at that rate. Up to this point it has been implicitly assumed that aggregate demand is kept equal to full-potential output. The behavior of aggregate demand in a growing economy must now be considered.

If output grows at the equilibrium rate, the entrepreneurs in the aggregate will want the capital stock to grow at the same rate. The desired growth of the capital stock will be sY/K, which means that intended investment will be equal to sY, the intended saving. Thus, aggregate demand will be equal to output. What is required to keep aggregate demand growing at the same rate as output is that entrepreneurs should *expect* output to grow at the equilibrium rate, and, therefore, should want to increase the capital stock at the same rate. So long as entrepreneurs expect output to grow at the equilibrium rate, they will invest an amount that will make output grow at that rate, fulfilling their expectations.

One aspect of the concern about maintaining sustained growth is thus the question of a sustained rate of growth of aggregate demand. Will entrepreneurs expect long-run growth at the equilibrium rate? Before examining this question, we should note and dispose of a common confusion between this problem of sustained growth and the general problem of economic instability.

Growth analyses frequently point out that a disturbance which causes aggregate demand to deviate from the equilibrium growth path will produce an economic fluctuation. The mechanism which generates the fluctuation is nothing but the familiar accelerator-multiplier interaction. An alteration in the present rate of increase of output is said to affect expectations about future output which, in turn, affect the demand for investment, and so on, through the accelerator-multiplier cyclical pattern. The extent of the swing will depend heavily on the extent to which expectations are affected by the current behavior of output. If a current change in the rate of growth is expected to be of brief duration, and expectations about the longer-term rate of growth are unaffected, investment projects with medium or long gestation periods will be unaffected (see pp. 108–9) and the accelerator effect will be small. But, small or large, the accelerator mechanism does subject the economy to some degree of instability. However, the relevant point in the present discussion is that there is nothing peculiarly associated with the growth process that makes for instability. The accelerator-multiplier model is equally applicable to an economy where the equilibrium rate of growth is zero.

Imagine an economy with a constant supply of labor and unchanging technology. In equilibrium, the capital stock and output will be constant. As capital wears out, it is replaced. Now, introduce a disturbance which creates expectations that aggregate demand will be lower in the future. Replacement is postponed and the accelerator-multiplier cycle follows. It is true that the amplitude of the cycle will be smaller in an economy with a constant long-run capital stock, since the maximum fall of investment will be limited to the amount of replacement demand, but the nature of the instability problem is the same as in a growing economy.

The aggregate-demand problem which is peculiar to a growing economy is not, therefore, the instability of demand, but the need for a mechanism assuring that aggregate demand will grow over the long run at the same rate as potential output. We have noted that if entrepreneurs expect the economy to grow at the equilibrium rate, aggregate demand will grow at that rate and the expectations will be fulfilled. The necessary ingredient for sustained growth of aggregate demand is sufficient entrepreneurial optimism or "buoyancy" to maintain expectations of long-run growth.[22] If the expected

---

[22] "Without assuming a certain minimum of 'buoyancy,' the mere accrual of fresh investment opportunities through technical progress will not alone ensure the continued growth in production—since the latter requires in addition that effective demand and profits increase sufficiently to match the growth of potential supply, and thus keep the process of accumulation going." Nicholas Kaldor, "A Model of Economic Growth," *Economic Journal*, Vol. LXVII, No. 268 (December, 1957), pp. 601–2.

growth is steady, the growth rate will tend to be stable. If expectations are of the type assumed in accelerator models, output may be subject to fluctuations, but the trend will be upward and output will bump along the ceiling set by the long-run growth of potential output, given the necessary minimum entrepreneurial buoyancy.[23] A deficiency of entrepreneurial buoyancy has not been observed in most advanced economies. Where such a problem appears, it may be necessary to bolster entrepreneurs' spirits by government assurances that expanding demand will be maintained by monetary and fiscal measures when required.[24]

PUBLIC POLICY AND GROWTH RATES

The model of economic growth presented in this chapter provides a basis for some general comments on appropriate government policies affecting the growth rate. For purposes of this discussion we will restore the assumption that aggregate demand can be kept equal to the potential output of the economy. Policies affecting aggregate demand are assumed to be optimal, and the sole issue is that of policies affecting the rate of growth of potential output.

Saving Policy

The saving rate is one variable in the growth process which can be adjusted by public policy. To reduce the complexities of the

---

[23] See R. C. O. Matthews, *The Business Cycle* (Chicago: University of Chicago Press, 1959), chap. xiii, for further discussion of the mechanism of long-run growth of aggregate demand.

[24] It has been suggested by T. C. Schelling, "Capital Growth and Equilibrium," *American Economic Review*, Vol. XXXVII, No. 5 (December, 1947), pp. 864–76, that sustained growth with less exuberant entrepreneurship can be explained by an accelerator formula in which the desired capital stock in the present period is the stock which is optimal for the production of the level of output of the previous period. An increase of output in the previous period induces entrepreneurs to increase the capital stock by the same proportion in the present period, causing output to rise by that proportion in the present period, and inducing an increase of the capital stock of that proportion in the next period, etc. Sustained growth at the warranted rate, in this formulation, does not require that entrepreneurs forecast the warranted rate of growth but merely that they expect the present level of demand to continue in the next period. (See the earlier discussion of accelerators, pp. 101–2.)

The notion of entrepreneurs' persistently keeping the capital stock trailing behind the optimum strains the imagination somewhat. One would suppose that eventually they would attempt to catch up. However, the lagged capital stock model might be descriptive of how growth can be sustained during a phase of timid entrepreneurship.

analysis, assume that, by fiscal and credit measures, the saving rate can be adjusted to any level desired, with neutral effects on incentives and the efficiency of the mechanism of resource allocation. (In reality, there are limits to the extent to which government policies can raise the saving rate without adversely affecting incentives and distorting resource allocation. The principal instrument for raising the saving rate must be taxation, and even the most nearly neutral types of taxes increasingly diverge from neutrality as tax rates rise.)

From the growth model and the theory of the optimum saving rate we learn that (1) an increase of the saving rate is likely to have a relatively small effect on the growth rate; (2) an optimum saving rate—one that will keep the output-capital ratio at the point which gives the highest growth-path of consumption—can be chosen, given the other parameters of the system; (3) the analysis of the optimum saving rate does not indicate what the saving rate should be during the period when the output-capital ratio is brought to the optimum level, i.e., it does not specify how rapidly the adjustment to the optimum output-capital ratio should take place; (4) the lower limit of the output-capital ratio is set by the point at which secular stagnation occurs; the saving rate should not be so high as to drive the output-capital ratio down to that limit.

The correct policy with respect to the saving rate depends on the empirical findings about the position of the economy. It has been argued that in the economy of the United States, the output-capital ratio is considerably above the optimum; that private savings decisions are, because of imperfect capital markets, based on lower rates of return than the true return on investment, and that this miscalculation leads savers to underestimate their optimum saving; and therefore public policy can increase welfare by raising the saving rate and increasing the rate of growth of capital.[25] The evaluation of these propositions must await further investigation of the facts. However, we can say that even if the facts should warrant government intervention to increase the growth of capital, it will probably not be sufficient merely to increase the rate of saving. The pure interest rate (the interest rate on riskless debts) is low and has not much scope for further reduction. If the growth rate of capital is increased, causing the rate of return on investment

---

[25] See Tobin, "Economic Growth as an Objective of Government Policy," and discussion by Johnson and Stein, *op. cit.*

to fall, and if the interest rate cannot be correspondingly reduced, it will be difficult to keep investment demand equal to saving at full-potential income. In those circumstances, an increase in the saving rate will lead to secular stagnation rather than faster growth, unless measures are also taken to sustain investment demand as the margin of the rate of return on investment over the pure rate of interest narrows. The excess of the rate of return over the pure rate of interest which is necessary to induce investors to invest depends on the risks of lending and the risks of investing. To sustain investment when the margin is shrinking, either the risks would have to be reduced, or offsets to risk provided by subsidies, or investment increased in the public sector.[26] Keeping in mind the small contribution which an increase in the rate of growth of capital can make to the rate of growth of output in a developed economy and deducting for the negative effects of government involvement in the economy, one wonders if the results would justify the fuss.

Policies to Accelerate Technical Progress

Increasing the rate of technical progress is potentially a source of substantial increase in the growth rate, and, as a policy objective, it is free of the limitations and objections that apply to saving policy. Unfortunately, very little is known about how to accelerate technical progress or whether it can, in fact, be much increased by public policy.

One obvious approach to accelerating the rate of technical progress is to increase the rate of investment in the production of technical knowledge. Technical knowledge can be divided into two types, according to whether the full value of the knowledge accrues to the producer of it or whether the value accrues only partially or not at all to the producer. In the case of the first type, the market supplies the inducement to invest in the production of knowledge, and unless the market is functioning defectively no argument can be made for the allocation of additional investment by the government. In the case of investment in the second type of knowledge, where part or all of the gain accrues to society rather than to the investor, the market motive to invest will be inadequate. Investment of this type, commonly known as basic research, is carried on in the United States by businesses which hope to capture part of the gain or for

---

[26] See *ibid.*, pp. 13–14.

a variety of nonprofit motives by businesses, universities, government agencies, and research organizations. In addition, the basic knowledge produced in other countries is available to the U.S. economy. Nevertheless, despite these various sources of support, it is possible that we are investing less than the optimal amount in basic research.

The possibilities of increasing technical knowledge through investment in research may easily be exaggerated. Like other forms of investment, investment in the production of knowledge is subject to diminishing returns. The supply of personnel with the abilities and personality characteristics for scientific discovery is limited. Moreover, a crucial input in the production of knowledge is the existing stock of knowledge; in any one time period the stock of knowledge is fixed and the application of additional investment to that stock results in diminishing returns.

Miscellaneous Growth Policies

Any policies which overcome defects in the functioning of the economic mechanism will add to the growth of potential output. Immobilities of inputs, restrictions on technological change, imperfect information for producers and consumers, and other causes of the waste and misallocation of inputs exist in varying degrees in any economy. To the extent that malfunctioning of the economy can be corrected, the potential output can be increased. The improvement may be a once-for-all change, or, if it permits an increase in the rate of technological progress, it can increase the equilibrium rate of growth.

Growth-Policy Conclusions

The possibilities of increasing the rate of growth through public policy depend upon the extent to which the economy is currently deviating from the optimum output-capital ratio and the optimum saving rate, the extent of its failure to use the best technology available, the extent to which it falls short of the optimum allocation of resources to the production of technical knowledge, and the extent of its other misallocations of resources. An economy doing a poor job in these respects has great scope for increasing the growth rate through corrective policies. An economy which has been doing a good job is rather in the position of the clean-living lady described by Mark Twain, who, when she became sick, had no bad habits to discard and could not be saved.

RECOMMENDED READINGS

ABRAMOVITZ, MOSES. "Economic Growth in the United States," *American Economic Review*, Vol. LII, No. 4 (September, 1962).

DENISON, EDWARD F. *The Sources of Economic Growth in the United States.* New York: Committee for Economic Development, 1962.

HARROD, R. F. *Towards a Dynamic Economics.* London: Macmillan & Co., Ltd., 1949.

SOLOW, ROBERT M. "A Contribution to the Theory of Economic Growth," *Quarterly Journal of Economics*, Vol. LXX, No. 1 (February, 1956).

SWAN, T. W. "Economic Growth and Capital Accumulation," *Economic Record*, Vol. XXXII, No. 63 (November, 1956).

QUESTIONS

1. Explain why, in the model presented in this chapter, the equilibrium rate of growth is independent of the saving rate.
2. How does the "embodiment effect" influence the relation between the saving rate and the equilibrium growth rate? Why is the "embodiment effect" especially significant for an underdeveloped economy?
3. Some empirical studies find that about half of long-run growth in the United States is explained by the growth of total input. What are the various factors which might explain the other half?
4. Explain what is meant by secular stagnation and why it might occur.
5. Why might a conflict arise between the objective of an optimum saving rate and the objective of preventing secular stagnation? Assess the policies available to reconcile this conflict.

Chapter 11 INTERNATIONAL ASPECTS OF INCOME ANALYSIS

National income analysis, as the name suggests, is oriented toward the problems and policies of an economic unit defined by national boundaries. Each nation, however, exists in an international setting; its economy interacts with other economies. These points of international contact and their effects on the functioning of the economic system have been touched on only lightly in earlier chapters. Here they are brought together for more complete examination.

THE PROBLEM OF INTERNATIONAL MONETARY BALANCE

The national income accounts, showing outlays for current product and current input, are not concerned with how those outlays are financed. Each spending unit will see to its own financing; otherwise its expenditures cannot take place. In the case of international transactions, however, there is the peculiarity that, though each unit may arrange the financing of its transactions in terms of its domestic currency, there remains the need for financing international transactions in terms of foreign currency. The fact that each country has its own monetary standard introduces the problem of obtaining an aggregate supply of foreign currency adequate for the net payments that individuals must make in foreign currency. This concern about the demand and supply of foreign means of payment requires that the account of international transactions be broadened from the foreign-sector account of the national income accounting system, which includes only exchanges of current product, to an account which includes *all* transactions involving a monetary exchange between the home country and the rest of the world. Such a statement is known as the "balance of payments" of a country.

The transactions in a balance of payments statement can be divided into those that make foreign exchange available to the home country and those that make home currency available to foreigners. Transactions that increase the supply of foreign exchange are "credits" or "plus items"; those that increase the supply of home currency to foreigners are "debits" or "minus items."[1] An illustration of a balance of payments statement, greatly compressed, is given in Table 11–1.

TABLE 11–1

United States Balance of Payments, 1968
(billions of dollars)

Current account:

Exports of goods and services	50.6
Imports of goods and services	−48.1
Net unilateral transfers	−2.9
Balance on current account (Net foreign investment)	−0.3

Capital account:

Net capital movement (import +)	1.9
Change of gold and foreign currency reserves (increase −)	−0.9
Balance on current and capital account	0.7
Errors and omissions	−0.7

Source: *Survey of Current Business*, June, 1969.

The first set of items, making up the current account, is the foreign sector account of the national income accounts.

The capital account lists all other transactions involving monetary payments between the United States and the rest of the world. Capital exports, which are loans and investments to the rest of the world, are a debit item because they increase the supply of dollars to foreigners. Capital imports, which are foreign loans to and investments in the United States, are a credit item because they increase the supply of foreign currency to the United States. The change of gold and foreign currency reserves refers to the government's holdings of those reserves, which constitute liquid assets that can be used as an international medium of payment.

The balance of payments statement is an account based on double-entry bookkeeping and, like any such account, it must "balance":

---

[1] The same distinction can be made by describing credits as transactions that increase the demand for home currency and debits as transactions that increase the demand for foreign currency. Since foreign-exchange markets exist to exchange home for foreign currency, an increase in the supply of home currency can be readily translated into an increase of demand for foreign currency, etc.

The sum of the credits must equal the sum of the debits. If it fails to do so, it can only be because of errors and omissions in the statistical data. Hence the "errors and omissions" item is added and the whole statement sums to zero. This accounting balance tells us nothing about whether all is well with the balance of payments. It may be that there is a fundamental deficit, arising from trade or capital movements, which is being covered by paying out gold or foreign currency reserves. Or perhaps the deficit is being covered by borrowing foreign exchange purely for that purpose. Since reserves and foreign credit are not inexhaustible, a country which has a fundamental deficit in its balance of payments must eventually face up to the question of how to eliminate that deficit. Such a basic maladjustment is known as a balance of payments disequilibrium.[2]

THE EQUILIBRATING DEVICES

A disequilibrium in the balance of payments can be closed by price changes, income changes, or direct public intervention to shift demand and supply curves. Equilibrating devices will be

---

[2] Defining and measuring a balance of payments disequilibrium is a complex matter having a number of possible approaches. The currently prevailing approach in the United States is that it is the international liquidity position of the country which is crucial. That is, it is the stock of liquid international reserves held by the United States and the stock of U.S. liquid liabilities (to foreigners) that determine whether the United States can maintain the exchange rate of the dollar. A balance of payments deficit is, therefore, defined as a worsening of the liquidity position (a decline of reserves or a rise of liquid liabilities), and a surplus is defined as an improvement of the liquidity position.

In defining the relevant liquidity concept, a major disagreement arises over the treatment of private holdings of international liquid assets and liabilities. If private holdings of liquid claims against foreigners are considered available as part of the defensive reserves of the country and private foreign holdings of liquid claims against the United States are considered as part of the potential threat to the dollar, then the total liquidity position, private plus official, is the relevant liquidity concept. If private liquid holdings are considered not to be part of the reserves or the potential threat to the dollar, the relevant liquidity concept is the state of official reserves and foreign official holdings of liquid claims against the United States.

The United States publishes estimates of its balance based on both liquidity concepts. The condition of the balance as measured by the change of total liquidity is known as the "liquidity basis," and as measured by the change of official liquidity only, as the "official reserve transaction" basis. (Certain nonliquid liabilities to foreign official agencies are also included in official reserve transactions.) The difference between these two bases can be substantial. In 1968, for example, there was a surplus of $93 million on the liquidity basis and a surplus of $1,600 million on the official reserve transactions basis.

Another facet of definition and measurement is that a fundamental disequilibrium may be disguised or suppressed by restrictions on trade or capital movements (restrictions which were imposed because of the balance of payments problem) or by a depressed level of income (which depresses imports). The definition and measurement of the true balance of payments disequilibrium must correct for these distortions.

described from the viewpoint of a country with a balance of payments deficit.

Lowering the Price Level

A reduction of the general level of domestic prices relative to foreign prices will increase the quantity of exports demanded and decrease the quantity of imports demanded. Unfortunately for the practical value of this device, it is extremely difficult to lower the general price level. In view of the stickiness of many prices, a policy of depressing aggregate money demand in an effort to reduce prices is likely to have as its main effect a fall of *real* output.

Devaluation of the Exchange Rate

A method of lowering domestic prices relative to foreign prices without the risk of depressing real output is to devalue the exchange rate, i.e., lower the price of domestic currency in terms of foreign currency. Prices of domestic product, measured in domestic currency, need not change; but the exports of the devaluing country will be cheaper, measured in foreign currency, and the prices of her imports will be dearer, measured in domestic currency. For instance, if the U.S. dollar were devalued from an exchange rate of 5 francs per dollar to 4 francs per dollar, an American commodity selling for $1 in the international market would cost the French buyer 5 francs before devaluation and 4 francs after; a French product selling for 5 francs would cost the American buyer $1 before devaluation and $1.25 after. The effect of devaluation, therefore, will be to increase the quantity demanded of the devaluing country's exports and to decrease the quantity of imports she demands.[3]

---

[3] The possibility has been extensively discussed that the elasticities of demand for exports and imports may be sufficiently low that a devaluation will increase the balance of payments deficit of the devaluing country. (A similar proposition can be developed for the case of lowering the price level of the deficit country.) The drift of the discussion in recent years has been toward a dampening of the belief in the possible instability of foreign-exchange markets (i.e., that a fall in the price of a currency will increase the excess supply of it) for the following reasons: (1) the statistical studies of elasticities contain downward biases; (2) the simple elasticities analysis is a partial equilibrium technique applied to a general equilibrium problem, and therefore omits much of the adjustment process that accompanies devaluation; (3) instability in the foreign-exchange market implies instability in at least one

Interest-Rate Changes

A deficit country might, by raising interest rates, attract a sufficient inflow of capital to close the balance of payments gap. The use of this adjustment device is severely limited by the fact that interest rates also have a role to play in maintaining domestic equilibrium. An increase of interest rates to assist in equilibrating the balance of payments may conflict with the need for lower interest rates to help maintain full-potential aggregate demand. The responsiveness of capital movements to interest rates, which will depend on the countries involved and the attendant circumstances, may be a further limiting factor.

Income Changes

Imports are dependent on, among other things, the level of national income. A fall of aggregate demand will be divided between the demand for domestic product and the demand for foreign product. The relationship between the demand for imports and the level of national income is expressed by the marginal propensity to import—the ratio of the change of imports to the change of income.

A fall of income, by inducing a fall of imports, will tend to reduce a deficit in the balance of payments. The extent of the reduction will depend on what happens to exports. Since we are abstracting from price changes in order to examine income effects, the demand for exports will be determined solely by the level of foreign income. If, as domestic income falls, foreign income is kept unchanged, exports will be constant and the balance of payments deficit will be eliminated by a reduction of income sufficient to induce imports downward by the amount of the deficit.

If foreign income is not sustained by stabilizing policies, the fall of domestic income will induce a fall of income abroad. Domestic imports are the exports of foreign economies, and, therefore, the reduction of imports constitutes a drop of aggregate demand in foreign economies. The fall of income abroad will reduce exports of the deficit country, which will lower her income, induce a fall of

product market, and, hence, the general presumption that product markets are stable leads to a presumption that foreign-exchange markets are stable. See, for example, E. Victor Morgan, "The Theory of Flexible Exchange Rates," *American Economic Review*, Vol. XLV, No. 3 (June, 1955), pp. 279–95.

her imports, reduce income abroad, etc. This series of repercussions means that for the balance of payments deficit to be reduced, the deficit country's imports must fall more than her exports, and that the fall of income required to eliminate a given deficit will be greater than if foreign income had been maintained constant.

The closing of the balance of payments gap, with and without foreign repercussions, is illustrated in Figure 11–1.[4] Assume all

FIGURE 11–1

Balance of Payments Equilibrium through Income Change

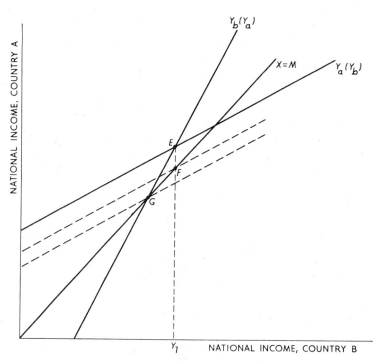

determinants of aggregate demand for the output of Country A to be given, except for the income of Country B (the rest of the world). Then the income of Country A can be shown as a function of the income of Country B: The greater B's income is, the greater is the demand for A's exports, and therefore the greater is A's income. A's income as a function of B's is shown by the line $Y_a(Y_b)$. Similarly, the line $Y_b(Y_a)$ shows the income of B as a function of A's income.

---

[4] This graphical method is derived in part from Charles P. Kindleberger, *International Economics* (rev. ed.; Homewood, Ill.: Richard D. Irwin, Inc., 1958), pp. 190–91.

The line labeled $X = M$ shows all the combinations of income in A and income in B that will equilibrate the balance of payments. Given the income in A and given all other determinants of balance of payments transactions except income in B, there is some one level of income in B that will bring about equilibrium in the balance of payments. The higher is A's income and thus the higher A's import demand, the higher must be B's income to raise A's exports enough to prevent a balance of payments deficit; hence the $X = M$ line slopes upward to the right.

The initial intersection of $Y_a(Y_b)$ and $Y_b(Y_a)$ at point E indicates the mutually determined income levels in A and B. That point does not lie on $X = M$, i.e., this combination of incomes in A and B does not equilibrate the balance of payments. The balance of payments can be equilibrated by reducing A's income—shifting $Y_a(Y_b)$ downward until the intersection of $Y_a(Y_b)$ and $Y_b(Y_a)$ lies on the $X = M$ line. If B's income were maintained at the initial level, Y_1, A's balance of payments deficit could be eliminated by reducing A's income from E to F. But, with B's income dependent on A's, A's income must fall to the level indicated by point G to erase the balance of payments deficit.

Direct Intervention in International Markets

Restrictions on imports through tariffs, quotas, or exchange controls can be used to suppress a deficit in the balance of payments. When an outflow of capital is contributing to the deficit, restrictions on capital export can also be applied.

The effectiveness of restrictions on imports depends upon the willingness of the trading partners to accept this method of dealing with the deficit and to refrain from retaliatory restrictions. These policies will also be more effective if foreign countries sustain their income levels and stifle the income repercussions of the deficit country's reduction of imports.

SOURCES OF BALANCE OF PAYMENTS DISEQUILIBRIUM

Disequilibria come in a variety of shapes and sizes. The choice of the appropriate corrective measure depends upon the type of disequilibrium to be treated. In the following highly condensed discussion, balance of payments disequilibria are divided into five main types.

Cyclical Disequilibrium—Fall of Income Abroad

A balance of payments problem may originate from income fluctuations either abroad or at home. Let us start from a point of
balance of payments equilibrium and full-potential output in the
domestic and foreign economies. Then a fall of income abroad or a
rise of aggregate domestic demand will produce a deficit in the
balance of payments.

A fall of income abroad will, through the foreign marginal propensity to import, reduce the demand for the home country's exports. That fall of exports will create a deficit in the balance of
payments. It will also tend to transmit the foreign depression to the
home economy. Domestic income may be supported by compensatory
policies; but, in that case, the balance of payments deficit will be
even larger.

The effect of a fall of foreign income is illustrated in Figure
11–2. The lines marked $Y_a(Y_b)$, $Y_b(Y_a)$, and $X = M$ are the same as

FIGURE 11–2

Cyclical Balance of Payments Disequilibrium

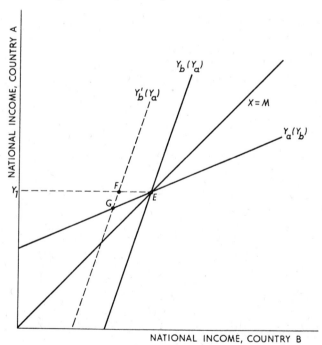

those in Figure 11–1. At the initial income levels, indicated by E, the balance of payments is in equilibrium, since E lies on the $X = M$ line. An autonomous drop of spending in Country B shifts $Y_b(Y_a)$ leftward to $Y'_b(Y_a)$. If income in Country A is permitted to fall, the new equilibrium position is G. The balance of payments deficit of A is shown by the fact that G lies above the $X = M$ line. If A's income is maintained at the original level Y_1, the equilibrium position is F. F is still further from the $X = M$ line than G; A's balance of payments deficit is greater if A's income is sustained than if it is allowed to fall.

Cyclical Disequilibrium—Increased Demand at Home

An increase of domestic aggregate demand will induce an increase of imports. The balance of payments deficit that will result can be shown by shifting upward the $Y_a(Y_b)$ line in Figure 11–2.

If, as we assumed, Country A was initially at the full-potential output, the additional demand cannot be satisfied by domestic production. The demand can be satisfied only by increasing imports. If the added imports are not covered by a capital inflow, a balance of payments deficit equal to the excess of demand over domestic output must develop. Alternatively, if imports are prevented from rising, unsatisfied demand persists until the excess demand is eliminated by the means previously discussed in the chapter on inflation.

A recapitulation of these points in simple algebraic terms may be useful. Let Y equal total output, D equal total domestic demand, and B equal the balance on current account of the balance of payments. Then

$$Y - D = B.$$

If D exceeds Y, and Y cannot be increased because it is at its upper limit, then the economy is attempting to "absorb" more than it can produce, and that absorption can only be fulfilled by borrowing abroad $(-B)$. Any part of $-B$ not covered by intended lending from abroad is a balance of payments deficit. To reduce that deficit, absorption (D) must somehow be reduced, either by reducing intended spending or by preventing part of the intended absorption from being actually fulfilled.[5]

---

[5] For a complete presentation of the "absorption" viewpoint, see S. S. Alexander, "Effects of a Devaluation on a Trade Balance," International Monetary Fund, *Staff Papers*, Vol. II, No. 2 (April, 1952), pp. 263–78.

Price Maladjustment

A relative rise of the general price level, through either an increase of the domestic price level or a fall of prices abroad, will tend to stimulate imports and depress exports, thus generating a deficit in the balance of payments. Little amplification of this source of a deficit is required, except, perhaps, to point up the distinction between the case of an increase in the domestic price level and the case of excess demand just previously discussed. First, the two need not be concomitant; the price level may rise without excess demand (push inflation), or excess demand may exist without a rise in the price level (suppressed inflation). Second, even when excess demand and a rising price level are conjoined, they are still separate and distinct sources of balance of payments disequilibrium. That can be most readily seen by noting that elimination of the excess demand alone will not correct the balance of payments problem, since the price maladjustment introduced by the relative rise of the home price level continues after the excess demand is gone.

Structural Disequilibrium

A structural disequilibrium in the balance of payments is one which originates from some nontemporary shift of demand or supply of imports or exports. The demand for exports may fall because of the expansion of the production of the same products abroad, the innovation of substitutes abroad, or a change of foreign consumers' preferences. The demand for imports can be increased by a change of domestic consumers' preferences or by a change in the structure of production which enlarges the demand for foreign-produced materials or capital goods. A country's export supply can be reduced by such events as the depletion of a natural resource, or the wartime loss of some asset like the shipping fleets or foreign investments destroyed or used up during World War II.

In essence, a structural disequilibrium is a condition in which the existing allocation of the factors of production has become incompatible with equilibrium in the balance of payments. Adjustments of relative prices can correct the disequilibrium, but they must operate by stimulating a reallocation of factors toward industries that can produce more exports or substitutes for imports.

Disequilibrium Arising from Capital Movements

When the residents of a country intend to export capital, the transfer of capital can only be effected if there is a corresponding positive balance on current account. For the purpose of illustrating this difficulty, imagine that it is statistically possible to separate intended from unintended capital movements, and that the balance of payments statement shows the following:

Balance on current account	2
Capital account	
Intended capital movement	−5
Unintended capital movement	3

The intended lending abroad was 5. Because the balance on current account was only 2, the balance of payments had to be balanced (*ex post*) by an unintended inflow of capital of 3. The net amount of capital successfully transferred to abroad was therefore only 2. The intention to lend abroad 5 when the balance on current account was 2 resulted in a balance of payments deficit of 3.

A special case of the disequilibrating capital movement is the speculative capital "flight." Transfers of liquid funds abroad on a large scale may occur because of some threat to the security of domestic asset holdings or because of the development of expectations that the domestic currency will be devalued. Such capital flights are ordinarily temporary phenomena; but while they last, they may impose a severe strain on the country's foreign-exchange position.

DIAGNOSIS AND PRESCRIPTION

The authorities of a nation with a balance of payments deficit must choose corrective measures from among the equilibrating devices outlined above. In so doing, they must recognize that different types of disequilibria require different types of policies, and that the prescribed treatment must be based on a diagnosis of the disequilibrium.

The policy-makers must further recognize that the policies applied in pursuit of the objective of equilibrating the balance of payments may impinge on the attainment of other objectives of national economic policy. One such objective is full-potential output without inflation. Another is the benefits of international specialization of production and international trade.

The job of dealing with a balance of payments disequilibrium, therefore, is one of determining the nature of the disequilibrium and of selecting a policy which is both appropriate to the type of disequilibrium and which involves a minimum of conflict with other objectives.

The policies available for equilibrating the balance of payments are not highly flexible instruments, but there is no urgent requirement that they should be. The balance of payments need not be in equilibrium continuously; deficits owing to seasonal or irregular fluctuations in receipts and outlays of foreign exchange will occur; but, if they are temporary and interspersed with surpluses, so that there is no persistent deficit, no policy action is called for. However, each country must have a sufficient reserve of international liquid assets (gold or foreign exchange) or sufficient borrowing ability to tide it over the deficit periods. In that respect, countries are like households or firms which hold money for transactions and precautionary purposes.

An attempt to summarize the relation between five varieties of disequilibrium and five equilibrating devices is presented in Table 11–2. The crosses indicate those policy applications which must be

TABLE 11–2

Policies for Varieties of Balance of Payments Disequilibria

Source of Disequilibrium	Policy				
	General Reduction of Price Level	Devaluation	Reduction of Domestic Demand	Increase of Interest Rate	Restriction of Trade or Capital Movement
Cyclical fall of income abroad	X	X	X	X	X
Excess demand at home	X	X			X
Price maladjustment	X		X	X	X
Structural change	X	?	X	X	?
Capital movement	X		X	X	?

considered unsatisfactory either because they will not function or because they conflict with other objectives. The number of acceptable applications, it appears, is rather small.

One policy, a general reduction in the price level, is ruled out entirely. The sheer mechanical difficulty of carrying out a lowering of prices without seriously conflicting with the objective of maintaining full-potential output makes this policy most unattractive. Under certain conditions, a *relative* reduction in the general price level can be carried out without disruptive effects, i.e., by keeping domestic prices stable while foreign prices are rising. Such a policy, however, requires the collaboration (intended or not) of other countries. It is not a dependable unilateral instrument, though it may on occasion come to the rescue of deficit countries.

1. For one type of disequilibrium—a deficit arising from a cyclical fall of income abroad—there appears to be no suitable policy. Reduction of domestic demand or increase of the interest rate permits or encourages the spread of recession from abroad to the home economy. Restrictions on trade violate the objective of maximizing the gains from international specialization. To put it more completely, if a country has imposed all those restrictions on trade which it believes necessary to achieve the optimum degree of international specialization, then any additional restrictions imposed purely because of the balance of payments deficit must worsen the country's allocation of resources. The argument that restrictions on balance of payments grounds can do little harm because they are "temporary" is not reassuring; strong pressures build up to retain restrictions once the resource allocation has become adjusted to them. Devaluation, aside from the fact that it is likely to be least effective when foreign economies are depressed, seems inappropriate for dealing with a deficit that will be corrected in the not-very-distant future by the cyclical recovery of foreign income. To be successful, devaluation must instigate a reallocation of resources to the production of exports and import-competing goods. The reallocation requires time, and the short-run effects are likely to be limited. The subsequent revaluation when foreign economies recover will require a reverse movement of the factors of production. Large devaluations and revaluations of the exchange rate to meet cyclical needs hardly seem advisable.

The most satisfactory policy in the case of a balance of payments deficit originating from a cyclical fall of income abroad is "no policy"—that is, to let the deficit run its course, using foreign-exchange reserves to fill the gap until foreign income recovers and the reserves can be built up again. In effect, this approach views as the proper period over which to equilibrate the balance of payments, not the annual or other arbitrary short span, but the whole income-cycle period from peak to peak.

This treatment of a cyclical deficit requires adequate foreign-exchange reserves, "adequacy" being dependent on the length and severity of the foreign recession. To help assure nations of a supply of foreign exchange sufficient to meet cyclical needs without the application of inappropriate policies, the International Monetary Fund was established. The Fund stands ready to lend (technically, to sell) foreign exchange to deficit member countries to meet cyclical needs.[6]

2. In the case of deficits traceable to excess demand at home, most policies are rejected because they will not work. The deficit, as we have seen, is the excess of domestic absorption of product over national product. If national product cannot be increased, the deficit can be reduced only by reducing absorption. Devaluation does not reduce aggregate demand, except perhaps in certain minor and quite indirect ways. Restrictions on imports similarly cannot be relied on to reduce the deficit—the unsatisfied demand that cannot buy imports flows over into domestic products, absorbing products that would have been exported or diverting inputs from the production of exports to the production of goods for the home market. The attempt to reduce imports will be accompanied by a fall of exports, unless the excess demand is eliminated. The first step in correcting this type of balance of payments deficit must be the reduction of domestic demand. A second, less promising, policy is an increase in the interest rate, which (besides its contractionary effect on demand) may serve to alleviate the deficit problem by attracting an inflow of capital.

3. When the balance of payments deficit is attributable to price maladjustment, the objections to the rejected policies are clear enough. They will reduce real income unnecessarily, since there exists a policy—devaluation—which will equilibrate the balance of payments without either depressing output or restricting international trade. That a devaluation will correct the deficit is tautological; if the relative height of the domestic price level accounts for the deficit, then devaluation, which adjusts relative price levels, must erase the deficit.

---

[6] The amounts drawn from the Fund for strictly cyclical needs have been quite small—a token of the success with which nations have avoided serious cyclical instability since the Fund was established.

4. Disequilibrium due to structural change is perhaps the most difficult type of balance of payments problem to prescribe for. The solution demands a reallocation of resources. The mobility of resources and the alternative productive opportunities available to the resources that must be shifted will determine the speed with which the reallocation can be carried out; but, at best, it is a slow process. Policies that will assist in the transfer of resources will make the greatest contribution. Devaluation, through changing relative prices, may encourage or facilitate the reallocation—hence the question mark on that policy in Table 11–2. Trade restrictions, undesirable though they are, may be necessary both to facilitate the movement of resources and to help to manage the deficit problem during the transitional period.

5. The transfer of capital can be assisted by devaluation when a sufficient balance on current account has not developed. A policy of raising interest rates, while it will act to retard the outflow of capital, will also have a depressing effect on national income.

In the special case of a speculative capital flight, it may be necessary, if the country's international reserves are not large enough to last until the speculators' expectations are reversed, to impose exchange controls on capital movements.

FLEXIBLE EXCHANGE RATES

The difficulties encountered in the attempt to reconcile the objective of equilibrium in the balance of payments with the objectives of full employment and freedom of international trade and capital movements have led to renewed interest in a long-standing proposal for reform of exchange-rate policy.

The prevailing exchange-rate policy, generally called a "fixed exchange rate," might in fact be better described as an adjustable parity rate. That is, the official parity rate is kept at a fixed level (or within a narrow band), but it is recognized that the authorities may adjust this rate when circumstances warrant.

The alternative to this adjustable parity rate is a *self-adjusting* exchange rate. This type of policy may take the form of a freely flexible rate, where the country's monetary authorities make no direct intervention in the foreign-exchange markets (by buying or selling foreign currencies) for the purpose of influencing the exchange rate. Or it may take the form of limited flexibility where the rate is permitted to vary, without official intervention, within a wide band (e.g., plus or minus 5 percent of the parity rate). This limited flexibility plan may also provide for gradual self-adjustment of the parity rate. For example, the "crawling peg" proposal determines the parity by some formula like an average of the exchange rates of a number of previous months. This formula would permit the parity rate (together with the band around it) to fall or rise slowly in response to market forces.

The chief advantage of exchange-rate flexibility is that it provides a method for dealing with fundamental balance of payments disequilibria without sacrificing other macroeconomic objectives. We have noted that if exchange rates are to be kept fixed, the available policies for correcting a persistent balance of payments deficit entail domestic underemployment or restrictions on international trade and capital movements. Under a system of exchange-rate flexibility, the exchange rate equilibrates the balance of payments without interfering with full employment or free trade.

Though it might be thought that under fixed (adjustable) exchange rates balance of payments disequilibria could be easily corrected by devaluing the exchange rate, that mechanism in fact works only very poorly. Periodic devaluations of a currency encourage speculation against that currency. That is, when a devaluation is expected, it pays speculators to sell their holdings of the weak currency and hold gold or another currency which is not expected to devalue. Speculation is encouraged under fixed exchange rates, for several reasons. First, there is no risk to the speculator because the currency he is speculating against can only move in one direction, downward. (By contrast, a flexible exchange rate is liable to move in either direction.) Secondly, the devaluation, when it does come, will provide an overnight gain which gives the speculator a large enough rate of return to make speculation attractive. (Under flexible exchange rates, the continuous process of adjustment spreads the change out over time, reducing or eliminating entirely the attractiveness of speculating.)

In view of this vulnerability of fixed exchange rates to adverse speculation, countries are most unwilling to consider a devaluation, preferring to take all possible measures to defend the exchange rate in order to put down rumors of devaluation. Consequently, we frequently see episodes of countries' depressing their economies and restricting their international trade to postpone a devaluation of the exchange rate, only to be forced, in the end, by mounting speculative pressure, to devalue. When the devaluation does come, not only do the authorities lack a clear idea of what the equilibrium rate is, but they may feel compelled to overdevalue to ensure that speculators are convinced that no further devaluation is likely.

In view of the comparative advantages of flexible exchange rates, why are they not adopted? The opponents of flexibility raise the following arguments against it:

1. A flexible exchange rate adds an element of risk to international transactions, thereby increasing their costs and reducing their volume. Though there is also an exchange-rate risk under fixed exchange rates, since the rate may be adjusted, there is a presumption that the risk cost is somewhat greater in a flexible system.

In response to this argument, the proponents of flexible exchange rates point out that there is also a great saving of costs under flexibility—the saving of the costs of unemployment and trade restrictions that are imposed under a fixed rate system in order to maintain the rate. It is probable that, for many countries, the social costs would be lower and the volume of trade greater under flexible exchange rates than under fixed exchange rates.

2. Opponents of exchange-rate flexibility fear that speculators would create disturbing fluctuations if exchange rates were free to vary widely. However, if speculators were to have an unstabilizing effect, they would in the aggregate suffer a loss. Speculators profit by buying in low-price periods and selling in high-price periods, an activity which tends to equalize the price over time, or, in other words, which has a stabilizing effect. If speculators have a destabilizing effect, raising the price higher in high-price periods and making the price lower in low-price periods, they must be buying at high prices and selling at low prices, an unprofitable business. Speculators maximize their profits by having the maximum stabilizing effect. It is true that speculators may be unstabilizing by making errors; but, since speculators will not continue speculating unless they are making profits, there is a strong presumption that they will have a net stabilizing effect.

In any event, any possible speculative disturbances under flexible exchange rates must be considered in comparison to the serious speculative disturbances generated by fixed exchange rates.

3. It is feared that flexible exchange rates will eliminate one of the restraints on inflationary monetary and fiscal policies. With flexible exchange rates, a government would no longer have to worry about a balance of payments deficit resulting from inflationary policies. On the other hand, it would have to worry about a falling ex-

change rate. There is no reason why concern over the exchange rate should exert any less discipline over monetary and fiscal policy than concern over the balance of payments. In fact, the exchange rate, being a more visible signal of the consequences of inflation, may well exert a stronger disciplinary effect than balance of payments disequilibrium.

4. The final objection to flexible exchange rates is that they could lead to competitive devaluations. The motivation for competitive devaluations would presumably be to increase domestic employment at the expense of the employment of other countries. However, now that countries are acquainted with the use of monetary and fiscal policies for eliminating unemployment, the less effective and more costly method of devaluation has little, if any, appeal. The threat of competitive devaluations, which may have been real in the depression of the 1930's, no longer is relevant to the international economy.

In some countries, the costs of fixed exchange rates are very high indeed. The United Kingdom, for example, has dealt with its recurrent balance of payments problem by restricting international trade and by periodically retarding economic growth. In such countries, the case for flexible exchange rates merits serious consideration.

THE TERMS OF TRADE

The various economic changes that occur within countries and the international economic policies that they pursue will affect the relative prices at which nations trade. A rise of import prices relative to export prices, i.e., a worsening of a country's terms of trade, reduces the aggregate real income of the country. If, for example, the average price of imports should rise by 10 percent, export prices remaining unchanged, a country would have to give up (in exports) 10 percent more of its product than before in order to buy the same quantity of imports. In that respect, a change in relative international prices has a distinctly different effect from purely domestic relative price shifts. Internal price movements do not *per se* alter the real national income. They may change the distribution of income and that may be a cause for concern, as in the case of the terms of trade between the agricultural and nonagricultural sectors of the economy. But from the aggregate viewpoint, income is unchanged and the redistributional effects are part of the process by which necessary reallocations of factors of production are brought about. But a change in the international terms of trade alters aggregate real national income; and, because of the immobility of factors of production between countries, the reallocation of factors that might be the *raison d'être* and the mitigator of the redistribution of income cannot take place.

Seasonal or cyclical fluctuations in the terms of trade need not detain us. While there are problems associated with fluctuating prices, there is no terms-of-trade problem when purely seasonal or cyclical price movements are averaged out.

A worsening of a country's terms of trade may occur because of a structural change—a fall of foreign demand for the country's exports, a rise of home demand for imports, a decrease of foreign supply of imports, or an increase of the domestic supply of exports. These structural changes will also disequilibrate the balance of payments, and the restoration of equilibrium by devaluation may entail a further deterioration in the terms of trade. The correction of a balance of payments deficit arising from an outflow of capital may also require some worsening of the terms of trade. However, whether devaluation will worsen or improve the terms of trade depends on demand and supply conditions in each country, and it is very difficult to generalize.[7] The most useful general proposition that can be offered is this: The more mobile are an economy's factors among alternative uses, the less will be the impact of structural changes or devaluation on the terms of trade. While the factors cannot move easily from countries where income has been lowered by the terms of trade to countries where income has been raised, they can move internally in response to the fall of export prices or the rise of import prices to industries offering better export opportunities or industries supplying substitutes for imports. In flexible economies, the terms of trade are unlikely to be a major concern; in

---

[7] A supposed advantage of trade restrictions over devaluation for eliminating a balance of payments deficit is that restrictions will not worsen, and may even improve, the terms of trade. But there is an income loss attached to trade restriction—the loss of real income that results from reducing international specialization. There is no *a priori* basis for knowing which policy will leave the economy with higher real income. See S. S. Alexander, "Devaluation versus Import Restriction as an Instrument for Improving Foreign Trade Balance," International Monetary Fund, *Staff Papers*, Vol. I, No. 3 (April, 1951), pp. 379–96.

economies with immobile resources or limited scope for shifting resources, the risks of terms-of-trade movements are more serious.

INFLATION IN AN OPEN ECONOMY

The international sector will be a moderating influence on a country with inflationary tendencies. If aggregate demand exceeds output, excess demand can be prevented by permitting demand to be satisfied by imports. However, unless the gap between demand and output is filled by capital inflow, imports are only a temporary solution to excess demand. The rise of imports substitutes external disequilibrium for internal disequilibrium. The balance of payments gap must eventually be closed and the excess demand then becomes manifest. Controls on international trade will be necessary to suppress the balance of payments deficit so long as the excess demand persists.

The distorting effects of excess demand on a country's resource allocation can be severe. Exports fall off as their prices rise. Imports must then be restricted. Factors of production are attracted to the production of substitutes for imports; and the supply of products for export is contracted, requiring a further restriction of imports, and so on. This threat to the gains from international trade increases the pressure on a country to eliminate its excess demand.

Inflation without excess demand (push inflation) will disequilibrate the balance of payments as rising prices depress exports and stimulate imports. The short-run effect of the international transactions will thus be to dampen the push process by reducing aggregate demand. In the longer run, the balance of payments must be equilibrated. If import restrictions are used, some gains from trade are sacrificed, aggregate demand is restored, and the inflation process can continue. Alternatively, the exchange rate can be devalued to restore international prices to their preinflation relationships, and the balance of payments can be equilibrated without loss of the advantages of trade. Devaluation also restores aggregate demand and permits the push process to resume.

The preceding comments all pertain to a country in which inflation is proceeding at a faster pace than in the countries with which it trades. In a world in which all countries are inflating, any one country can more easily reconcile its inflationary behavior with its desired freedom in international trade.

GROWTH AND THE BALANCE OF PAYMENTS

The growth of income is regarded in some quarters as greatly complicating the job of maintaining equilibrium in the balance of payments. It has been argued that because of differences among countries in the marginal propensity to import, growth will breed deficits in the countries with the higher propensities. It has been argued that when countries grow at different rates, the faster growing countries will find their demand for imports rising more rapidly than the demand for their exports, and they will suffer from a tendency toward a balance of payments deficit. And it has been argued that the faster growing countries will, because of their increasing productivity and falling costs, tend to export more and import less, and thus impose on the rest of the world a chronic deficit problem.

In all of these arguments, the conflict between growth and external balance is overstated by understating the adjustment mechanisms built into the economy. Growth increases not only the demand for imports but also the capacity to produce exports and substitutes for imports. Relative prices can adjust the allocation of resources and the rates of growth in the export, import, and import-competing sectors so as to equilibrate the external accounts. To assume away the adjustment functions of the price system is akin to assuming that automobiles have square wheels and then bemoaning the bumpy rides we shall have.

However, some countries do have "square wheels." Either because some less flexible allocative mechanism has been substituted for the price system or because the structure of the economy offers little scope for resource reallocation, it may seem very difficult to reconcile growth and external equilibrium without recourse to trade restrictions. More often, though, the balance of payments deficit is generated, not by growth itself, but by the program through which the country seeks to stimulate growth. Heavy investment programs which create excess demand and which raise the propensity to import are responsible for most of the balance of payments problems that are attributed to growth.

RECOMMENDED READINGS

Kindleberger, Charles P. *International Economics.* 4th ed. Homewood, Ill.: Richard D. Irwin, Inc., 1968.

Kreuger, Anne O. "Balance-of-Payments Theory," *Journal of Economic Literature,* Vol. VII, No. 1 (March, 1969), pp. 1–26.

Machlup, F. "Three Concepts of the Balance of Payments and the So-Called Dollar Shortage," *Economic Journal,* Vol. LX, No. 237 (March, 1950), pp. 46–68.

Nurkse, Ragnar. "Conditions of International Monetary Equilibrium," in American Economic Association, *Readings in the Theory of International Trade.* Philadelphia: Blakiston Co., 1949, pp. 3–34. Reprinted from *Essays in International Finance,* No. 4. Princeton, N.J.: International Finance Section, Department of Economics and Social Institutions, Princeton University, 1945.

———. "Domestic and International Equilibrium," *The New Economics* (ed. Seymour E. Harris), pp. 264–92. New York: Alfred A. Knopf, 1947.

Polak, J. J. "The Post-War International Cycle," *The Business Cycle in the Post-War World; Proceedings of a Conference Held by the International Economic Association* (ed. Erik Lundberg), pp. 246–65. London: Macmillan & Co., Ltd., 1955.

"Round Table on Exchange Rate Policy," *American Economic Review,* Vol. LIX, No. 2 (May, 1969), pp. 357–69.

QUESTIONS

1. Explain how net foreign investment acts as an automatic stabilizer. Why is its stabilizing effect more uncertain than that of induced changes in tax receipts?

2. Compare the effects of excess-demand inflation and cost-push inflation on the current account of the balance of payments, using the "absorption" equation (income − total domestic demand = balance on current account of balance of payments). In terms of this comparison, discuss the suitability of devaluation for dealing with the balance of payments deficit caused by the two types of inflation.

3. Assume that a country undertakes to accelerate its growth by increasing its rate of investment. A large proportion of the additional investment goods will have to be imported. What policies, other than imposing restrictions on international trade, can the country apply to prevent a balance of payments disequilibrium?

4. Compare a fixed (adjustable) exchange rate with a flexible (self-adjusting) exchange rate with respect to efficiency as a mechanism for equilibrating the balance of payments.

Chapter 12 | MACROECONOMIC POLICIES

THE OBJECTIVES OF POLICY

The public authorities who assume responsibility for administering macroeconomic policies must keep in view four economic objectives:

1. Full-Potential Output The first goal of policy is to prevent the loss of real output and the costs in the form of risk and insecurity that result from the failure to keep the economy up to its full-potential output level.

2. Avoiding Inflation Policy seeks to improve the functioning of the economy by preventing excess demand and inflationary price rises from imposing real costs on society.

3. Growth Policy aims to assist the economy to attain the optimum rate of growth, if such a thing can be defined and if policy-makers have the information necessary to make the definition operational. In particular, macroeconomic policy is concerned (*a*) with the determination of the rate of saving which is optimal for growth and (*b*) with measures to insure that investment demand is sustained at the level of optimal saving.

4. Balance of Payments Equilibrium Policy must correct any tendency of the economy toward a chronic balance of payments disequilibrium. Persistent deficits must be corrected because limited foreign-exchange reserves permit no alternative. Policies to reduce a persistent balance of payments surplus, i.e., to assist other countries to eliminate their deficits, will be pursued by foresighted nations to head off the restrictionist policies that deficit countries may feel impelled to pursue.

These four macroeconomic objectives cannot be isolated from certain other goals. First, there is the fundamental microeconomic goal of the optimum allocation of resources. Macroeconomic policies are not always neutral in their effects on the composition of output or factor combinations. The mutual satisfaction of macro and micro aims must be sought.

Finally, a noneconomic objective—the establishment or maintenance of the political forms that the society prefers—must be taken into account. Societies committed to democratic processes and individual freedom will be restricted in their choice of policies to those that are consistent with the preservation of those political values.

CONGENIAL AND UNCONGENIAL OBJECTIVES

Certain economic objectives are mutually reinforcing, in the sense that the pursuit of one will contribute to the attainment of the other; these can be termed "congenial" objectives. Among the four macroeconomic objectives, balance of payments equilibrium and the avoidance of inflation are congenial in that the attainment of the latter will assist in the achievement of the former. Also, full-potential output and growth are congenial objectives.[1]

The other pairings of macroeconomic objectives, numbered 1 to 4 in Figure 12–1, are likely to be uncongenial.

FIGURE 12–1

Macroeconomic Objectives

	AVOIDANCE OF INFLATION	BALANCE-OF-PAYMENTS EQUILIBRIUM
FULL-POTENTIAL OUTPUT	1	3
GROWTH	2	4

1. The zone between excess demand and the aggregate demand necessary to maintain full-potential output is narrow and indistinct. Overzealousness in pursuing one of these objectives may result in failure with respect to the other. If the fear of inflation arises from some push process rather than from excess demand, the reconciliation of the objectives will be even more difficult, since the maintenance of full-potential output at the same time creates a more friendly climate for push inflation.

---

[1] See pp. 234–36

2. Anti-inflation efforts, if they involve a persistent dampening of aggregate demand, may inhibit investment and adversely affect the growth rate. As an offset, there will be some gain in efficiency through the elimination of excess demand, but the risk of an incompatibility between the two objectives must be faced.

3. A balance of payments deficit can be reduced by permitting or causing national output to fall. The objectives of full-potential output and balance of payments equilibrium are at odds in the sense that the goal of full-potential output makes unacceptable one of the methods by which a balance of payments deficit can be diminished.

4. The possible strained relations between the objectives of growth and balance of payments equilibrium have been discussed in Chapter 11 (p. 261).

The statement that two goals of policy are "uncongenial" means only that it will be difficult, but not that it will be impossible, to find and manipulate a set of policies which will enable the economy to attain both. If, however, the goals are conflicting (that is, if it proves impossible to administer policies that will achieve both), then policy-makers will be in the unhappy position of having to choose which is to be sacrificed.

The macroeconomic objectives must be reconciled, not only with each other, but also with the microeconomic objective of an optimum allocation of resources. The efficiency of income-stabilizing policies is judged not only by their success in sustaining income but also by their effect, for better or for worse, on the composition of the national output. Balance of payments policies are appraised for their impact on international specialization and the international allocation of resources, as well as for their effectiveness in treating payments disequilibria. Policies affecting growth or inflation must be similarly evaluated.

Finally, all policies, macro and micro, must be considered within the context of the kind of political system the society wants. The relation between democratic institutions with a free price system and each of the economic objectives may be mainly congenial (optimum allocation of resources? growth?) or mainly uncongenial (control of inflation?) ; but, in any event, such values impose one more constraint upon policy.

Throughout the discussion that follows, in which each macroeconomic objective is taken up in turn, it should be kept in mind that policy-makers are not free to deal with objectives separately.

They must aim, insofar as it is possible, at a simultaneous achievement of all goals.

POLICIES FOR STABLE FULL-POTENTIAL INCOME

The Criteria for Choosing among Policy Instruments

One obvious criterion by which to judge a stabilization policy is its ability to affect aggregate demand. A good policy is one that can be depended upon to change demand in the right direction and adequately. More than that, the reaction to the policy should, within reasonable limits, be predictable, so that the proper dose of policy can be estimated.

A second criterion that applies to policies intended to smooth out income fluctuations is that they be flexible in administration and swift in producing their effects. The longer the time gap between recognition of the need for a change of policy and application of the new policy, or between application of policy and its effects, the wider are the swings of economic activity permitted. Under the worst conditions, lags in the timing of stabilization policies may reinforce the fluctuations of income by causing a policy to take effect after the state of the economy has changed and a reverse policy is in order.

Third, policies undertaken for any one objective must be evaluated in the light of their contribution toward or their interference with the accomplishment of other objectives.

Fiscal Policies

1. Government Purchases of Current Product   A change in the amount of government purchases acts directly on aggregate demand. It produces a predictable autonomous change, provided that the change of government demand does not have a contrary effect on any component of private demand. An increase of government expenditure to provide something ordinarily supplied by the private sector will have a depressing effect on private investment demand. To be fully effective in raising aggregate demand, the additional government purchases must either produce those services which are the sole responsibility of the government to provide or they must provide no services at all.

What the government should buy is one of the critical problems in using government purchases as an antirecession weapon. No doubt any purchase, even one yielding no useful service, would be of net benefit because of the induced increase of useful product it would generate through its multiplier effect. Nevertheless, policy must aim at the maximum benefit. The purchases should be within the scope of accepted government activity so as not to discourage private investment. They should be expenditures that can be varied anticyclically without disruptive effects on the allocation of resources or the flow of services to the public. They should yield a marginal utility to the community at least as large as would be yielded by an equal increase in private consumer purchases.

In view of these limitations on the range of government purchases and the difficulty of determining their relative marginal utility, it might be thought best to leave government purchases to be determined by noncyclical considerations, and to fill in cyclical deficiencies in aggregate demand with private consumption. But an argument for an increase of government purchases can be made on the grounds that if consumer demand is to be used to compensate for a drop of investment, total utility is likely to be greater if the increment of consumption is divided between private and public consumption than if the entire increase is devoted to private consumption. A stronger case can be made if it can be shown that in prosperous periods public consumption falls short of its optimum proportion of total consumption, and that the antirecession use of government purchases offers an opportunity to make good a part of the deficiency.

The type of government purchases suitable for cyclical variation is restricted. Certain kinds of equipment might be replaced or expanded in a countercyclical pattern. Military purchases might to some extent be varied to counter economic fluctuations, though, for obvious reasons, national security rather than economic stability sets the limits for the appropriate level of defense spending. The great bulk of any countercyclical government expenditures would have to be for public works such as roads, dams, or public buildings.

A possible advantage of added expenditure on public works in a recession is that it will employ the resources of the construction industry, which are particularly likely to be underemployed in a slumping economy. But a general rule for all recessions cannot be laid down; construction activity may remain high, as in a pure inventory cycle, and expansion of public works would only create excess demand in the construction sector.

A serious disadvantage of public works expenditures in combating fluctuations is their relative inflexibility. A rather long lag between the decision to undertake a project and the beginning of actual construction is imposed by the requirements of drawing up plans, obtaining land, letting contracts, and other problems of organization.[2] Once the project has been begun, expenditure on it may have to continue well past the recovery phase in order to complete it. The awkwardness of their timing makes public works a rather poor anticyclical device except for fairly prolonged depressions. For short recessions of the type we have experienced since the war, the use of public works policy depends chiefly on the possibilities of accelerating the rate of expenditures on projects already under way.

2. Tax Policy   Changes in tax rates may aim to affect aggregate demand through either consumption or investment demand.

The effect of the change of rates on disposable income and of the change of disposable income on aggregate consumer demand is, within adequate limits, dependable and predictable. The precise impact will depend in part on which taxes are changed. Either personal income taxes or sales and excise taxes will reach a broad cross section of the population and have a direct effect on disposable income and consumption. The effect of a change of corporate income tax receipts on disposable income depends on the change of corporation dividends; the stickiness of dividends relative to corporate net income reduces the impact of the corporate income tax on consumption. The marginal propensity to consume of the groups affected by tax changes will also have a bearing on the relative effect of the various taxes, though this factor is often overstated by exaggerating the differences of the marginal propensity to consume among income groups.

Once the policy-makers have acted, tax policy for adjusting consumer demand has the advantage of flexibility and comparatively smooth timing. The spending decisions are left to the consumers, whose purchases will ordinarily be of a type that requires very little lag between decision and execution.

On the other hand, the tax effect on consumption has the disadvantage that it acts on the sector of the economy that most probably

---

[2] See, for example, Sherman J. Maisel, "Timing and Flexibility of a Public Works Program," *Review of Economics and Statistics*, Vol. XXXI, No. 2 (May, 1949), pp. 147–52.

needs the least correction. Instability is greater in the investment-goods than in the consumer-goods industries. In a recession, for example, it will be difficult to raise to full employment the factors of production in the investment sector by direct stimulation of the consumer sector alone. Factors are not sufficiently mobile in the short run for more than a minor shift from investment to consumer industries. The expansion of consumer demand will eventually stimulate the demand for capital goods, but not without a lag. The lag, however, will be shortened if tax policy generates *expectations* of high consumer demand.

Taxation can act on investment demand, as we have seen,[3] in two ways. First, taxing business income will, to the extent that the offsetting of losses is incomplete, reduce the incentive to undertake risk. Second, to the extent that firms' investment decisions are affected by their supplies of internal funds, business income taxes will influence investment through their effect on business saving. It is doubtful that cyclical tax policy will have any effect on investment by the first route, the incentive to invest. Investors must assume risks for longer than one phase of a cycle and are unlikely to be moved by temporary variations in tax rates. As to the effect on investment by way of the supply of internal funds, empirical studies indicate that this effect is quite small.

3. Transfer Payments   Increases or decreases of government transfer payments to individuals can be employed for stabilization purposes along lines broadly similar to the use of tax policy to change disposable income. An economy collecting only small amounts of tax revenue and therefore limited in its scope for tax reductions would find transfers a particularly useful stabilizing instrument. But few economies are now in that position. The chief current difference between tax and transfer policy is that transfers permit a greater increase in disposable income at the low end of the income scale than is permitted by tax-rate changes. The main drawback of transfers is that, as a form of "giving away," they raise controversial issues of social policy that distract from the immediate objective of stabilization in a way that tax reductions, which can be viewed as "giving back," do not. The timing of policy suffers when complex side issues are added to the other impediments to rapid stabilizing action.

---

[3] See pp. 116–20.

4. The Public Debt   Countercyclical fiscal policy will require a deficit in the public budget during depressed phases of the economy.[4] The prospect of a budget deficit disturbs some people and appears to them a hindrance to the practice of fiscal stabilization policy. The naïve fears that public debt makes the country poorer or that it passes on a burden to future generations have been easily and frequently answered by pointing out that an internally held debt (which is the only kind that need be incurred as a direct consequence of antirecession fiscal policy) is both a liability and an asset of the nation; that if "every man, woman, and child owes $1640 on the federal debt," the same people also own on the average $1640 of government bonds; that the interest payments are transfers and do not in themselves add to or detract from national income; that any payment by a future generation is paid to that same generation. However, at a more sophisticated level, certain questions about deficit financing arise which merit some analytical comment. These questions concern (a) the redistribution effects of the interest payments and debt retirement; (b) the inflationary impact on some later boom period of the debt accumulated in a recession; (c) the potential burden on the economy, in the form of a loss of incentives, inflicted by the tax-and-transfer process of making interest payments.

a) The redistribution effects of a debt incurred in order to raise national income depend on the distribution of the ownership of the debt, the distribution of the burden of taxes collected because of the debt, and the distribution of the additional income created by the deficit-financed fiscal policy. A large part of the national debt, 44 percent, is held in government accounts (Federal Reserve, government trust funds, etc.) and has no redistribution effect. Another 26 percent is held by banks, insurance companies, and other private corporations; the interest received on this 26 percent is shared by the owners and their customers. Estimates of the distribution of the interest payments on the national debt and of the burden of federal taxes show that the net effect on income distribution is progressive.[5]

---

[4] The "balanced budget" multiplier cannot be considered as a practical stabilizing device. It magnifies the size of the required changes in government expenditures, introduces distortions of abnormally high tax rates, and requires a shift of resources from the production of private consumer goods to public goods, all of which impede stabilization and impose serious costs.

[5] See Donald F. Vitaliano, "The Impact of the Interest of the Federal Debt upon the Distribution of Income in the United States," unpublished doctoral dissertation, City University of New York, 1969.

The income benefits of the deficit will, given the multiplier effects, be larger than the addition to the debt; the distribution of the benefits will be diffuse and are difficult to estimate. All in all, we have no reason to think that the overall redistribution effects of the deficit will be either significant or undesirable. Relative to the benefits to be obtained, the redistribution question seems trivial.

b) The growth of the privately held public debt adds highly liquid assets to the stock of private assets. In a growing economy, the demand for liquid assets will grow and some increase of supply will be desirable. But an overincrease of liquidity may, in a succeeding boom period, complicate the task of preventing excess demand. Much depends on the magnitudes involved. The great expansion of the public debt that occurred during the war left the economy with an amount of liquidity that monetary and fiscal policy found it difficult to cope with. The modest increases in debt required for anti-recession purposes ought not to strain the monetary-fiscal techniques for soaking up liquidity if the upswing proves too vigorous.

c) Taxes, with the negligible exception of a poll tax, fall on some form of economic activity. If the tax collection goes beyond draining off pure economic surplus or rent, it reduces the compensation for economic effort. Reducing the compensation reduces the willingness to substitute effort for ease. However, the reduction of income by taxes has the effect of inducing a larger supply of effort by increasing the attractiveness of a marginal increment of income relative to a marginal amount of ease. The individual who wants to maintain the same standard of living after the imposition of the tax must work harder. Thus the substitution effect (the result of the fall in the rate of payment for substituting effort for ease) reduces the supply of effort, while the income effect (the effect of the fall of income on the willingness to supply effort) increases the supply of effort. If the substitution effect outweighs the income effect, an increase of taxes will reduce the supply of economic effort.

The higher the proportion of national income taken by taxes, the more heavily must taxation fall on economic effort (rather than on economic surplus) and the more likely it becomes that the substitution effect will outweigh the income effect. The taxes collected for interest payments on the public debt, when superimposed on the taxes that are collected for other purposes, bring the total tax levy that much closer to the point where it will adversely affect economic effort. The interest payments, on the other hand, are not a payment for effort and so do not add to the incentive to supply effort. In fact, their income effect results in less effort. Thus, the interest payments, though pure transfers, do not have a symmetrical effect on the taxpayers and the interest receivers, and the net effect is likely to be a loss of economic incentives.

It is difficult to say at what level of taxation this effect would be felt. One can only say that the national debt, if it becomes sufficiently large relative to national income, can impose a real burden on the economy through the tax effect.

The growth of income weakens this threat of an eventual burden of the public debt. It would take quite pessimistic views about the budget deficits required over the long run and about the future growth rate of the economy for one to predict a rise of the ratio of national debt to national income to a burdensome level.[6]

Monetary Policy

1. General Monetary Controls   General monetary controls are the devices for affecting the quantity of money in circulation. The administration of these controls is ordinarily the function of a central bank equipped with such tools as open-market operations, central bank credit to commercial banks, and the regulation of commercial bank reserve requirements.

As a stabilizer, monetary policy suffers from uncertainty about its effectiveness. There is, first, some uncertainty about the exact

---

[6] It has been shown that if the annual government deficit is a constant percentage, d, of income and if income grows annually by a percentage, r, the ratio of debt to income will approach d/r. [See Evsey D. Domar, "The 'Burden of the Debt' and the National Income," American Economic Association, *Readings in Fiscal Policy* (Homewood, Ill.: Richard D. Irwin, Inc., 1955), pp. 489–92; reprinted from *American Economic Review*, Vol. XXXIV, No. 4 (December, 1944), pp. 798–827.] Assume that the economy fluctuates at regular intervals, so that over a long term, half the years are recession years and the other half are years of high demand. Assume that in the recession years, the government borrows; in the other years it balances the budget. Further, assume that investment is 16 percent of income, that in recessions investment demand falls 20 percent, that government fiscal policy operates by lowering taxes while holding government purchases constant, and that the marginal propensity to consume applicable to the tax reduction is 0.8. The deflationary gap created by the fall of investment is then 3.2 percent of income ($20\% \times 16\%$); and the tax reduction necessary to raise consumption to fill the gap is 4 percent of income ($3.2\%/0.8$). The deficit is then 4 percent of income in recession years, or an average of 2 percent of income in all years. Finally, assume that income grows at the rate of 4 percent per year. Then the ratio of debt to income approaches $d/r = 2\%/4\% = \frac{1}{2}$. On these assumptions, which are not particularly optimistic, the result of antirecession fiscal policy is a debt-to-income ratio of quite moderate size.

extent of the monetary authorities' ability to tighten or loosen credit conditions through general monetary controls. This doubt arises from the presence in the economy of large amounts of highly liquid assets which are close substitutes for money, particularly government securities and savings accounts. When there is a very elastic supply of substitutes for money, the impact of changes in the supply of money on the terms on which money can be obtained is reduced. Suppose, for example, that the supply of money is reduced. Those wishing to replenish their stock of money can do so by exchanging government securities for money. If the two are close substitutes, people can be induced by only a small rise in the yield on the securities to switch into them from money balances. Thus, large amounts of close money substitutes make the demand for money more elastic and cushion the effect of a change in the quantity of money. This defect in the mechanics of monetary control may eventually be dealt with by an expansion of the monetary authorities' regulatory powers over the supply of near-moneys and their degree of substitutability for money.[7]

Second, there is uncertainty about the effect of a tightening or loosening of credit on aggregate demand. These doubts are stronger in the case of the effort to raise demand during recessions than in the case of restraining demand during booms. In principle, there is no upper limit on the terms of credit. Monetary conditions can be made sufficiently stringent to achieve any desired reduction in aggregate demand, whether through the rise of interest rates or through credit rationing. In practice, there may be political limitations on how far a tight money policy can be pushed because of the discriminatory effects, actual or imagined, of credit restraints on certain groups of borrowers such as farmers, small businesses, or house buyers. In the case of an easy money policy, there is a limit to how low interest rates can fall or how loose credit rationing can become. The increase of aggregate demand that can be achieved will then depend on the interest-elasticity of investment demand and the extent to which the investment-demand function has fallen during the recession. The relative contribution monetary policy can make toward sustaining income will depend heavily on the state of investment demand through the course of the depressed phase.

The chief advantageous feature of general monetary stabilization

---

[7] See, for example, Albert Gailord Hart, "Making Monetary Policy More Effective," American Assembly, Columbia University, *United States Monetary Policy* (New York: Columbia University, 1958), pp. 171–95.

policy is that it acts directly on private investment—the most unstable sector of the economy. Measures that can reach immediately into the areas of fluctuating demand can stabilize output more quickly and with less dislocation of the factors of production than those that must use the roundabout approach of affecting the more stable consumer sector.

The flexibility of monetary policy is generally regarded as one of its strong points. The timing of monetary controls benefits mainly from the greater speed with which the central bank can take action, once the need has been recognized, than is possible for a legislative body in applying fiscal policy. But monetary policy has no conspicuous timing advantage in the phase between the adoption of a new policy and the final effects of the new policy on aggregate demand.[8] Credit conditions affect a wide range of investment categories, from inventories, which can respond to a policy shift quickly, to construction, which reacts with a considerable lag. In rapidity of response, monetary policy on the average apparently lies somewhere between government spending policy and a tax policy to affect consumer demand. The lag between policy action and spending washes out much of the popular picture of monetary policy as an extremely sensitive instrument which can be raised or lowered gradually until precisely the right level is found. Because of the lagged responses, the "right" level must be anticipated, in much the same way as with a public spending program. Moreover, the monetary authorities may hesitate to pursue a policy strong enough for the near-term needs of the economy for fear of the delayed effects of the policy that may be felt after the economy has reversed its direction.

2. Selective Credit Controls   The demand for particular types of products may be expanded or contracted by controlling the terms of credit that apply specifically to those products. Consumer credit and housing loans are examples of types of credit that have been subjected to selective controls.

The use of selective controls requires the government to assume an allocative function which, under general monetary controls, is left to the market. The presumption in favor of a market mechanism for directing the allocation of resources is sufficiently strong that a showing of serious shortcomings in the working of the credit market is needed to make a convincing case for supplanting it to any

---

[8] See Thomas Mayer, "The Inflexibility of Monetary Policy," *Review of Economics and Statistics*, Vol. XL, No. 4 (November, 1958), pp. 358–74.

extent with selective controls. The alleged imperfections in the credit market on which the case for selective controls is based are (1) that general monetary controls have selective effects, reaching some types of credit and leaving others virtually untouched, so that selective regulations are necessary for those credit areas out of reach of the general controls in order to redress the balance; (2) that certain types of credit may be subject to wide swings, possibly inspired by speculative motives, which have an unstabilizing effect on the economy.

Both of these imperfections have been ascribed to consumer credit. The demand for consumer credit is said to respond primarily to the size of the original down payment required and the amount of the monthly payment as determined by length of time over which the debt is to be repaid, rather than to the interest cost of the loan. The supply of credit is also said to behave in a way which favors consumer over investment borrowing during periods of tight money; it is alleged that the high rate of return on consumer loans attracts sufficient funds to satisfy demand in that area, and any restriction of credit due to tighter rationing falls upon business borrowing. If the unresponsiveness of consumer credit to general monetary controls is not simply an expression of a highly interest-inelastic demand for borrowing but proceeds from some failure of rational economic calculation by consumers, selective controls can be used to bring the economy closer to an optimum combination of consumption and investment than would be achieved by the market.

A wide swing in demand for some type of consumer good may occur and inject into the economy an element of instability which might have been moderated without significant inconvenience to consumers. The automobile boom of 1955, for example, is often cited as a case of a rapid rise and decline of consumer demand which could have been smoothed out to the advantage of practically everyone. An unusual fluctuation in one sector of the economy can best be treated by a selective device that will bear directly on the misbehaving sector. However, if selective controls are to be used on special occasions, some method will have to be found to prevent expectations of a tightening of regulations from setting off a speculative burst of demand.

3. Management of the Public Debt   The public debt is the meeting point of fiscal policy and monetary policy. The size of the public debt is determined by fiscal policy. The *composition* of the public debt—the structure according to the length of time to maturity—is determined by the type of securities issued by the fiscal authorities when they add to the debt or refund it. The monetary authorities, by their purchases and sales of government securities, can affect the size and composition of the public debt which is held by the private sector. Management of the public debt refers to the determination of the composition of the privately held public debt.

The relevance of debt management to income analysis lies in three links between the composition of the debt and aggregate demand:

a) Shortening the maturity of the debt increases the liquidity of the owners of the debt. The increase in the liquidity of the private sector tends to increase the demand of that sector, while the increased liquidity of the public sector's liabilities has no effect on public demand. The net effect of shortening the debt, therefore, is to increase aggregate demand; and of lengthening the debt, to reduce demand. However, about the magnitude of these effects very little is known. The response of spending to liquidity is probably very small; and, since the difference in liquidity between short-term and long-term government debt is not great, the liquidity effects of debt management on aggregate demand are not likely to be of much importance.

b) Shifting the debt from long-term to short-term tends to lower short-term interest rates and raise long-term interest rates. This change in the interest-rate structure may have selective effects on credit, but not enough is known about the reaction of different types of borrowing to the structure of interest rates to make debt management a usable instrument of selective control.

c) Shortening the debt increases the quantity of close substitutes for money. The high degree of substitutability between money and short-term public debt means that holders of money are willing to exchange into short-term debt in response to a very small increase in the interest rate. When the monetary authorities attempt to tighten money, money can be obtained by selling short-term debt to the holders of cash balances, with slight increase in the interest rate. Thus, a large supply of short-term debt introduces considerable "slack" into the financial system and increases the tightening operations which the central bank must carry out in order to affect aggregate demand. An important objective of debt management, therefore, is to lengthen the debt enough to eliminate unnecessary "slack." The maintenance of a debt structure that will not weaken monetary policy appears to be the chief contribution that debt management can make to economic stability.

Automatic Stabilizers

Some lag between an economic turning point and action by the policy authorities seems unavoidable so long as forecasts of fluctuations cannot be made with enough certainty to provide a basis for policy decisions. This lag makes particularly attractive stabilizing mechanisms which are automatically set in operation by the fluctuation of the economy.

The fiscal automatic stabilizers consist primarily of those induced relations which cause tax receipts to fall and government transfer payments to rise as income falls, and to do the reverse as income rises. The effect of these induced changes is to make disposable income more stable than national income and thus to reduce the fluctuation in consumption brought about by any given change in national income.

Among the taxes, the personal income tax is the most responsive to income fluctuations because of its progressive rate structure. Corporate profits taxes, sales and excise taxes, and social security contributions will behave in a stabilizing way. The property tax is the only important form of taxation that does not react automatically to income fluctuations.

Among the transfer payments, unemployment compensation is the principal automatic stabilizer. Programs to support farm prices or incomes by supplementary payments to farmers or government purchases of agricultural "surpluses" will also produce counter-cyclical movements of transfer payments. During moderate fluctuations, little automatic change in public assistance and relief payments occurs. In major depressions, where the need for public assistance may rise sharply, the automaticity of the payments cannot be relied upon, since the programs are administered at the state and local levels and a large expansion of aid would probably hinge upon a discretionary increase of federal grants-in-aid to the states.

In addition to the fiscal automatic stabilizers, there are three other induced variables—business saving, imports, and the demand for money—which may be stabilizers, though their effects are somewhat more problematical than those of the fiscal type.

Since dividends change slowly, fluctuations of corporate profits affect mainly business savings and cause relatively little change in disposable income. As an insulator of disposable income, business savings help to reduce the fluctuations of consumption. But, to the extent that there is an internal-funds effect on the level of investment, fluctuations of business savings accentuate the fluctuations of investment. Whether business savings are, on balance, stabilizers or destabilizers depends on the cyclical relationship of investment to business saving. If the reaction is small or occurs with a substantial lag which carries into the next phase of the cycle, business savings will be a stabilizer.

The induced change of imports will act as an automatic stabilizer, raising net foreign investment as income falls and decreasing it as income rises, provided exports are stable. Much depends, however, on the behavior of foreign income and foreign trade policy. The possibility that exports may fluctuate with imports makes induced imports an uncertain stabilizer.

The induced change in demand for money tends to lower the interest rate as income falls and raise it as income rises. Thus, income fluctuations will automatically tighten or ease monetary conditions in a stabilizing manner. On the other hand, demand for money may act as an automatic destabilizer if the risk attached to illiquidity rises in recessions and falls in booms, shifting the liquidity-preference function upward or downward in a procyclical pattern.

The operation of the automatic stabilizers can be most easily described by saying that they make the income multiplier smaller. A multiplier containing terms for all the automatic stabilizers has been developed in earlier chapters:[9]

$$\frac{1}{1 - b\,(1 - t - p - z) + m + \dfrac{lk}{f}}$$

where b is the marginal propensity to consume and the remaining terms are the induced changes in: taxes (t), transfer payments (p), business saving (z), imports (m), and investment via the rate of interest (lk/f)—all expressed as a proportion of the change of income.

The automatic stabilizers can substantially reduce the multiplier, but they cannot reduce it to zero. It is extremely doubtful that they can reduce the multiplier to one.[10] An autonomous fall in spending

[9] See pp. 52–53 and p. 149.

[10] Estimates of the automatic stabilizers cannot be exact, since the induced effects depend on how the change of income is distributed, how the change of employment is divided between layoffs and shortening of the workweek, and

will reduce income by at least the amount of the autonomous change, so that purely automatic stabilizers cannot eliminate fluctuations.

Formula Flexibility

The timing difficulties of discretionary fiscal policy (policies requiring a government action) and the inadequacy of automatic stabilizers have led to proposals to blend discretion and automaticity into a hybrid form of fiscal policy known as "formula flexibility." The basic idea of formula flexibility is that government expenditures and tax rates shall be geared to some cyclical indicator so that spending will be increased and tax rates will be reduced when the indicator signals a downturn. It would be possible, by the use of a formula, to make the fiscal response to the indicator completely predetermined. However, since cyclical indicators are somewhat irregular and require interpretation in each situation, complete automaticity has not been seriously advocated. Practical plans for the United States have proposed that the response to the indicator shall be a matter for decision by the President. This type of plan can be illustrated by the proposal made by the Kennedy Administration in 1962.[11]

The President's plan used the unemployment rate as the cyclical indicator. When the unemployment rate had risen in at least three out of four months (or in four out of six months) and upon finding that expansionary fiscal policy would be required to meet the objectives of the Employment Act, the President would be empowered to commit a total of $2 billion to accelerate direct federal expenditures previously authorized by Congress and to make grants and

---

other possible differences among fluctuations. But a rough estimate of $(t + p)$ puts it between 26 and 40. [See Albert Gailord Hart and Peter B. Kenen, *Money, Debt, and Economic Activity* (3d ed.; New York: Prentice-Hall, Inc., 1961), pp. 465–68.] Applying Hart's method, I estimate z at between 0.08 and 0.1. If we assume a marginal propensity to consume of 0.7, and omit m and lk/f, the multiplier employing the above estimates becomes $1/.54$ to $1/.65$ or between 1.9 and 1.5.

The U.S. marginal propensity to import has recently been estimated at about 0.06 [Mordechai E. Kreinin, "United States Imports and Income in the Postwar Period," *Review of Economics and Statistics*, Vol. XLII, No. 2 (May, 1960), pp. 223–25]. If we assume that the import stabilizer is fully effective, i.e., that there are no repercussions on exports, the multiplier including m becomes $1/.58$ to $1/.69$ or between 1.7 and 1.4.

No estimates are available for lk/f.

[11] See *Economic Report of the President, 1962* (Washington, D.C.: U.S. Government Printing Office, 1962), pp. 17–20.

loans to state and local governments for high-priority projects which would represent a net addition to their expenditures and which could be started and completed quickly. In addition, it was suggested that the President be granted stand-by tax reduction authority under which, when expansionary fiscal policy should be required, the President would submit to Congress a proposed temporary uniform reduction in all individual income tax rates, the reduction not to exceed five percentage points. If not rejected by Congress, the reduction would take effect for six months and could be reconsidered by Congress thereafter.

Though these proposals were not accepted by Congress, the rejection was not on grounds of impracticability. Presidents have already applied this idea, within the limits set by their present powers, in recent recessions. The President is able to accelerate the expenditure of existing appropriations for authorized programs and that has been done in each of the last three recessions.[12] The proposed legislation would have expanded this presidential power by providing additional appropriations during recessions.

The potential for formula flexibility with respect to expenditures is, in any event, limited by the relatively small capacity for rapidly accelerating outlays on existing projects. Nevertheless, a full utilization of the opportunity for speed-up, when combined with a temporary tax cut, can make a substantial contribution toward smoothing out the small fluctuations which have been the typical cyclical pattern.

A Concluding Comment on Stabilization

The government has an adequate set of antifluctuation policies, fiscal and monetary, which can effectively adjust aggregate demand. But the timing problems of these policies are such that it appears impossible for fluctuations to be entirely eliminated. Even if, immediately upon recognition that a downturn had begun, monetary or tax action were taken, the lag of its initial effect on demand could easily be three months or more, and the full effect would be spread over an even longer period. While government purchases

---

[12] See Wilfred Lewis, Jr., *Federal Fiscal Policy in the Postwar Recessions* (Washington, D.C.: Brookings Institution, 1962), pp. 18–19, 177–82, 220–25, 269–73. These administrative speed-ups were applied to outlays on construction, modernization and repair of public works, defense, stockpiling, forest service, water resource projects, and procurement of supplies.

have an immediate effect on demand, most government expenditure cannot be quickly increased or decreased. Only a very small amount of government purchases is capable of rapid adjustment.

If the fluctuations to be dealt with were long and deep, fiscal and monetary policies could unquestionably make them smaller. But the outlook is for, at most, quite short, shallow, contractions; and the potential contribution of policy to making them still smaller, appears rather limited.

However, the important function of fiscal and monetary policy is not in counteracting fluctuations once they have begun, *but in not starting them:* The review of fluctuations in Chapter 8 shows the overwhelming importance of fiscal and monetary shocks as a cause of contractions. Almost all the contractions can be accounted for by an unstable monetary system (before the Federal Reserve Act), some mismanagement of monetary policy (since then), monetary and fiscal disturbances during wars, monetary and fiscal mismanagement of postwar adjustments, and some recent peacetime fiscal disturbances.

Most of the past destabilizing monetary and fiscal policy can be explained simply by ignorance and incompetence. But the more recent episodes grew out of the difficulty of reconciling economic objectives. A concern for rising prices, and to some extent a balance of payments deficit, led to the tight fiscal and monetary policies which initiated the contractions of 1957–58 and 1960–61, and which maintained the stagnation of 1956–64.[13]

If macroeconomic policy will cease to be destabilizing, we need not be overly concerned about the limitations to its capabilities for stabilizing. A pound of prevention will relieve the anxiety about the ounce of cure.

POLICIES TO PREVENT INFLATION

If inflation were of the excess-demand type only, the previous discussion of stabilization policy would include anti-inflation policy as well. The same policies that can keep aggregate demand from becoming deficient can also be used to keep it from becoming exces-

---

[13] The postwar recessions of European countries have also been the product of monetary and fiscal tightenings undertaken to mitigate inflation and balance of payments problems. See David Williams, "What's Left of the Business Cycle in Europe?" *Finance and Development* (Washington, D.C.: International Monetary Fund and International Bank for Reconstruction and Development), Vol. V, No. 1 (March, 1968), pp. 42–47.

sive. But wage-push inflation confronts policy-makers with a different sort of problem. The conflict, created by the wage-push process, between the objectives of full employment and stable prices, requires a choice or a compromise. This conflict has spurred the search for a new policy instrument to reconcile the two objectives.

Some European countries have tried programs of wage and price controls, but without conspicuous success. The antagonisms and inefficiencies engendered by the imposition of a rigid set of controls have led to either nonenforcement or abandonment of the programs.

Guideposts

A recent American approach to reconciling full employment and stable prices has been the program of "wage-price guideposts" of the President's Council of Economic Advisers. It is a program of education, persuasion, and voluntary cooperation, aimed at keeping wage increases within a noninflationary limit and keeping price changes within the limit set by changes in labor cost per unit of output. Though suspended for the past several years, during which the problem has been excess demand rather than wage push, the guidepost program can still be considered one of the policy instruments available for reactivation at a propitious time.

The basis for the guidepost for wages is the expected average increase in productivity of labor.[14] The reasoning is that if wages are increased by a percentage equal to the percentage increase in product per man-hour, there will be no increase in labor cost per unit of output and therefore the wage increase will exert no upward pressure on the price level. Unions and managements are urged to hold wage increases to the guidepost figure. Note that the same guidepost—based on the average productivity increase of the whole labor force—must apply to each labor group, regardless of what the group's own productivity change has been. For to base wage increases on the productivity increases of separate groups or bargaining units would be not only inequitable but unworkable as an anti-inflation program. Widening wage differentials favoring those fortunate enough to be working in industries having relatively rapid technological progress would not long be tolerated and wage in-

---

[14] When the Council of Economic Advisers first proposed the guidepost program in 1962, it gave no specific figure for the productivity increase. In 1964 the council's report cited 3.2 percent per year as the trend of labor productivity in the preceding five years, and that figure came to be adopted as the guidepost.

creases would tend to be equalized at the rate set by the sectors with the fastest rise of productivity.

The guidepost pattern for prices (assuming that wages adhere to the guidepost rule) is stable prices in industries whose trend of productivity is close to the average, rising prices in industries whose trend of productivity is below the average, and falling prices in industries whose trend of productivity is above the average. The overall result would be a stable price level.

It might seem improbable that a voluntary program could materially affect wage settlements, and the popular impression is that it did not. It is striking, therefore, to find statistical investigations offering strong evidence that the guideposts program was effective in retarding the rate of wage increase. Two studies,[15] both using the technique of applying a wage equation of the type presented on page 200, find that the rate of wage increase in the years 1962–66, when the guideposts were in effect, was lower than would be predicted in the absence of the guideposts. No plausible alternative explanation for the slower rate of wage increase being forthcoming, it appears that the guideposts did succeed in shifting the inflation-unemployment trade-off curve downward. This statistical evidence offers some basis for the hope that when excess demand is eliminated a resumption of the guidepost program can contribute to the reconciliation of the goals of full employment and price stability.

POLICIES TO PROMOTE GROWTH

The analysis of the growth process marks four points at which policy can be applied to raise the rate of growth: saving and investment, the growth of labor, technological progress, and improvement of resource allocation. If it is *per capita* growth we are interested in, we can omit the growth of labor, which depends primarily on the growth of population.

The main conclusions about saving and investment policy can be briefly summarized. (1) A policy of increasing the saving rate is valid only if a corresponding increase of investment demand can be counted on. An increase of the rate of growth of capital, with given rates of technological progress and growth of labor, means a falling

[15] George L. Perry, "Wages and Guideposts," *American Economic Review*, Vol. LVII, No. 4 (September, 1967), pp. 832–40, and Gail Pierson, "The Effect of Union Strength on the U.S. Phillips Curve," *American Economic Review*, Vol. LVIII, No. 3, Part 1 (June, 1968), pp. 456–67.

rate of profit. Consequently, raising the rate of investment requires either a decline in the interest rate, for which there is little scope in an economy with a low interest rate, or a decline in the margin of profit in excess of the interest rate which investors require as a risk allowance. (2) In an advanced economy with a capital stock which is comparatively new in terms of the technology it embodies, an increase in the rate of growth of capital is likely to make a relatively small contribution to the rate of growth. (3) Further study of the present saving rate in relation to the optimum saving rate is needed to determine whether an increase in the saving rate, even if it increases the rate of growth of output, would increase the rate of growth of welfare.

Policies to increase the rate of technological progress are, in the present state of our knowledge, primarily matters of conjecture. To the extent that the economy is failing to allocate investment in research in an optimal way (e.g., for basic research), public encouragement of research may make a contribution. Another approach to stimulating research which has won some adherents is to encourage greater concentration of industry on the grounds that a firm's research outlays increase more than proportionately with the size of the firm. On the whole, the evidence we have does not appear to support this view; neither the size nor success of firms' research efforts seems to be systematically related to firm size.[16] Moreover, to the extent that greater concentration reduces competition, which is one of the most effective stimuli to research, the result is likely to be adverse to technological progress.

Technological progress depends not only on the development of new knowledge but also on the rate at which the new knowledge is introduced into the productive process. Impediments to technological change, which may arise from government regulation (as in the case of building codes), labor union opposition, or insufficient entrepreneurial initiative, will both discourage research and retard its application. Policies which remove obstacles to change and which increase competition so as to spur more rapid change can contribute toward an acceleration of the rate of technological advance.

The correction of resource misallocation is a vast subject, which

---

[16] See Jacob Schmookler, "Bigness, Fewness, and Research," *Journal of Political Economy*, Vol. LXVII, No. 6 (December, 1959), pp. 628–32; Edwin Mansfield, "Industrial Research and Development Expenditures: Determinants, Prospects, and Relation to Size of Firm and Inventive Output," *ibid.*, Vol. LXXII, No. 4 (August, 1964), pp. 319–40.

lies, for the most part, outside the scope of this book. We can only touch on a major allocation problem in a growing economy—the mobility of resources. Growth requires continuous change. The productivity of factors increases, new industries develop, old industries may decline. Labor and capital are released from some uses by the rise of their productivity relative to the demand for their output or by an absolute decline of the demand for their output, and they must be continuously reallocated to the uses which are expanding. Obviously, policies which break down the barriers to the movement of factors or which positively encourage factor mobility will facilitate economic growth.

Policies to increase the rate of investment, the rate of technological progress, or the mobility of factors are not easy to devise or apply. But we do have one macroeconomic policy ready at hand which can make a powerful contribution to all three of those growth determinants, and that is the maintenance of high aggregate demand. The stabilization of demand at the full-potential level serves both to raise the rate of saving by maintaining higher incomes and to raise investment demand by reducing the risks of investment and sustaining entrepreneurs' expectations of growth. Stable high demand encourages research for and the introduction of technological improvements and reduces labor resistance to innovation. High demand for inputs increases the mobility of factors by making it easier for factors to move and by eroding the barriers to movement that develop under conditions of unemployment.

RECOMMENDED READINGS

FELLNER, WILLIAM. *Trends and Cycles in Economic Activity*, New York: Henry Holt & Co., 1956, chap. xiv.

FRIEDMAN, MILTON. "The Role of Monetary Policy," *American Economic Review*, Vol. LVIII, No. 1 (March, 1968), pp. 1–17.

HART, ALBERT GAILORD, and KENEN, PETER B. *Money, Debt, and Economic Activity*, 3d ed. New York: Prentice-Hall, Inc., 1961, chaps. xxiii–xxv.

MILLIKAN, MAX F. (ed.). *Income Stabilization for a Developing Democracy; A Study of the Politics and Economics of High Employment Without Inflation*. New Haven, Conn.: Yale University Press, 1953.

MUSGRAVE, RICHARD A. "The Optimal Mix of Stabilization Policies," in United States Congress, Joint Economic Committee, *The Relationship of Prices to Economic Stability and Growth; Compendium of Papers Submitted by Panelists Appearing Before the Joint Economic Commit-*

tee, 85th Cong., 2d Sess. Washington, D.C.: U.S. Government Printing Office, 1958, pp. 597–609.

UNIVERSITIES—NATIONAL BUREAU COMMITTEE FOR ECONOMIC RESEARCH. *Policies to Combat Depression.* Princeton, N.J.: Princeton University Press, 1956.

QUESTIONS

1. Compare the merits of fiscal and monetary stabilization policies with respect to timing.
2. Outline a stabilization program for an economy which is willing to tolerate a small rate of inflation in order to minimize fluctuations.
3. Are economic growth and the avoidance of inflation congenial or uncongenial objectives? Explain.
4. Review and evaluate the use of fiscal policy for stabilization during income fluctuations since 1929.
5. Assume that monetary policy can be effectively used as a substitute for fiscal policy for purposes of economic stabilization. Compare the effects of the two policies on consumption, saving, investment, and the rate of growth. What part should considerations of growth play in the choice between the two types of policy?

Index

INDEX

United States—*Cont.*
  unemployment rate of, and inflation,
    1948–68, 197–98

V

Value added, 4
Velocity of money, 164–65
Vietnam War, 185
Vitaliano, Donald F., 270 n

W

Wage-price guidelines, 200 n, 282–83

Wage-push inflation, 188–90, 195–96
War
  Korean, 196
  Vietnam, 185
  World War II, 196
Watts, Harold W., 69 n
Wealth, redistribution of, through in-
  flation, 204
Welfare and national income, 24
White, William H., 122 n, 125
Williams, David, 281 n
World War II, 196

*This book has been set in 10 point Century
Expanded with Century Bold, leaded 3
points, and 9 point Primer, leaded 2 points.
Part numbers and titles are in 18 point
Helvetica Regular. Chapter numbers and
titles are in 18 point Helvetica. The size of
the type page is 27 by 45¾ picas.*